Madhavi S. Mahadevan has published two collections of short stories, *Paltan Tales* (Indialog, 2005) and *Doppelganger* (Alchemy, 2014). *The Kaunteyas* is her first novel. Her most recent work is *Bride of the Forest: The Untold Story of Yayati's Daughter*. She has also written fiction for children. She lives in Bengaluru.

PRAISE FOR *THE KAUNTEYAS*

'Every chapter ends with a cliffhanger, the dialogues are realistic and there is no dead-air...Such balance and sobriety makes *The Kaunteyas* less of a controversy to talk about, and more of a book to actually read.'

—*New Indian Express*

'In the oeuvre of retellings on the epic, *The Kaunteyas* is not just another retelling. In time, it will carve a special place in the epic fantasy genre.'

—*The Pioneer*

PRAISE FOR *BRIDE OF THE FOREST: THE UNTOLD STORY OF YAYATI'S DAUGHTER*

Winner of the Special Jury Award for Best Book, Fiction, JK Papers/Times of India AutHER Awards 2021

'...a harrowing saga of grace about a woman who managed to be generous, kind and compassionate even while held hostage to the feckless notions of dharma adhered to by powerful men...The author does an admirable job of handling the sensational material with sensitivity even as she infuses it with the gentle beats of a pain-wracked heart.'

—Anuja Chandramouli, *The New Indian Express*

'The book is balanced and nuanced. It is defiant and outspoken against a gendered society, without ever seeming out of place for its time of setting. With lyrical prose, interesting characters and side characters and strong philosophical points, this book is a must-read.'

—Times of India.Indiatimes.com

'In [*Bride of the Forest*], Drishadvati is a delicately poised figure while tracing feminist lineage...Mahadevan sensitively focuses on Drishadvati's radical character instead of projecting her as a helpless woman, as in earlier adaptations.'

—*Hindustan Times*

'This was a delight to read! The writing sparkles with its word flow—there is wit, there is a poetic lilt and a lot of humour tinged with sarcasm...Would recommend this for readers who love Indian mythology, strong women characters and writing that leaves you thinking.'

—Wordpress.com

The Kaunteyas

MADHAVI S. MAHADEVAN

SPEAKING
TIGER

SPEAKING TIGER BOOKS LLP
125A, Ground Floor, Shahpur Jat,
Near Asiad Village, New Delhi - 110 049

First published by Westland Ltd 2016
This edition published by Speaking Tiger Books 2022

ISBN: 978-93-5447-365-4
eISBN: 978-93-5447-372-2

10 9 8 7 6 5 4 3 2 1

Printed at HT Media Ltd, Greater Noida

Contents

Know that it is the womb
From which all beings arise;
The universe is born within me
And within me will be destroyed.

–7.3-7, *Bhagavad Gita.*
A new translation. Stephen Mitchell

Prologue

The best stories have always been men's stories, and what men regard as the best stories are often war stories. The tale of the Kurukshetra War will be sung for a long time. Fields of blood, wondrous weapons, subtle strategies, bold tactics, courage, cowardice, trickery, treachery, brutality, death and glory. It has all these. Above all—honour. Men place great value on honour, but along with it comes anger. Aggression is a sign of manliness.

After the war, Yudhisthira accused me. 'You kept this a secret for so long. *How could you?*' Furious, he spurned the crown. 'This victory tastes like defeat,' he said.

It turned out exactly the way I had imagined. His brothers' faces reflected shock, disappointment. To them it was a betrayal. I wanted to ask: Did you not want to get back your kingdom? Would you have got it back if I hadn't kept silent for so long? But I had no words. Without my secret, I was naked, revealed to the world—but also to myself. It was then that I realized I no longer needed the protective colouring of words. I was not afraid of being judged. Being men, they would all probably reach the same conclusion. The tale would be told as men saw fit.

Yes, women's tales, too, have been told by men, but with an important difference: they are cautionary. They warn men that women are clever, conniving, deceitful and, frequently, the cause of dissension. They tell women how they should be and, more importantly, *not* be. A common theme is retribution for breaking rules that are invariably manmade. Speaking out of turn, laughing at the wrong time, keeping a secret. Crossing the line.

Men's stories are the bones of a bygone age, sanctified as relics, preserved in stone. Women's stories are written in water. Passed in silence from mother to daughter. About things perishable: flesh, blood, feelings, tears. Suffering. Endurance is a sign of womanliness. But what men overlook is that endurance is a crucible, it changes the existing state.

I wonder what would happen if women started telling their own stories. Like water that grinds down the hardest rock, would these stories change the shape of the world? Would Truth then become something else?

This story, of which I have long been a keeper, begins with the arrival of a visitor.

PART ONE

Kuntibhoja

1

What astral combination presaged his entrance in our lives we could not say, but one thing we knew for sure: the future would be filled with turbulence.

'One year,' he had assured, as if bestowing a benediction upon us.

'One *year!*' we had echoed—in horror.

The calendar would now read differently. The temperature would rise and fall as per his disposition for the day. For weeks preceding his arrival the question uppermost in everyone's mind was: how were we going to survive? We even made nervous jokes about it.

'Not for nothing is he called Durvasa,' the *rajmata* said.

Purujit looked up from the toy chariot he was playing with. 'What does it mean, Daadi?'

'Badly dressed,' I supplied.

The rajmata frowned at me for speaking out of turn. 'Badly *behaved*,' she said. 'He's a dreadful guest.'

'Who invited him?'

Hidden in the branches of the neem tree in the courtyard, a crow cawed, as if repeating the question: *Kaun? Kaun?*

The rajmata glared in the crow's direction. Turning

to Purujit, she said, 'Invited? Does bad news wait to be invited?'

Her tone surprised me. It was unlike her to be curt with Purujit, who she always referred to as her *eldest* grandchild, the point being made that I, though two years older, was merely the foster child—the one who had been foisted on the family. There were others ways in which she displayed her hostility: Purujit and his brothers were encouraged to call her daadi, but I had to always address her by the honorific rajmata. 'You may be our relative, but that doesn't mean you should forget your place,' she had said to me. What place? I had wanted to snap back. I am no more a dependant than you are. But I held my tongue, never uttered a word. Not only did I not want to start a quarrel with her, but I also had no real desire to address her by anything more intimate. Rajmata she was, rajmata she would remain.

We were sitting on the balcony outside her chamber, soaking up the diminishing warmth of the afternoon sun. Below us in the courtyard, where the rajmata could keep an eagle eye on them, the kitchen maids were cleaning greens, sifting grain and pounding spices for the evening meal. The month of Maagh had begun and a passing spell of bad weather, cold, wet and windy, had worsened her arthritis.

A *dasi* appeared with a copper bowl.

'What's that?' the rajmata asked.

'It's the poultice that the *vaidya* wanted you to apply,' I replied. 'Would you like Kapila to do it?'

'Not her. You.'

I signalled to Kapila to leave the bowl. She kept her eyes lowered, but threw me a small smile of sympathy and fled.

The rajmata was a slave driver, clouting the maids if they displeased her, but she would not go so far as to raise a hand on me. I moved up her silk *antariya* to her thighs and exposed her stubby legs.

'*Gently*, girl!' she snarled through gritted teeth, although I was extra careful as I dabbed the paste on her left knee. 'What is this strange concoction?'

'Arandi leaves and warm oil.'

She wrinkled her nose. 'Smells foul.'

'Vaid ji says that it will bring you relief.'

She had the girth of the kettledrum that was beaten on festivals. The vaidya had recommended a weight-loss diet. When I had said that she would never agree, he had quoted a line from the *Taittreya Upanishad*. *From food all creatures are produced, and by food, when born, do they grow.* He had emphasized the last word.

As the warmth from the poultice sank in and brought relief to the inflamed joint, she leaned back, shut her eyes, and said, 'Fetch that almond oil the trader from Gandhara got us. You can give me a hand massage while you are here.'

I winked at Purujit and went to get the oil. Taking a few drops of it in my palm, I began to rub it into her skin which looked, and felt, like the inflated buffalo hide rafts that villagers used to cross the river. The massage and the poultice improved her mood. She gave a grunt of satisfaction. Coming back to the earlier topic, she said, 'It must be at least fifteen years since Durvasa *rishi* honoured us with a visit, but I haven't forgotten.'

Purujit immediately asked, 'What did he look like?'

The rajmata grimaced in disgust. 'Dirty and scruffy, his

skin was shrivelled and you could count his very bones. He was dressed in tatters that even a beggar would refuse. He had just finished performing a penance in a cave god-knows-where.'

'A cave with bats?'

'Probably.'

'How long was he in there?'

'Twenty years, we were told.'

'You mean he didn't have a bath for *twenty* years?'

'He certainly smelled like that…It was the worst fortnight of our lives.'

'Why?'

'*Nothing* pleased him. He complained that the kheer was not sweet enough, the rotis not soft, the bath water was never the right temperature, the deer skin on which he sat for meditation was infested with fleas.' She raised her eyebrows to show scepticism at this last objection.

Grumbles from guests were not unknown to us. Our land was uninteresting: arid, dun-coloured, surrounded by giant rocky outcrops and low hills covered with sparse vegetation. Summers scorched us, winters froze, and the brief rainy season brought mugginess, mildew and mosquitoes. The palace, too, was not built to any grand design. Instead, it was a jumbled sprawl, a labyrinth, with wings added, altered or broken as the need arose. No one could remember precisely how many rooms it had. There were shrines for deities big and small, a number of gardens, kitchens, granaries and store rooms. There were separate stables for horses and elephants, and several long rows of cowsheds where the precious royal herds were housed. Visitors often complained of how they would take a wrong turn and find themselves hopelessly lost in an unfamiliar courtyard or a derelict passage; occasionally we even had to send search parties to rescue a guest gone astray. Despite that we had house guests year round, mostly pilgrims on their way to a *teertha sthan*, but also others who came for a few days of hunting as there was plenty of game in the scrub forests nearby.

'Is that all?' Purujit asked, slightly disappointed.

'*All?*' echoed the rajmata. 'No, that is not all…He came and went at will. After all, who would dare question the famous maharishi? Sometimes he'd disappear for the entire day and return at some odd hour during the night after the kitchen had been closed and demand a meal. Nothing as simple as puffed rice, seasonal fruits and plain milk, which is the appropriate food for a brahmin, but a full meal with steamed rice, roti, dal, three vegetables, fried tidbits, chutney, and at least *two* types of sweet, one of which had to be cooked in milk!' She paused to let this sink in. 'The entire meal had to prepared from scratch, but before the cooks could start on their work they had to cleanse themselves by having a bath—at midnight! On top of that, he hated to be kept waiting. The servants ran helter-skelter to do his bidding, no one shirked in the effort to please him, *yet* he lost his temper. They say that a brahmin should be mild and forgiving; above all, he should be self-controlled; but Durvasa's anger was something to behold.'

'Did he hit someone?' Purujit asked.

'*Hit someone*?' The rajmata widened her eyes. '*Arre*! That is what a normal person does. When a sage gets into a rage he does much worse. He curses.'

'Whom did he curse? '

The rajmata was silent for a long moment. 'He uttered a *shaap* that turned two of the servants into crows.'

Purujit's mouth fell open. 'And then?'

'The entire staff fled that very day.'

'And then?'

The rajmata sent him a look that was part affection, part exasperation. 'Then what, my little parrot prince? You tell me...Who was there to do the chores? Do you even know how many different jobs are done by the servants daily, not just in the house, but in the *gaushala* too? Nine hundred cows waiting to be milked! Such a racket they made with their bellowing, as if the world was about to end.' She shuddered at the memory. 'The milkmaids from nearby villages had to be called in. Your mother, and *even I*, had to pitch in. The creatures were so distressed that they were kicking and butting left, right and centre. Calming them down was a nightmare!' She scowled. 'I *can't* understand why that man has chosen to descend upon us. He is nothing but trouble.'

The crow cawed again as though in complete agreement with her. Purujit glanced at it and then at me, his eyes two question marks.

I gave a brief nod. 'The servants,' I said in a sepulchral tone. 'They know he's coming back—the Angriest Man in the World.'

Purujit caught the joke and grinned but the rajmata gave me an icy stare.

'Don't be impertinent, Pritha,' she said, 'and don't just *sit* around. Make yourself useful! Go down to the kitchen and tell them to send up some fresh roasted green gram. It's a long time to dinner.' She looked at Purujit and her expression melted into one that was soft and adoring. 'Is there anything else you'd like?' she inquired tenderly. 'Til laddus? You don't eat enough, my moon. How will you become big and strong?'

I wished fervently that I knew a curse that would turn her into a crow or, better still, a short-nosed fruit bat, the species she closely resembled in looks. As usual, by calling me Pritha, the name my birth father had given me, she was driving home the point that I did not belong. Keeping my face deadpan, I stood up. Her gaze, travelling over me, froze. 'Cover your chest,' she said tersely.

Glancing down, I saw that the plain cotton bodice had slipped and the dark brown tips of my nipples were revealed. The cold air had made them rigid. I looked up in confusion. Purujit was staring at me curiously. Blushing, hastily adjusting the cloth, I mumbled an apology.

The rajmata's broad homely face clouded with displeasure. Antipathy glittered, like the sharpened edge of a knife, in her narrowed eyes. 'Those aren't lemons you have growing there, shameless girl!'

The sting of hot tears pricked my eyelids. I tucked my chin down. As I turned and walked away, I felt her hostile stare branding my back.

Not lemons, I thought angrily, *but they are still a long way from being dry, shrivelled fruit like yours.*

2

A name, Pritha, that was all my biological father, Shura, thought to bestow on me. It means *She-who-upholds-and-supports-all-things*. It also means 'the palm of the hand'. Maybe they are one and the same. After all, don't the lines of our hand support our fate? It could also be that I was named thus because I was so tiny that I fitted in the palm of Shura's hand when he offered me to his cousin Kuntibhoja.

Shura was the *sangha mukhiya*, elected chieftain, of the Vrishni Yadavas. The Vrishnis were herdsmen who, with their kin, the Andhakas and the Bhojas, had formed a confederacy of clans. In the Dwapara *yuga*, a very long time ago, our common ancestors had settled in the fertile Vraj *bhumi* on the banks of the river Yamuna. Subsequent generations had prospered and this flourishing territory came to be known as Shurasena. Kuntibhoja, who told us this, said that we were all descendants of Yadu, the eldest son of Yayati, a legendary king of Aryavarta.

Shura and Kuntibhoja were best friends. The latter, older by a few years, had got married before Shura, but he and his wife remained childless. Kuntibhoja was over six feet tall, thin and weedy, with a slight stoop. That, combined with the look of apology permanently etched on his features, made him appear inconsequential. He believed in moderation in all things but, as time passed, became increasingly despondent and was heard to repeat several times: 'Despite all the special sacrifices I have performed, including the arduous Putrakameshti *yajna*, the gods have not seen fit to bestow the blessing of an offspring on me. The Puranas say that a man who dies without clearing the debt to his ancestors in Pitr Loka by fathering a child, will be denied entry into that very heaven. Instead, he is doomed to go in the opposite direction—to Put.'

This place Put was a particularly difficult hell to endure because anyone unfortunate enough to go there had to hang upside down for eternity. 'Could there be a fate worse than that?' Kuntibhoja asked, with such a downturn to his mouth that it seemed to everyone that he was already suspended by his heels. 'How will I answer my forefathers when they demand to know why I failed them? The thought of what awaits me is so terrible that I have no interest in living any more.'

His words, with their overtones of impending suicide, alarmed Shura enough to make him promise that as soon as one of his wives delivered, he would give the newborn to Kuntibhoja to bring up as his own. And that is exactly what he did. In my childhood, Shura visited Kuntibhoja's kingdom on a few occasions. My biological father had a dark, narrow face like a fox, with deep-set eyes, slivers of agate, hard and glittering, viewing the whole world with suspicion. When I was presented before him, his glance flicked over me without interest and moved away. I did not inherit Shura's eyes, nor, thank God, did I get his hooked nose and thin mouth.

My eyes, I have been told, are my exceptional feature. Wide-set, almond-shaped, with thick, curling lashes. I have heard them described as rainwater pools in a sal forest. No one in Kuntibhoja's palace had eyes like mine. I used to wonder if I got them from my birth mother Marisha, a princess of the forest-dwelling Nagavansh tribe. The Nagavanshis are serpent-worshipers. Their women are reputed to be strong, clever and stunningly beautiful. Was *she* beautiful, my mother? When I was growing up, I would study my reflection and try to divine her visage in it. *Did I inherit this narrow nose from her? This full mouth? The square jaw? Were her eyelashes, too, thick and long? Did she weep when she had to part with me?*

Even before Marisha became my mother I was pledged away. Yet, didn't she see me draw my first breath and hear my first cry? As I took form within her, some deeper compassion would surely have arisen to bring on that strange welter of feelings—tenderness, concern, hope, anxiety and anguish—that are a child's return gift to its mother for giving it life. Gift, or maybe the very opposite. After all, what is a mother deep down but a bundle of raw nerve endings? The baby may leave her body, but it is as if her heart, having learnt to keep time for nine months with the new being's inner rhythm, must now beat differently lifelong.

Whenever someone from Mathura visited, I used to hover around waiting to hear if anyone there had inquired about me. Thus I got news of my siblings, my brother Vasudeva and my four sisters. With so many children to care for, my mother probably just put me out of her mind altogether. She had married into the Vrishnis, and their women were known for being pragmatic and unsentimental; perhaps she felt she had to live up to this reputation.

I was barely a few weeks old when I journeyed in a covered bullock cart from Mathura, accompanied by a wet nurse. After two days we arrived at Kuntibhoja's palace. The wet nurse returned home and a new one, a local woman, was appointed for a few months. I had a succession of nurses, but was there anyone who cared to celebrate the rites of passage in my infancy? Who held me in her lap as I was fed my first spoon of rice? Who saw me take my first step? Who was there to rejoice over the first word I ever spoke?

My foster father's welcome of me started with a change of name. At the insistence of the royal astrologer, he renamed me after himself and his realm Kunti. I was his *manasaputri,* he said, the child born of his wish. Pritha, pledged away before her birth, had no place to call her own, but I, Kunti, belonged to a kingdom. On my part I always addressed him as *pitaji.* The *patrani*, senior of Kuntibhoja's two wives, however, was indifferent to the change of name. 'Pritha or Kunti, it doesn't matter what name you give her,' she is supposed to have said. 'This child will belong only to herself.' No one knew what to make of this remark, but no one took it seriously either: the patrani had a reputation for eccentricity.

To everyone's surprise, a year after my arrival, the patrani conceived. So did the junior *rani*. Both gave birth to boys. Kuntibhoja was overjoyed. He insisted that it was all due to the good luck I had brought with me. If anything, after Purujit's birth, his belief that I was auspicious for his family only deepened. I suspect this was partly why the rajmata disliked me from the beginning. What she hated even more was that Purujit and I grew up to be closer than most real siblings. The patrani's attitude to me was a mix of absent-minded affection and mild interest. Strangely, Purujit's birth did not bring on any stronger maternal feeling towards him either. She treated him in exactly the same casual way that she behaved with me. She was a spare woman with an erect bearing, gaunt, dark-eyed, with thick black tresses that flowed down to her knees. She stayed away from the lively atmosphere of the women's quarters.

Lively is too mild a word for the clamour and colour generated by the coming and going of beads- and bangle-sellers, silk weavers, vendors of scented oils and exotic spices, bird-catchers, bright-eyed tribal women selling wild honey, bunches of herbs and berries, jugglers, animal entertainers, snake charmers, itinerant musicians, storytellers, sharp-eyed astrologers and spare-bodied wandering religious mendicants looking for alms. During the day, the corridors of the women's quarters buzzed with constant chatter and noisy arguments interspersed with gusts of laughter. At night it was a vast dormitory for the many dasis who served us.

The running of a royal household is an enormous and challenging task that falls to the chief queen. There are armies of servants that must be supervised, religious and social rituals that must be observed, important guests who must be received and looked after. Whether it was out of deference, tact, or plain lack of interest, the patrani had nothing to do with any of this: she left it entirely to her mother-in-law. Thus it was the rajmata who went about ordering the purchase of provisions; overseeing the storage of grains, lentils, oil; checking on the cooks in the kitchen; looking over the accounts; and assigning duties to the servants.

The older staff in the palace whispered that when the patrani failed to have a baby, the rajmata made her life miserable. She delivered barbs in everyone's hearing about her daughter-in-law's unfruitfulness, advised her to eat 'hot' foods, tied amulets on her wrists, and even suggested sexual positions she could take. Driven by the compulsion to have a child, Kuntibhoja and the patrani went through a great deal of self-mortification: they swallowed potions and powders suggested by the vaidyas, made pilgrimages to distant shrines, bathed in sacred rivers and ponds, assumed vows and undertook difficult fasts. There were the endless sacrifices, *pujas* and *havans* that went on for months, consuming gallons of ghee, grain and milk as oblations to the gods and leaving the palace's walls darkened by the smoke for years. They fed thousands of brahmins and gave away several times that number in cows as *daan-dakshina*. While they undertook all this jointly, the constant cycle of hope rising, falling, rising again had disparate effects on the couple. Kuntibhoja became more anxious for an offspring while the desire for one ebbed in the patrani. She withdrew from the outer world and its concerns, turning to her gods for comfort. The rajmata pressed Kuntibhoja to take other wives who would help him father a son. This caused a rift between her and the patrani, but I have to say that in all my years in Kuntibhoja's palace, I never heard the two women exchange an acrimonious word. In fact, the patrani was scrupulously polite on the occasions that she had to deal directly with the rajmata, and the rajmata, on her part, maintained a veneer of civility that she didn't deign to show anyone else. However, contact between the two women was rare.

❖

The patrani had her own apartment in the palace. A set of spacious rooms, a kitchen where she preferred to do her own cooking, and a large garden in which she spent her time. It was where Purujit and I loved to while away our free hours. The garden was named Nandana, after the god Indra's garden in the heavenly city of Amaravati. Over the years the patrani had stocked it with saplings that she brought back from her various pilgrimages. These had thrived and become full-grown trees. 'You two are Kuntibhoja's children,' she used to say in a slightly disparaging manner to Purujit and me, 'but these plants are *my* babies.'

She would tell us the name of each one and why it was special. The palash with its flaming red flowers was the god of fire, Agni, born of Dyaus Pita, the sky, and Mata Prithvi, our Mother Earth. The large asvattha tree in the centre of the garden was the bridge between heaven and earth, and below its roots was the source of the secret river Saraswati. The ancient, broad-canopied vata vriksha in the corner was the three-storied family home of the holy trinity itself: Brahma lived in the tangle of roots that gripped the dark wet soil, Vishnu in the thick trunk and Shiva in the lofty green canopy.

'Where do their wives live?' we asked, for we knew that the three gods were married to goddesses powerful in their own right.

'Right here for one,' the patrani said, caressing the leaves of the flourishing tulsi shrub under which she lit a terracotta oil lamp every evening. 'This is Sri Lakshmi herself. Isn't she beautiful?'

Besides the sacred trees and the ponds filled with pink lotuses, the garden also held several shrines that the patrani tended herself. The palace had a rich and elaborate temple dedicated to Mahadeva, where Kuntibhoja offered fresh bilva leaves every day. The rani's garden housed the simpler *grama devi* and *devata*, the village deities of our land. Though she never had much to say about everyday life lived on the human plane, she was always willing to talk about the teeming universe of her gods and goddesses. She would display the fine cloths that she had ordered from the weaver, or the bangles and the ruby nose ring that the jeweller had made. She would tell us that if we wanted to please Mahadeva we should offer him the fragrant, coral-centred little white flower called parijata; if it was his son Ganesha whose blessings we needed, then the offering was a garland of durva grass; if we wanted to curry favour with Varuna, lord of the ocean, presenting him with a coconut would do the trick. Sometimes she would allow me to do small chores for her: I'd string the pearly blooms of jasmine and glowing orbs of marigold into colourful garlands; scrape a block of sandalwood to make the sweet-smelling paste for anointing the idols; wash and polish the bronze and copper puja vessels. Away from the formal world of the palace, secure in her own domain, the patrani was easy to talk with. I cherished the conversations we had because she always treated me as an equal.

I have a vivid memory of one such conversation that occurred when I was about ten years old. We were in the kitchen. It was a festive day and I was helping her prepare the *bhog* that was to be presented to the gods in a set of silver dishes reserved only for such occasions. As she placed the food on the trays, I asked her, 'Do your devis and devatas eat all this?'

'They do.'

'Then where does it all go?'

She looked down her long nose at me without speaking for several minutes. 'They are satisfied by the piety of the cook and the love with which the food is offered,' she said.

'So, they don't actually eat it, do they?'

'They feed on the aroma. It is enough to satisfy them.'

Her answer, however, was not enough to satisfy me. 'So, are they different from us, or aren't they?'

'Different from *us*?' She wrinkled her brow as if considering the question for the first time in her life. 'Well, they *are* immortal.'

'That's only because they outwitted the asuras and drank all the *amrita*,' I said, cleverly. 'If you look at it that way, then you can say that they are *richer* than us because they have the *kalpa vriksha*. It is a wish-fulfilling tree and it gives them whatever they ask of it. You can also say that they are more powerful than us because they control the rain and the sunshine. Otherwise why would we pray to them or make offerings to please them?'

A smile began to play on her lips, but she nodded.

Encouraged by her interest, I continued. 'Except for these one or two things, immortality and magical powers, the devis and devatas are just like us human beings.'

'They behave just like us—is that what you mean?'

I nodded. 'Some of them even *hate* each other. You always tell us that Indra bhagwan, the lord of rain, and Surya, the sun god, don't get along. They are jealous of each other because both are equally strong. Doesn't that show that the devas are *exactly* like us? They like to display their strength.

They marry and have children, sometimes favouring one child over another. They quarrel and make up. Some of them play harmless jokes, while others play mean tricks. They steal from each other and from us, cheat at games. They can also be greedy. And sometimes they can simply be very difficult.'

'True,' she said. 'But they are also fair, kind and generous. In return for all the joys and comforts they bless us with, all they ask for is that we remember them.'

I didn't quite agree with her that it was *all* they asked but I didn't want the discussion to be diverted: she had a habit of drifting into silence in mid-conversation. 'Pitaji says that dharma must guide our actions,' I said. 'Do they even have anything like it in Deva loka?'

'Doesn't the sun rise every day?' she asked quietly. 'Don't the clouds bring us rain? Doesn't the bee give honey? Don't the cows give us milk?'

'But all this will happen anyway,' I said, suddenly impatient with adult illogic. 'If we stop praying, the sun won't stop rising and the cows won't stop giving milk either.'

'The natural order in our world is maintained because the gods, too, are bound by their functions,' she said. 'Even when we forget ours.'

I looked out to the peaceful garden sunbathing in the morning brilliance. A soft breeze rifled through the leaves of trees, ruffled the surface of the lotus pond and sent a delicate shiver through the clustered blooms of the madhavilata. Their fragrance rode on the breeze. Was it carrying our conversation to the gods? Were they laughing at us, or frowning in displeasure? The shrines in the patrani's garden were simple, even crude, made mostly from wood or clay.

Some of them were plain with flat roofs, others had modest shikharas and embellishments. There were several open-air shrines too, each with its own deity, and sometimes entire households of them—father, mother, children, attendants, gatekeepers, pet animals and birds—sculpted in stone or terracotta. There were sinuous serpent gods, mysterious devatas with animal heads, fierce devis with six arms, *gandharvas* who loved music, graceful dancing *apsaras*, ugly *yakshas* who guarded hidden treasure and curvaceous *yakshis* to whom women prayed for babies. Surya and Chandra had their shrines, as did the seven planets who ruled the seven days of the week.

'Why are there so many?' I asked.

'I think of them as the colours of the rainbow,' she said. 'If all those shades were not there would the rainbow be as beautiful? It could also be because we *need* them. Indra and Surya may not want to have anything to do with one another, but *we* mortals cannot do without either of them. Without timely rain would our fields flourish? Without plenty of sunshine would our harvest ripen?'

'They exercise power over us,' I said flatly. 'Only *that* makes them superior.'

'They have more powers than humans, but we are not completely bereft. Don't we have intelligence and imagination? The gods have their own world on Mount Meru, filled with treasures like the kalpa vriksha, but don't we have wonderful plants like the banana and the coconut that give us *all* we need?' She pointed to the banyan tree. 'Just look at that vata vriksha. It's a world in itself, as complete as our own.'

Complete? My world was nothing like the vata vriksha. It did not supply me with all that I needed. It barely gave me enough to keep myself together. However, I didn't say anything for fear of contradicting her a little too often. I opened my mouth to ask her something else, but she began to shake her head reprovingly. 'You are intelligent, Kunti, but like the learned Gargi, you ask too many questions. Doesn't the rajmata tell you that a girl must not do that?'

'I never ask *her* any questions. I just do whatever she tells me.'

'Intelligent and sensible,' she said with a wry smile. 'Obedience is the highest virtue.'

3

Kuntibhoja was taking no chances this time. He had ordered the building of a new guesthouse for Durvasa. It was in the middle of a mango orchard some distance away from the palace. Masons, joiners, painters had laboured day and night, and soon after the festival of Holi, it was ready. Now the carpenters were busy making the furniture, potters were firing the dishes, reed-workers were stitching together especially soft mats, and weavers were weaving fine cloths for the sanyasi.

'Make sure that the bed is wide enough,' the rajmata said. 'He had a lot to say about that the last time.'

'Let's not talk about that, Amma,' Kuntibhoja cast an oblique glance at Purujit and me. 'We are, indeed, fortunate to have such a great *tapasvi* as our guest. He is one of the greatest seers of all time.' The rajmata gave a derisive snort. Ignoring her, Kuntibhoja went on. 'He is the son of an illustrious father, the great brahmarishi Atri, who was born of the mind of the great god Brahma. In fact, he prefers to be known as Krishnatreya rather than—'

'Durvasa suits him much better,' the rajmata interrupted.

'His mother Anusuya, too, was a—a—' Kuntibhoja floundered for lack of a suitable word.

'*Great* mother?' supplied Purujit with a look of limpid-eyed innocence. I hid a smile. Family histories of the ruling houses of Aryavarta were our father's hobbyhorse. If he started on the stories of ancestors or antecedents, he could go on for hours.

'Besides, *munivar* is also related to us.' Kuntibhoja would allow nothing to break his flow. 'The connection goes all the way back to the earliest forefather of our line, the Chandravanshis, and some may even say that it is tenuous, nevertheless—'

'Nevertheless, the man has a vile temper,' declared the rajmata.

Kuntibhoja stroked his chin. 'They say that he is a part of the Mighty Howler, the great god Rudra himself. Just as his brother Dattatreya is—'

The rajmata clapped her hands on her ears. '*Enough!*' She glared at Kuntibhoja. 'Tell me, what are you going to do about the servants? They are not gods but mere mortals. Not *one* among them dares to serve this exalted man with his godly connections and ungodly temper. They are frightened to death of his reputation of uttering horrible curses at the mildest provocation.'

'Let's not talk about that, Amma,' Kuntibhoja said, with another meaningful glance in our direction. 'It's an old story.'

'What story?' Purujit asked. 'The one about the servants who were turned into crows?'

Kuntibhoja sent the rajmata a look of consternation. She turned upon him in exaggerated anger. 'How many mouths can you order to shut up? Of course, the servants are talking. They are terrified. Can't you put off this man? Say there's an epidemic in a village nearby—small pox, tell him that.'

Kuntibhoja was shocked. 'Amma, I can't *lie* to mahamuni Durvasa! He has *divya drishti* and knows everything about everyone. Past, present, future.' To Purujit he said, 'You may not know the entire story, *Putr*. Did your daadi tell you *why* Durvasa got angry the last time he was here?'

Purujit shook his head.

Kuntibhoja gave a grim nod. 'Well, let me tell you…The great muni is the very soul of dharma. He attaches the utmost importance to good behaviour in everyone, be it an ordinary mortal or even Indra, the king of Deva loka. He loses his temper only when he sees someone transgress, when he sees an action that is clearly adharma.'

The rajmata shook her head from side to side. 'Don't blow up the story. What transgression? One servant was a bit late in getting him his bath water, so what? It happens now and then.'

Kuntibhoja ignored her and continued to address Purujit. 'The servant was late because he was out drinking and gambling the previous night. Consequently he overslept. To hide his misdemeanour he told a lie and asked the other servant to back him. You see how one small action of adharma breeds more such actions?'

'Well, what are we to do? Servants are servants, after all,' the rajmata said with a philosophical shrug. 'They have so much to do. Who has the time to mull over questions of dharma–adharma? That is for kings and maharishis.' Turning to the problem on hand, she said, 'Someone has to look after that man for one whole year. The question is, who?'

Kuntibhoja's gaze flitted around the chamber, ricocheting off the walls and ceiling like a trapped bumble bee. It settled on me briefly and then moved away. I felt a prickle along my skin.

'I was thinking of Kunti,' he said, in such a calm, normal voice that it took a minute for his words to register.

The rajmata was dumbfounded. 'Are you in your senses?'

Kuntibhoja winced at her sharp tone, but replied evenly. 'Yes, Amma. I have thought it over and discussed it with the maharani. She believes, like I do, that Kunti is the right person. She is my foster daughter, a princess. I know she is only fourteen, but she is mature enough for the responsibility. She is circumspect and knows how to conduct herself with dignity, but at the same time she is respectful towards elders.' He made his speech deliberately slow for emphasis. 'It is all due to the training *you* have given her. Not only have you taught her deportment, she is skilled in all the household arts. Truly, Amma, she is a credit to you.'

'But—'

Overriding her protest, Kuntibhoja went on. 'She will not be alone. There will be a full complement of reliable servants to help her, all handpicked, of course. No calamity will befall us, trust me. Durvasa muni will shower blessings on us not curses.'

For a while the rajmata fulminated in silence. When she finally spoke, her tone was detached. 'Kuntibhoja, in the matter of this girl, Pritha, you have never heeded my advice. Girls in our family are taught how to run a household, trained to be good, dutiful wives in the future, but you have encouraged her to study the shastras because she has a sharp mind—that was what you said. How does a sharp mind reveal itself but through a sharp tongue? In a woman is that a virtue or a vice? Pritha may look big for her age, but she is a child. A wilful child. I have tried to tame her, but I'm not sure—' She broke off. 'With all this knowledge that you've filled in her head, she has a tendency to show off. She speaks without thinking. What if she inadvertently does or says something that annoys Durvasa? We know what his temper is like. He can ruin anyone's life. What will her fate be? Who will marry a girl with a shaap on her head? As her foster father, it is your duty to protect her while she is in your care, not put her in a difficult and, probably, dangerous situation just to suit your own ends.' Her tone hardened. 'And don't pretend that it isn't the case!'

A hangdog expression came over Kuntibhoja's face. 'Amma, you know how uncertain the times are,' he said on a whiny note. 'Although we Yadavas are a republic, Ugrasena, the mukhiya of the Andhakas, has been called our raja. He is a decent man, but his son Kansa is extremely brutal, with far more ambition than is healthy for him, or for the rest of us. Ugrasena cannot control him. Kansa listens to no one but advisors who share his worldview. You know that ever since his wedding to the two princesses of Magadha he has grown arrogant because his father-in-law Jarasandha is the most influential monarch in Aryavarta. Jarasandha is of the same ilk as Kansa. *Worse*, in fact, as he wants to conquer the world and is amassing an army for the purpose. This does not augur well for a small, peace-loving kingdom like ours.'

'And you think Durvasa can protect you?'

Kuntibhoja rubbed the back of his neck. 'There's no denying that the rishi is a powerful man. Even Jarasandha would not dare risk his anger. Besides, just his presence is enough to bring us good luck.' He tapered off under the rajmata's stony stare. 'It's only for one year,' he pleaded.

'One year is a long time in the life of a young girl,' the rajmata said. 'Pritha is growing up. Fourteen is a vulnerable age. Your guest may be a brahmin rishi, but he is still a man, isn't he?' My ears burned at her insinuation, but I felt gratified as well. She had never taken my side before. Unmindful of me she continued, 'She will soon be eligible for marriage. It isn't as if she's showing any sign of becoming a great beauty. Nor are you, for that matter, a powerful king with whom everyone in Aryavarta is likely to seek an alliance. Besides, it's common knowledge that she is only your foster daughter. If we are able to find a minor chieftain among our kinsmen for her we should consider ourselves lucky. Have you thought of all these matters?'

To my surprise, Kuntibhoja gave a vigorous nod. 'Actually, yes, I have. It is to her advantage if it becomes known that she served the great Durvasa. It raises her reputation above any looks, wealth, connections and all that.'

I felt offended. They were talking about me as if I was a slightly inferior breed of cattle that they expected to have difficulty getting rid of, when the time came to sell.

'Who knows? Maybe Durvasa muni will be so pleased with her service that he may even grant her a *vardaan*,' Kuntibhoja said.

'A boon instead of a curse? Coming from Durvasa, would that be a good thing or a bad one?' the rajmata countered sharply. She looked away into the distance. After a moment, she said in a tired, indifferent tone, 'Do as you please, Kuntibhoja. When have you ever listened to me anyway?'

Kuntibhoja chewed his lower lip. 'I think the only way to resolve this is to let Kunti decide for herself.' He turned to me, '*Putri*, it is a question of my honour. Will you do this for me?'

Kuntibhoja's request placed me in a quandary, as it was meant to. What could I reply? There was a dryness in my mouth, as if the answer had evaporated on my tongue. I looked at the three pairs of eyes trained on me, their scrutiny as intense as the midday sun. In the child's eyes I saw trepidation: would I say yes, and risk being turned into a crow? In the man's eyes there was a keen look, partly speculative partly expectant. But I was completely taken aback by the old woman's expression. Eyebrows drawn together, eyes clouded with apprehension, she stared at me with something like pity, a look of genuine concern, as if she was worried about my fate.

In an instant it was gone, replaced by her habitual aloofness. The reserve was nothing more than a mask for the unmistakable hostility she had harboured against me all these years. I would never be anything to her other than a poor female relative, cast off by her own parents. A mouth to be fed, a body to be clothed, a pair of hands to be put to use, a girl to be married off. *A burden*. I clenched my jaw, swallowing the bitterness that flooded my mouth, blinked back the tears and, forcing a smile on my lips, looked only at Kuntibhoja.

'Yes, Pitaji,' I said. 'I will do my best.'

4

The sun had burned off the day when he emerged out of the tawny twilight in orange-red robes, as if conjured by the final blaze of the dying orb. His presence seemed to affect the surroundings: the air grew leaden, the sky turned green with the rush of parrots winging their way to the nests in the mango grove, massifs of glowering clouds appeared on the horizon foreshadowing a storm. A hot wind began to blow through the trees, lifting up columns of powdery beige dust, twisting them into ghoulish shapes. As the last light faded, the freshly-painted walls of the guesthouse glowed with the effulgence of a pearl. I stepped forward to greet the traveller with the *arghya,* water to wash his feet.

'My foster daughter,' said Kuntibhoja by way of introduction.

The seer removed his wooden clogs so that I could perform my duty. His feet were big, callused, covered with dust. His legs were long and spindly as an egret's. I kept the water jug aside, knelt in front of him and touched my head to his feet.

'*Ayushmati bhava.*' The customary blessing for a long life had the heavy cadence of a sentence.

There was no way of gauging *his* age. Going by the tales, he had been around for aeons. Long ago, he had lost his temper at Indra, king of the devas, and cursed him so that the gods began to lose all their power. This led to a big event in our *itihasa*, the churning of the Ocean of Milk, an endeavour in which the devas and their sworn enemies, the asuras, had collaborated. The churning had brought forth amrita, the magic drink that conferred immortality on the devas and made them supremely powerful. All this had happened so far back in the archives of time that even the silver-haired *sutas* who roamed the land, singing the tales of gods, demons, kings and powerful sages, made it clear that they had only heard about The Churning from their grandfathers who, in turn, had got it from their ancestors. Despite being handed down so many times, no one doubted that the tales were true.

While the story was age-old, Durvasa showed none of the usual signs of old age. It was the month of Jyeshtha. He had travelled in the searing afternoon heat, but his appearance was pristine. He was tall, ramrod straight, lean to the point of being emaciated, but hard-muscled. His chest was bare, revealing every bone of the ribcage. His skin shone like burnished copper. His features were chiselled—an aquiline nose, full lips, a sleek moustache that united with a luxuriant black beard that cascaded down his chin. The forehead was high and sloping, the brow marked by three horizontal white lines with a fiery red dot in the centre. Surmounting it was a magnificent three-tiered top knot, circled by a string of the dark-ridged seed of the rudraksha tree. His water pot was a dried gourd.

'O, illustrious Mahamuni Krishnatreya, we are honoured by your visit,' began Kuntibhoja in a sonorous tone. He had prepared a fulsome speech of welcome, but our guest cut it short with a curt gesture of his hand.

'Do you have a name?' he asked me, with some degree of irritation.

'Yes, of course, Munivar,' said Kuntibhoja nervously. 'We call her—' His voice faded as the seer quelled him with a look.

'They call me Kunti,' I said.

He laughed silently, the white of his teeth flashing briefly through his beard. What about my answer had amused him? I sneaked a glance at his face. His eyes were sunken. In their depth was a glow, like a banked fire. At that moment he looked like an eagle, untamed, waiting to pounce on its prey.

'Why are you here, Kunti?'

Kuntibhoja opened his mouth but, at a warning look from me, quickly closed it.

'Because it is my duty to take care of you,' I said. 'You are our honoured guest. We are blessed to have you here.'

His gaze swivelled to Kuntibhoja's face. 'A mere child to take care of me?' Though his tone was one of polite curiosity, there was a sting in it. 'Can you do no better than that?'

Kuntibhoja's shaky composure gave way entirely. He looked like a centipede that had been knocked onto its back and was helplessly waving its legs in the air. 'Sh—she is my adopted daughter, M—Munivar. She will spare n—no effort in making your stay here comfortable.'

Without looking at me, the seer said, 'Go, Kunti, take care of my disciples.'

'Your *disciples*?' said Kuntibhoja, paling.

'Haven't they arrived?' Durvasa asked, without too much concern. 'They started out hours ahead of me.'

And suddenly they were pouring into the grove, an unkempt, ash-smeared, grumbling, jabbering mass of half-naked sadhus, the young and middle-aged trudging along, features blurred with exhaustion, while the ancient, silver-haired, corrugated with age, burnt black by the sun, were carried in on creaking bullock carts or on litters. They had been normal men once, each one belonging to the *jati* that would determine his *gotra* and name, which god he would worship, how he would make a living, who he would marry. But they had forsaken that fate, those names and homes, died to their families and been reborn for a lifetime of wandering. Now they belonged only to their guru. On seeing him, they jabbed the air with their tridents and set up a jubilant cry that rose towards the darkening sky, resounding with the splendour of a drum roll.

Bum bum Bhole.

Hara hara Mahadeva.

The seer raised his right hand, palm outward. The gesture was an acknowledgement, a blessing and a sign to be quiet. A moan ran through the crowd like a summer wind blowing over the dunes. The disorderliness of the last few moments disappeared. All was calm.

'They will be here for a few days,' he said casually. The words were for Kuntibhoja, but his eyes were on me. Was he testing me?

Kuntibhoja's face was chalk-white. 'Yes, of course! Why not?' he croaked. Turning to me, he said, half pleading, 'Putri, will you see to it?'

'Yes, Pitaji,' I said. 'The south wing in the palace has been repaired. It is empty. We can make arrangements for their stay.'

Relief washed over Kuntibhoja's face. 'Oh yes! I hadn't thought of that.' To the sage, he said, 'It's only a short distance from here, Munivar. By the time they bathe in the river the evening meal will be ready.'

A snide smile tugged at the sage's lips. He nodded and turned away.

5

The seer was up an hour before dawn. I heard him tramping down the wooden staircase, stepping out of the front door, the dead leaves crunching as he walked beneath the mango trees down the path to the ghat. It would take him a while to complete his ablutions, offer prayers to the rising sun and get back. I hopped out of bed and shook the dasi who was asleep on a reed mat on the floor.

'He's up.'

Shanta reluctantly opened her eyes. 'Does he *ever* sleep?' she grumbled.

'Tell the cook to light the fire,' I said. 'Then come up and help me tidy his room.'

Though he had stayed in it barely a fortnight, the room upstairs had acquired a patina of the sage's personality. In the murky half-light of the pre-dawn hour it was like the silent, pungent-smelling lair of feral creatures, the dimming oil lamps around the room glowing like wary amber eyes in sunken sockets: suspicious, watching, waiting. Ready to pounce. Compared to other rooms in the guest house, in here it was like a furnace. From the stale air, sweaty dampness, turmoil of the bedclothes and the empty, overturned water jug, I made out that, once again, the sage's sleep had been troubled.

On seeing the suite for the first time he had found it unusual enough to remark, 'My room is on the *top* floor?'

'Only to afford you more privacy, Munivar,' Kuntibhoja had said with the fawning air, the false bonhomie of an innkeeper trying to persuade a prospective customer to rent his most expensive room. 'The ventilation is much better too. You'll sleep soundly at night. And the view is incomparable! You can see all the way to the river.'

In response to this spiel our guest had merely raised an eyebrow and stared at Kuntibhoja till he'd foundered and thrown me an anguished look. This was *your* idea, it said. Recognizing that I would have to take care of a demanding and temperamental guest, I had suggested that some changes be made in the accommodation for him. Though Kuntibhoja had qualms he had agreed when I explained that if the seer's room was directly above mine, I'd know when he was awake and I could attend to him quickly.

I cleared my throat. 'If you are not comfortable, we have other rooms downstairs, Munivar. Pitaji will be disappointed, though. He went to a lot of trouble to make this room perfect.'

That sardonic half-smile appeared again, but he inclined his head.

The first few days passed without a hitch. He seemed quite satisfied with the arrangements, even the bed passed muster. Though his meal timings were irregular, he liked the food and tasted nearly every dish that was presented before him. He particularly relished mangoes and asked to be served aamras for breakfast and fresh sliced mangoes with milk in the evening.

He had a few peculiarities, such as a fondness for oil massages. He also liked to rub sandalwood paste all over himself. During certain hours of the day he'd meditate and we all had to observe strict silence. Sometimes he'd call me in and ask me to sing a particular song; if I said that I did not know it he'd spend an hour teaching me the words and notes, practising the lines again and again. At other times, he'd mimic different bird calls and ask me to do the same. 'Pay attention to the vibration,' he would say. '*Become* the sound.' I found it all a bit tiresome, but not particularly difficult. He was odd, I decided, but not, as I had feared, mean. In fact, I was beginning to believe that the rajmata had embellished the story of Durvasa's last visit. But one night, a week after his arrival, something happened that shook me out of my growing sense of complacency.

He was, I discovered, a light sleeper. The cry of a night bird outside his window was enough to awaken him. When this happened, I would hear the floorboards above creak. I would wait for him to call. He never did. An hour or two would pass while he paced restlessly. Then he'd lie down again and sleep till just before dawn.

That night, however, it was very dark when I opened my eyes. Still as death, sweltering. I lay in bed wondering what it was that had awakened me. The sound came again. A scrape of the floorboards above, followed by the noise of something heavy crashing to the floor. Was he having a nightmare? Was he unwell? Had he fallen off the cot? I was in a dilemma.

His instructions had been clear. On no account was he to be disturbed at night. When the noise continued, I ran upstairs, pausing on the threshold of his room. He was on the bed, but without a stitch of clothing on him. Instinctively, I averted my gaze. He whimpered as though in terrible pain and brought his knees close to his chest in a tight curl. Steeling myself, I approached the bed and knelt by his side, eyes trained on his face, but uncomfortably aware of his nakedness.

'Rishivar,' I whispered.

'Go away,' he said hoarsely. His eyes were bloodshot, unfocused, his breath hot and fetid. Sweat trickled down his face.

'Are you all right?' After a moment I laid my hand on his forehead.

He flinched. 'Don't touch me, silly girl. Don't!'

'Your body is on fire,' I said. 'I am going to send for the vaidya.'

He laughed, a harsh, grating sound. 'Fool! What can he do for me that I cannot do for myself?'

'I don't understand.'

'This is what I have inherited from Rudra.'

Inherited from Rudra? Was he delirious? Was he having a fit? An even more frightening thought came to me: was he possessed?

As if to lend credence to my fears, he began to tremble violently, eyes bulging till it seemed that they'd pop out of their sockets. His jaw opened and closed several times, the tongue finally moved, a voice emerged, unfamiliar, dull and slurred. 'The headaches of elephants, lava of volcanoes, moss in the water, sloughed skin of serpents, sore hooves of bulls, sting of scorpions, barren cracked earth, cataract of cattle, eye diseases of cuckoos...This is what he has deposited in me. This burning fever! Burn, burn...*I burn*!'

At the last word his body arched upward like a bow stretched to its limit. It would surely snap in a moment. Hardly aware of what I was doing, I darted across the room to the open window. A large earthen pot stood by it, full, cooled by the night air. I lifted the pot, carried it across to the bed and tipped it over, dousing him in cold water. He gasped in shock, his frame arched one last time, fell back, and lay still. His eyes were closed.

Fear gripped my heart. My voice came out in a desperate rasp. 'Please—please forgive me—I didn't know what else to do. Vaid ji once said that when the fever is very high, this is the only method that works.'

He remained motionless. Was he breathing? I stared at his chest. Outside in the trees an owl hooted thrice. Its cry, a bad omen, sent a chill through me. Was he *dead*?

'Munivar, please open your eyes,' I wailed. 'O deva, what have I done?'

The baleful silence around me shouted back. *Brahmahatya*! You've killed a brahmin.

Ignoring the seer's earlier warning, I shook his arm. To my relief, he mumbled something. Though I couldn't make out what it was, I noticed that he was breathing normally. After a few minutes it looked as if he was sleeping. I sat by his bedside all night, watching the steady rise and fall of his chest, till I too fell asleep. The next morning, except for the ashen look on his face and a sluggishness in his movements, he was fine. Though he did not refer to it even once, I knew that he did not want me to mention the previous night's episode to anyone.

❖

While waiting for the dasi to come up, I opened the windows to rid the room of its smells. Framed in the square of the east-facing skylight, the indigo sky above the trees was fading to a soft slate grey, brush stroked with peach and carmine. It seemed like a signal that the birds were waiting for. Pure, low notes—the soft *guturr guturr* of doves, the lilting trill of a lone bulbul—raised a paean to the day. As the sun's rays set fire to the treetops, an asylum of cuckoos began their daily practice, hysteria plaintively rising from the first trembling note, running up and down the musical scale: Koo...*koooo. Kooh...ooh.* Silence followed. And then it would start again.

Shanta came in with the broom and began to sweep the floor. She picked up the previous day's discarded garments and made a face. 'Where does he go that they get so soiled?'

I had wondered about these mysterious disappearances too. He would tell me in the morning: 'I'm going to take a head massage today. I will be in for all meals.' When I returned with the oil, he'd have vanished for the rest of that day, sometimes longer. On his return he would look battered and ravaged, as though he had been dragged backwards through the dry brush, clothes in tatters, or completely soaked and shivering as if he had taken a dip in an ice-melt stream. On several occasions he brought back souvenirs from his travels. A piece of bark, a bunch of herbs, or a solitary flower, the like of which I'd never seen before: round, dense petals, purplish pink. A snow lotus, he called it.

I mentioned these odd comings and goings to Kuntibhoja, but he shushed me saying, 'Sages as illustrious as him have *siddhis*. He does not feel heat or cold like ordinary humans. He can see and hear things that are happening far away. No doubt, our munivar can also travel in space and time without even leaving his room.'

'*Our* munivar? When did he become ours?'

'He has brought the kingdom good fortune,' Kuntibhoja said. 'That makes him ours.'

Once the room was ready, I went out to pluck flowers for the sage's puja. On the riverbank, there was a shiva kamal tree. I walked down to it, broke off several blooms and added them to the basket. He hadn't said it outright, but I knew that when he had first seen the round orange flowers with leathery petals that I'd placed on the shivalinga, he had appreciated it. There had been an almost imperceptible easing in his usual remote expression that I deciphered as a sign of approval. I was gradually learning to discern these signs, as if mapping a new country. The angle of his head, the quick upward movement of his eyebrows, the flare of his narrow nostrils told me when he was thoughtful, amused or curious.

From a high branch of the shiva kamal tree, a roseate bloom broke off and sailed gently through the air into the gurgling river. It bowled along the waves, the brisk current taking it further and further away. Though it was high summer and the river was not in full spate, it was, nevertheless, energetic. We called her Ashwa *nadi*, our Horse River. Later, as she flowed through the Kuru lands, she would merge into the mighty Ganga and conform to a more stately pace. But now she was young and restless.

Reflecting the crimson sky in her wavelets, she seemed like a slim, young dancing girl, adorned with jewels, carefree, artless and graceful in her movements. Look at me, she said with a provocative sway of hips, am I not lovely?

The sound of anklet bells jolted me out of my reverie. A gaggle of village women had arrived at the ghat to fill their mud pots. Their scarlet skirts flashed in the soft morning light. I turned away from the river and made my way back to the house, plucking a twig of the thorny babool tree to clean my teeth. By the time the seer returned, I had finished arranging everything he would need for the puja.

While he completed the prayer ritual, a line of visitors formed outside. This happened every day. They were a motley group made up of priests, landed gentry, merchants, artisans, cultivators, even hunters from the forests in the region. While waiting for the seer to make an appearance, they chatted quietly among themselves. In this way I picked up news of what was happening in the larger world outside the grove. Everyone, it seemed, was happy that Durvasa had chosen to spend a year in our kingdom. The milk from the cows had tripled—they said such a thing was unheard of in the dry season. There had been fewer dust storms and the mango crop had been very good. The wells had not dried up and it even looked as if the rains might come on time. So this was what Kuntibhoja had meant when he said that the seer's arrival had brought good fortune to the realm.

What had it brought me? I looked at the pale, tired sky, already exhausted by the sun's relentless blaze. What did fate have in store for me? At best, marriage to a minor chieftain from the Vrishni clan, just as the rajmata had predicted. Well,

I told myself, minor he may be, rich or not, his house would be *my* home, my rightful place where I'd bring up my own family. I would make sure no one felt left out. And even if I had a dozen children, I would love them all equally. I would never do what my parents had done. I would not give away a single child.

6

The stupefying heat of summer did not let up. Perspiration flowed in rivulets, clinging to the body in a sticky embrace. In the last week of Ashadh, the heat only became worse. Even the flies became comatose. We looked up to the sky almost hourly for a reprieve.

The month of Shravan came; armies of rain clouds, bulging with moisture, began to amass. Borne forward by gusts of wind, Indra's cavalry rumbled across the sky. Any day now, we said to one another. One evening, the wind grew stronger, it sang. Trees thrashed their branches about in a wild dance. Flashes of lightning and the sweeping crescendo of thunder announced his arrival: magnificent Indra riding on Airavata, his spotless white pachyderm, had appeared for a final inspection of the assembled hordes. Late that night the roiling heavens opened their gates and the fraught clouds released their load. The next morning I woke up to a world awash in the torrent.

How many ways are there for rain to fall? The clatter of fat drops on the roof, the driving rain that pitted the earth, the fine spray that had entered through the open window and pooled on the floor, the soft gush in the gutters that ran along the walls of the house—it was pouring in every nook and cranny. I listened with quiet joy to the constant drip, drip. I looked out of the window at the mystery of this world. The trees were soaked to the skin, their bark darker. Glistening leaves clung lovingly to translucent droplets that, nevertheless, glided away to quench the thirsty soil below. Turtle doves, scruffy and wet, cooed softly in clusters as they shook themselves dry under the eaves. A bedraggled grey owl peered mournfully from a hollow in the jamun tree. And there was our munivar, baring his chest, out in the open, bathing in the rain. *Am I dreaming?* He tilted his face to meet the steady shower, held out his arms in front of him, palms facing upwards as if receiving a blessing. He opened his mouth to the falling rain. There was something curiously vulnerable about the gesture, as if he was moving back in time, seeking an old connection with an earlier ingenuous, pure self.

❖

During the long weeks of the rainy season, the seer remained indoors. He was sleeping better and his temper seemed considerably improved. Visitors still came, but their number had fallen; travel during the rainy season was difficult as the rivers were raging and the bridges swept away.

The seer only left the house for brief expeditions into the forest to gather the seasonal herbs and grasses that he used in medicinal preparations. On these trips he would use the services of the forest people, the lean and swarthy Nishadha tribe. Their language was one among the many he spoke fluently. The Nishadhas lived off the land, on wild tubers, forest honey and the game they hunted down with crude bows and arrows. They knew every inch of the jungle, were adept at using it to camouflage themselves, merging into bushes, twisting their agile, well-oiled limbs into the semblance of tree stumps and branches. They were also expert thieves: the story went that a Nishadha could steal the eggs from under a nesting bird.

One day the sage returned from his usual foray into the forest. It was late afternoon, the kitchen fire had been put out, the hearth cleaned of ashes. It had been raining quite heavily and there was no sign of it letting up. He was drenched, but in good spirits. Also, he was not alone; there were at least two dozen tribals with him, bare-bodied except for the thin sheets of bark that covered their loins. They swarmed all over the house, gaze flitting over every object, fingers acting swiftly in making them disappear.

'They are hungry,' he said. 'Make khichadi for them.'

'Would you like something for yourself, Munivar?' I asked.

He shook his head, then nodded. 'I'll eat whatever you serve them.'

Cursing under his breath, the cook sent off a minion to fetch dry kindling from the palace. Other servants ran to get a pile of leaf plates and cups, clean the rice and lentils, grind garlic into a pungent chutney, churn and spice the buttermilk.

'Is it ready?' I asked the cook, an hour later.

'Almost done,' he replied, beads of sweat glistening on his forehead as he squatted at the hearth and puffed at the bellows, reached for the long-handled ladle and stirred the pots.

'I can't wait,' said a familiar voice. I whirled around.

Aware that the cook and his assistants had turned into stone through sheer fright, their eyeballs glazing over, their tongues frozen, I said quickly, 'Rishivar, I'll bring a dish to your chamber.'

'I cannot wait,' he repeated, a manic gleam in his eyes. 'I want it *now*.'

Not knowing what else to do, I did something that seems incomprehensible even today. I picked up the pot with the ladle in it. He stood and calmly ate while I held up the pot before him. His tongue did not burn, but can I say the same of my hands? The heat seared the flesh of my palm, a red-hot sword slicing all the way through the layers of skin and sinew, burning up nerve and charring bone. It felt as if the fire was devouring me. How long did the ordeal last? Three minutes, five or ten, I cannot say. All my senses contracted to a pinpoint that glowed white hot. I was not aware of falling, but when I opened my eyes, the world seemed different, skewed, peopled by unfamiliar faces wide-eyed with shock, mouth rounded in horror, staring at me. The seer was gone. I looked down at my hands, as if they were things unconnected with me. They did not seem anything like hands, but more like remains: swollen, raw, scalded, whitish pink blisters erupting like volcanic islands out of a purple ocean. A scream rose in my chest, caught in my throat, emerged as a pathetic mewling cry of distress. *Help me!* And then, mercifully, I fainted.

❖

'You showed endurance,' Kuntibhoja said, with the solemn air of someone awarding me a prize. 'It means that you are destined for great things.'

'Hunh!' the rajmata snorted. 'What great things? Have you seen those scars? Now we'll be saddled with her forever.'

'Nonsense, Amma,' Kuntibhoja said. 'Kunti has the fortitude and the courage of a true *kshatrani*. That is what those scars prove.'

Fortitude. A woman's strength is measured by her capacity to bear suffering, but is it a sign of courage? They are not one and same, are they? It would be many years before I learned the difference. It would be another woman, much younger than I, who would teach me that.

A month had passed since the incident.

'Just continue to apply the juice of the ghritakumari plant,' said Vaid ji. 'The scars will fade.'

7

The year had aged, spending longer hours in bed. At dawn the grass was bejewelled with tiny dew pearls. The light had a blurring smokiness to it. This was the time of the year I loved best. Vast flocks of geese and ducks had begun to arrive in our land to winter by its rivers and *jheels*. The air smelled clean and fragrant. The parijat bloomed, scenting the night air, leaving a pool of tiny white flowers that I picked every morning. In the world beyond the grove, life went on as it had done for centuries. The women of our land fasted and sang the melodious songs of Teej, they prayed to the goddess to bless their husbands with a long life, decorated the altar and hung swings from the branches of trees. The world prepared for the arrival of the Mother Goddess and the Festival of Nine Nights.

On Bhau-beej, Purujit came to see me. He was now three inches taller, almost shoulder-to-shoulder with me. His chest had filled out. There was the faint shadow of a moustache on his upper lip. He was learning wrestling and he was full of it, describing the various ways to grip an opponent, and the advantages of each method. How different he sounded from the boy I had known! It wasn't just that his voice was now deep, or the formal way of speaking that he had developed, it was the look in his eyes, assessing and guarded. Listening to him, I had an indescribable sense of despair mingled with regret: my baby brother was lost to me.

His gaze fell on my hands. The skin had peeled off and was growing back. The palms were pale grey in some patches and pink in others, like underdone meat. My fingers were stiff. Purujit stared aghast. I made no effort to hide my scars, but silently held them open in front of him.

He swallowed hard, reached out and briefly stroked my hands. 'I miss you, Didi,' he said, without looking at me. 'I haven't played *gitta* with anyone else since you came here.' His words were meant to console me, but all they did was leave a sour taste in my mouth. After a while he asked, 'When is the Angriest Man in the World going to leave? When will you come back to the palace?'

Sudden tears pricked my eyelids. I wasn't sure that I even wanted to return to the palace and my old life, but where else was there for me to go? I stared at my hands as if they were a mirror in which I hoped to see myself. Were new lines forming? Was Pritha's fortunes about to change? I felt the strain of months gone by, the loneliness, fatigue and anxiety that had begun to dog my waking hours.

'I wish I knew.'

❖

The remaining months passed uneventfully. The year was new again. I turned fifteen, but no one except me cared to remember the day. One morning in the beginning of Chaitra, the seer, after his prayers, sat down for his meal. The servants brought up the array of dishes. I served him as usual. He ate in silence, chewing slowly. The only hint of something abnormal came when he refused a second helping of kheer, a favourite dish of his.

'Is everything all right, Rishivar?'

He did not reply. I signalled to the servant to bring water for him to wash his hands. As the dishes were cleared away I, too, turned to leave.

'Stay,' he said. He was standing by the window, his back to me. He sat down cross-legged on the deer skin before the altar.

'Sit.'

I felt a stirring of fear in my belly, but sat down, a little to the side.

'Sit opposite me, facing east.'

I complied.

Fixing his enigmatic gaze on me, he said, 'You have served me well, Kunti.'

I lowered my eyes to hide my feelings. I had carried on with my duties as before, but my heart wasn't in it. Ever since the day my hands had been scalded, I had felt a nugget of resentment against him. Over months it had burned inside me like a chunk of glowing firewood. The heat it gave out fired up all the grievances I had against those in this world who should have spared a thought for me: my birth parents, my foster father, the rajmata and the patrani. Were my feelings of no consequence?

'I am pleased with you,' he said. 'I wish to grant you a boon. Ask of me what you will.'

I looked up, not believing my ears.

'I don't just give curses,' he said sardonically. 'When I see someone truly deserving, I grant them a boon. My boons are even more powerful than my curses.'

What could he possibly bless me with? The thought came to me that if he could curse humans and turn them into crows, maybe he could transform me into a creature of the wild, a swan. At that moment I had a very real vision of wide open skies. I was flying over the northern peaks to faraway lands. The silent swirling air currents gave lift to my wings. As I rose, I could feel the air cooling. Below lay the slowly spinning earth, its unpeopled continents and teal brown deserts, the mountain walls that bounded our land, the gushing cataracts formed by melting snows. I flew low over empty plateaus as flat as plates, hovered above the iridescent blue-green of a vast solitary lake. It was what I wanted: to fly away.

'Hurry up,' he growled as though aware of my runaway thoughts and suddenly losing patience. 'I haven't got all day.'

My vision and all its certainties melted away. I could have been a wild bird, but fate had made me a human. A girl. It had given me this existence, its constraints, and all its ambiguity. The years thus far had not brought me much happiness, of the years that stretched ahead each one was an unopened page in the book of my life. Were they blank or had the story already been written? Who had written it? How would it play out? How did I want it to end? What could I ask for? I was no longer sure of anything.

Once again he displayed that uncanny ability of reading another's mind. 'Humans have a knack for choosing precisely those things that are the worst for them,' he said drily. 'Before choosing, be aware that it is bound to produce not just a result but a reaction.'

Was there a warning in his words?

'I want nothing, Munivar,' I said.

'*Ask*!'

I took a deep breath to control my unease. 'They say you can read the future.'

A look of contempt entered his eyes. 'You want me to tell you your future—is that it?' Like a simple-minded village girl who shows her palm to an astrologer for a few coins, his tone said.

I shook my head. 'I don't want to know my future, but if you really can foretell what will happen in my life, then give me a boon that will rescue me in my worst hour.'

He nodded slowly. 'I couldn't have put it better myself. *Your worst hour*. Hmm. Hard to choose. It will be a long life and there will be quite a few of those. Let's see what we can do.'

He closed his eyes and sat so still that it was as if something had left him, a seed pod emptied of its contents. Where had he journeyed to this time? What was he seeing behind those lowered eyelids? Was he really sifting through the moments of my yet unlived life? Had its deepest mystery opened itself to him?

Is he playing a trick on me? He isn't to be trusted. A man who could burn the hands that serve him should not be depended on.

A butterfly with wings of azure flew in through the open window. It weaved its shimmering zigzag dance across the room and came to rest on his thigh, antennae twitching, wings swaying open and then shut. The fine black lines on its wings deepened the blue shade. I had never seen a butterfly so beautiful. As if my stare had intruded upon it, the butterfly took off suddenly, flying straight out of the window. When it was no longer visible I turned back to look at the seer. His eyes were open and fixed on me, their gaze calm.

'You will be the mother of heroes,' he said.

I tried to look suitably gratified, but I wasn't impressed. It was the standard blessing for a woman. Every kshatriya hoped to be called a hero, ergo every kshatrani hoped to be the mother of a hero.

'I have a set of mantras for you,' he said.

The doubts and disappointment must have shown on my face. He was going to teach me *spells*? Spells were chanted by holy men to whom a villager might plead for the recovery of lost cattle, cure a fever, harm an enemy, or lure a lover. As far as I knew, they worked, but only sometimes.

'I don't want—'

'One day you will,' he said firmly.

More than his tone it was the certainty in his words that cowed me. *One day.*

'Hold out your right hand.'

He dripped water on my palm, dribbled a few grains of rice, flower petals and tulsi leaves, all the while intoning a succession of mantras. Next he took a small brass bowl of water, covered it with his palm for a few seconds, whispered an incantation and lifted his hand. To my surprise the liquid in the bowl had turned a pale green. It smelled strange.

'Drink it.'

'What is it?'

'It will remove all your bodily impurities.'

'But—what *is* it?'

'Panchagavya.'

My heart sank. *Another test*. Keeping my face expressionless, I reached for the bowl and emptied the concoction of milk, curd, ghee, cow urine and cow dung into my mouth. It did not taste as bad as I had expected.

'Now the mantra,' he said. 'I want you to concentrate on the sound. Let the syllables sink in, one by one.'

I felt his loaded breath blow into my ear. *Om...hrim...* As the magic syllables pooled in my ear, time stopped, there was utter silence, the world receded. I felt as if I was being sucked into a void. There was a deep boom, a hot rushing wind. I had the feeling that my ear had exploded in flames. The syllables were strung on a thread of fire. They glowed white hot. They pierced my eardrum. They lodged themselves in my brain. They formed a shield around themselves. Then all was quiet.

'Each one is a *vashikaran* mantra,' he said. 'It gives you power over the gods. When you repeat it and meditate upon the god you wish to call, he will appear before you. You, in turn, will accept the *prasad* the divine being bestows on you.' He sent me a hard admonishing look. 'Don't use the mantra before its time.'

I don't intend to use it at all, I thought, but kept the words to myself.

The seer rose to his feet, held up his deer skin and shook it, as if shaking off all association with us. He wrapped it around his waist, gripped his water pot and made for the door. As he walked away, I heard the hard clatter of his clogs down the stairs. Somehow I knew that it was for the last time. He would not be coming back.

8

I was not afraid, not at first, when I heard the sound of hooves approaching, not even when the shining chariot came to a stop at the western corner of the garden, under the velvety yellow shade of an amaltas tree. It had never happened before. Seven mares white as polished silver. Creatures of magnificence, grace and luminosity. Their tails and manes were combed out so thoroughly they looked like sprays of sea foam. The horses put the chariot—a golden, two-wheeled open vehicle mounted with a plush orange seat—in the pale. Just below the seat was the charioteer's box. A man in red groom's livery jumped off the box and began to unyoke the horses. He led them to the water. The mares formed a semicircle at the edge of the pond and lowered their heads to drink. One of them moved away, rolled onto its side and began to rub its flanks against the grass. A second animal released a generous jet of urine.

'You!' I shouted, from the window of my bedroom. 'This is the king's land. Take your horses away!'

I knew he'd heard because he glanced in my direction. I gestured that he should leave, but he ignored me and stretched out under the shade of a tree, throwing the loose edge of his turban over his eyes. The nerve of him! Where were the guards?

After the sage had gone, the staff at the guesthouse had been rewarded for their service. They had returned to the palace and taken up their former duties, but I had been permitted to remain in the guesthouse. It was what I wanted; though the rajmata had objected, Kuntibhoja had overruled her. I had grown accustomed to the solitude of the place. With the sage's departure it had acquired an air of tranquillity that was like a healing balm for my despondent soul. But now, watching the intruder in the garden, I was suddenly aware that seclusion and the lack of activity had made the house, and me, vulnerable. 'Go away at once!' I shouted.

I heard a man's deep laugh. A voice behind me said, 'Oh, leave them be!'

I whirled around. 'Who—who are you?'

He tilted his head slightly and gave me a quizzical look.

The answer hit my brain like a dart. *No! Could it be—?* My heart began to beat faster. *It works! It actually works.*

It was still spring. The morning had started cool, fragranced, still dreaming. Its light poured into me, an amber glow, like honey gathered from wild flowers. The breeze fluttered through the garden with the restless energy of a whispered secret. The river, flowing in a preoccupied eager flurry at my feet, had been like a maiden on her wedding day, dressed in gold. Standing at the water's edge, drinking the splendour of this dawn, I had been filled with a longing for I know not what. An urgent ache, fierce in its intensity, yet so sweet and tender that it felt as if I was melting. Raising my eyes heavenwards, I had offered obeisance to the sun when the sage's words came to mind. *Meditate upon the devata you wish to call; he will appear before you, obedient to your command.* On an impulse I had uttered the incantation. Nothing had happened immediately, but that had been a while ago.

'Why—I mean, why are you here?' I asked.

'To light up your life,' he said, looking at me in a way that made my heart beat wildly. 'It's what I do best.'

Was he mocking me? No man had ever looked at me with such a direct gaze. It was like warm, scented oil, sliding teasingly over my body. There was a confident smile on his lips. It made him appear not just human, but very male. He was, I noted, a very handsome male. Tall and brawny, with a lean waist, well-formed calves, long, sinewy arms. Perfectly symmetrical face, narrow and angular, the mouth firm and full, the nose long, eyes large and wide-set, fringed with golden eyelashes. However, it was his thick mane, shoulder-length, untamed, incandescent as a sacrificial fire, that drew my breath away. What an aura of vitality it gave him! I wanted to touch it, comb it out with my fingers, run my hands along his thick neck, trace the line of his firm jaw.

A look passed between us that made my blood tingle. I felt a strange stirring, as if another woman, bold and feral, who had lain somewhere inside me was uncurling, sitting up, stretching her limbs. Was he reading my thoughts? To give myself time to recover, I repeated the question. 'Who are you?'

'Hmm,' he said, lowering his head to hide a smile and tapping his nose, as though in deep thought. 'At the last count I had a thousand and eight names. No doubt you, too, know some of them.'

'What arrogance!' The words were out before I knew it. I clapped my hands over my mouth and threw him a stricken look.

He laughed in pure amusement. 'Call me Mitra,' he said. 'It is one of my names. Besides, I am your friend. You called and here I am.'

'What do you want?'

'Devi, *you* called me. Don't you know why you summoned me?' He moved closer. I saw the glint of his heavy gold earrings. I felt a strange sensation, like a flame slowly licking along my spine, and stepped back.

He restrained me with his hand. 'Don't be afraid,' he said in a soft voice, slowly caressing my upper arm. 'I will be gentle.'

My hair stood on end. His words, the touch, the avid gleam in his eyes, as if he was not seeing *me* any longer, but was blinded by some deeper compulsion. Suddenly it hit me, the reason why he was here. I felt the blood drain away from my face.

'Deva,' I said. My voice shook. What was the right way to address him—O shining one? Or should it be O supreme lord? 'Prabhu, please forgive me. It was a misunderstanding.'

'A misunderstanding?' He frowned. The grip on my arm tightened.

'*Please*! Let me go!' I twisted from him wildly and freed myself. 'It was a mistake. I was just trying to see if I recalled the mantra. I didn't think for a moment that it—'

'Works?' he asked in a smooth voice. 'Yes, it does. See, I am here, standing before you. Ready to gratify your desire.'

'De–de–desire, Prabhu?' I brought my palms together in

supplication. 'M–my only desire, my sincere request, is that you leave me alone. I will never again repeat my mistake...I am a good girl, my lord.'

His look became unfriendly. 'A reckless girl. You used the mantra without thinking, but *I* am duty-bound by it. I have no wish to force myself on you, but I cannot turn back now. You called me here for a purpose, I cannot leave without accomplishing it!'

My tongue was as dry as charred wood. 'What purpose, my lord?'

The anger in his voice diminished a little. 'Your seed and mine are meant to be joined. The greatest warrior of all time will be born of the union.'

'Warrior? Born?' I repeated stupidly. 'You mean I will have a...*baby*?'

He gave a faint smile, a nod. 'You will become a mother, yes.'

The ground shifted beneath my feet. I stared at him in horror. 'I am a *kanya*! How can a maiden become a mother?'

He quirked an eyebrow as though he found the question mildly amusing. 'In the same manner as every other female.'

'An unwed mother is *not* a mother,' I cried. 'It is not her child, but her shame, her sin.'

He gave me a peculiar look. 'Bearing the child of a devata is a sin?'

'Devata, king, commoner or beast, it doesn't matter who the father is,' I said. 'An illegitimate child carries the sin of his mother.' His face was expressionless. Had I gone too far? A voice in me warned, *It will not do to cause an offence to a deva*. Yet, some deeper pent-up resentment led me to disregard that counsel, to persist. 'I am only telling you what has been dinned into me by my elders. A maiden who gives birth out of wedlock brings lifelong disgrace to herself. Worse, she brings dishonour to her entire family!'

'If you knew this, why did you call me?'

'I did not intend to call you...I was just...curious, that's all.'

'Didn't the sage warn you when he gave you the mantra?'

'He never said...' I wavered in confusion. 'He said that it was a vashikaran mantra. It would give me power over the deity I called.'

'A woman's power. Surely, you understood that.'

I was thinking hard. What *had* the sage said? 'Don't use it before its time.' Why had he chosen such ambiguous words? Why hadn't I thought to ask him what the right time would be? *He called it a boon, but it is worse than any curse.*

Sheer panic made me gibber. 'I acted from ignorance, my lord. It was a mistake, I admit—punish me, but not so cruelly. You can see the future...You *know* what this will mean for me.'

'All I know is that when you used the mantra you set the future in motion,' he said with quiet firmness. 'This son of mine must be born. He will have all of my glory.'

Glory! It is all men ever think of. 'Your son will have your glory, but will he have your name? By what name will he be called?'

The look he sent me was full of irony. 'Would it be wrong if he was called by *your* name—as Kaunteya?'

'How little you know of this world!' I said bitterly. 'By bearing a child before marriage, not only will I sully my name forever, but that of your son, too. Here, in *mrityu loka*, he will live and die ingloriously—as a *kanina*, an illegitimate! What rights will you, his father, assure him? By whose identity will he be known?'

'By his own,' he said. 'Courage, capability and conviction are all a real man needs. Through his commitment and energy he creates an identity for himself.' His gaze turned gentle, his voice, too, became soft and cajoling. 'Have the courage to break free of your fears, Rajkumari. Don't be cowed down by the opinions of others. Are you going to live only to please others?'

His words, addressed directly to the deepest part of me, brought tears to my eyes. 'What other way is there for someone like me? They say you are the Eye of the Universe. You've witnessed every day of my life, but do you understand its truth? You promise your son glory, but what of the daily humiliation? Surely, you know the fate of many an illegitimate child fathered upon a hapless maiden. Nobody will believe me if I say that a *god* fathered my child. They will mock me, shun me, shame me. Your son, too, will not escape the slander. You say that he will be in your image, but what good is that when there will be a slur on him? Honour is everything to a kshatriya. A life of dishonour for your son—is that what you want? Don't do this to him, my lord, don't do this to *me*!' I was weeping openly. 'You are a god. Have mercy on me. We humans pray to you for your grace so that our lot in life gets better. Don't ruin my life... Please—go away.'

'Do you know what it means to turn away a god?' The words, said in a quiet tone, were, nevertheless, full of menace.

'Not just you, but that careless brahmin who foolishly gave you a mantra, and that stupid king who placed a flighty girl like you in the service of the sage—I can burn all three of you to ash. Your entire clan, if I so wish.'

I knew then that there was nothing to be gained by beseeching him. He was a god. Gods were powerful. Gods were vengeful. Gods were merciless. Gods *were* what they were made of: stone. Hard, cold, unfeeling, they could never be moved by compassion; they had no heart. Themselves immune against sorrow and suffering, they thought nothing of heaping misfortune on mortals who displeased them. They had no sense of proportion either. He would curse not just me, but my entire clan. What harm had they done him? I stood there for a moment, letting resentment overtake my helplessness and slowly climb to the cool decision-making part of my brain. Blinking my tears away I looked at him. 'All right.' I could barely recognize the voice, angry and inflexible, as my own. 'This union, you say, is not a sin?'

'It is not,' he said. 'The boy is destined for greatness. He will be a hero. He will live among mortals, but he will outshine them. He will conquer death.'

'But *I* am a mere mortal.' They sounded so sad and forlorn, my own words, but they steadied me. Where there had been a fog of confusion, there was now a crystalline clarity. His son was destined for greatness, but my life was doomed to ignominy. *Unless I do something to prevent it. I have to protect myself. There is no one who will do that for me.* I took a deep breath. 'Taking a woman against her will is wrong, whether it is in your world or mine. Before I submit to you, you have to promise me that when the time comes for my husband to lie with me, I will be as pure as I was the day I was born.'

He smirked. 'Women don't need lessons in trickery. Any prostitute will tell you how to ensure that the sheets are stained on your wedding night.'

'Do I look as if I were the kind of girl who counts prostitutes among her friends? I have a reputation to protect.'

'*Reputation?*' he repeated scornfully. 'Is that all you care about? I travel from one end of the world to the other, day after day, and I hear the same story everywhere. Are you going to be all your life what other people want you to be?'

The scorn in his tone made me flinch. 'What other way is there?'

'You could be yourself.'

'What do you mean *be yourself*?' I cried. 'I am a kshatriya princess. My reputation matters to *me*! A good name sustains us in life and it is all we can hope to leave behind when we die.'

He laughed outright. 'Not just headstrong but priggish too.'

I blushed. My words had sounded sanctimonious even to my ears. 'Do you promise?' I asked.

'Promise what? The restoration of your virginity?' He gave a thin smile. 'You will not need to practise deception, my kshatriya princess. But, all right, I promise. Your reputation will not suffer. You will be blameless, pure as *gangajal*. And *now* are you ready to receive me?'

❖

When I awoke, the chamber was draped in shadows, still and empty, its blankness like the encounter that had just taken place. I remembered nothing, felt nothing, other than a strange lassitude. Looking out through the window, I saw that it was late afternoon and the garden had a quiet hushed air, as though in mourning for the world that had just died. Had it all been nothing more than a bad dream? I turned my head on the pillow. My cheek touched something soft. It was a cloth of gold. Fine spun, smooth and delicate. A vest meant for a babe. Beside it nestled a pair of earrings, miniature *kundala*, exactly like the pair he had worn in his ears. Why had he left this keepsake?

The patrani had once told me something, though, at that time, I had thought it was another of her stories. Surya's earrings, she'd said, were made from amrita, the nectar of immortality. His mother Aditi had given them to him. This was the immortality he had bestowed his son. The child whose journey had already started in my womb. A chill settled in my heart. *So.*

9

I did not show for several months. Only Shanta had remained with me. If she sensed a change in me, she did not probe. She was older by a few years, married at the age of twelve, but before she could leave for her husband's home, the husband, a herdsman, died of a scorpion bite. Her birth family did not cast her out, but they treated her only slightly better than an outcast. The patrani, hearing of her plight, offered her a place in her staff.

Shanta was given to speaking her mind. However, the year in the sage's service had taught her, as it had taught all of us, how to keep her mouth shut. Thus, when she caught me retching one morning, she did not ask any questions, but wiped my face with a soft cloth, made a drink of mint, ginger and lemon, and stood over me as I sipped it. Once or twice during the days that followed, I caught her looking at me sideways, a frown on her brow, eyes narrowed in speculation, lips pressed tight. One evening, while lighting the lamps in my room at dusk, she lingered over the task.

'There is a woman who can help us,' she said, her tone deceptively casual.

It was Vaisakh, the days were warming. The full moon,

slowly cresting the treetops in its solitary journey, was a perfect pearl set in the starry night. The air was a gauze veil, saturated with the fragrance of madhumalati and champaka. Outside the window, I saw pinpoints of golden light gliding through the darkness. Fireflies. In the tall grass and low bushes, in the trees. Burning themselves up. Were our words and thoughts, too, fireflies crisscrossing through the gloom?

'Help us with what?'

'She is reliable.'

The effulgence of something like hope lit up in me, but it, too quickly, burned out. The words of a god echoed in my ears. *He will live among mortals, but he will outshine them. He will conquer death.*

'Please think the matter over, Rajkumari,' she said urgently. 'Whatever needs to be done should be done quickly and quietly.'

Could I, a helpless mortal, deny a god his dream? I sighed. It was going to be one more long night. For the moon. For me.

❖

Purujit brought news: an invitation had come from Shurasena. My brother Vasudeva was to marry the niece of Raja Ugrasena.

'But he has just married Rohini,' I said. 'Isn't it a bit early for him to take a second wife?'

'It's a political alliance,' Purujit said. 'Devaki is Kansa's favourite sister. By marrying her, Vasudeva hopes to prevent a war between the Yadava clans.'

The Yadavas were a contentious lot, but they had managed to resolve their disputes in the past. '*Is* there going to be a war?' I asked.

'The clansmen are getting restive. Kansa's tyranny is unbearable. He levies unreasonable taxes, has spies everywhere, and uses his army to punish anyone who dares to resist.'

'And this alliance will change him?'

'Vasudeva hopes that it will restrain him.'

A cool breeze lifted off the river and tickled my skin. It had been another good year for the rains. Wasn't it enough that the grain was ripening in our fields, our cattle flourished, our forests were lush and green, our rivers full?

'Will you be going to the wedding?' I asked.

'Pitaji and I are going.' He gave a boyish grin. 'It's going to be a spectacle. Kansa will make sure of that.'

'And you'll get to see the mighty Jarasandha.'

His smile widened. 'So I will.'

'Maybe he has another daughter, or two, who might fall hopelessly in love with you.'

He shook his head. 'It's your turn next, Didi.'

The moment of flippant banter suddenly turned sour. I looked away, unable to meet Purujit's eyes. He was the one person who had brought a modicum of cheer to my life. He had been my brother, my friend, my comfort. But when I desperately needed kindness, I could not reach out to him.

'It's too quiet,' he said, looking around. 'How can you stand it?'

'I like it.'

He tilted his head and looked at me critically. 'You seem different.'

My skin prickled.

'Some weight on your bones,' he said. 'It suits you.'

A peacock cried in the forest. In the secret world inside me, for the first time, something moved. Very definitely it did.

❖

Agrahayana. Nesting season. The mornings were especially beautiful, filled with soft radiance. The earth itself wore the magical, lambent light of heaven. The sky was lapis lazuli, teeming with the rush of birds soaring over the trees, slowly gliding into the waters, paddling quietly among the reeds.

I rarely left the seashell of my room, its watery half-light a refuge for my inchoate thoughts. What was it that I dreaded—the end or the beginning? The shape of my distended belly had altered as the weight in it inched downwards. Shanta, too, had taken to remaining within earshot. One day she came in and placed a wooden box in my room. I gave a start. A cradle. She gave it a slight push to set it rocking. The inside was lined with layers of muslin.

'I could get it painted,' she said.

'Take it away,' I said tonelessly.

Her face fell. 'It will look nice once it's painted. What colours would you like?'

'None.'

'You will feel differently when it is born,' she said. 'A baby is no worse for being conceived out of wedlock. It is blameless, irrespective of what you may feel.'

I remained silent.

After a moment or two she said quietly, 'I only want to help you, Rajkumari.'

'In that case you can get me a cane basket,' I said. 'Not too big. It should have soft cotton lining and the joints must be sealed with wax.'

She looked at me in confusion. As the meaning of my words sank in she turned pale. 'You're going to be a *mother!*' she cried in horror.

I met her eyes squarely. 'Just do as you've been told.'

After a moment she lowered her gaze and left the room.

❖

The waters broke in the late afternoon. The pain followed: sharp, deep, dark. A trap that came crashing and clamped shut on a wild beast. Clawing. Snarling. Licking the base of my spine, it moved along the sides and travelled to my belly, digging in like a cleaver. Crushing through sinew and bone, nerve and soul. After it tore through me, there was a clear, clean moment of stillness. Sound and sight were restored. A windless day. Outside the window, the sun spread its light like a giant white bird unfolding its wings.

Again. It surged forward, a stronger wave than before.

'Rajkumari!'

Out of the red screaming mist enveloping me, I made out that someone was near me. Shanta's hands pressed my shoulders, mopped my brow, helped me up into a half-sitting position. I leaned against her body. Her face seemed a mirror image of mine, contorted, brow knitted in concentration. *Why does she look so worried?*

'Am I dying?'

'Don't be silly.'

'If I die, will you promise—?' The words left a trail in the air. A track going nowhere.

'Shh…Save your breath.'

'It's coming again—aaah!'

Stretching, burning pain. A radiant raging river of agony. I struggled to breathe, to break free of the swelling weight which was dragging me along in its impatient, angry push towards its own form.

Shanta's eyes rounded in wonder. 'Oh, oh, just see this! You can see the head—O deva! The hair, ears—*push*. Push harder, my princess…Here it comes!'

The first cry, a thin mewl, changed into a howl of indignation. A new sound had entered my life. Love speaks in the flesh before it forms in thought. Even before the spirit recognizes it, the body does. Of their own volition my arms reached out to greet it. He lay high on my belly, just below my heart. Slick with blood and slime that was mine too; tied by the life line that had connected him to me, he slithered his way up, blindly. The tiny bud-like mouth opened pink. Unerringly it closed on my nipple. The first tug. A trembling, and then an indescribable rush. Letting go, I floated away on a timeless sea. And slowly, slowly I surrendered my earlier self.

You are mine. Mine alone. I am a mother. Your mother.

❖

The night had paused outside my window. A night magicked away from the long procession of nights to come, all dark, a lifetime of silence. The moon hung mid-sky, an empty bowl seeking alms in exchange for a benediction; the light it shed was just enough to silver the gloom in my chamber. This half-light I have never forgotten. The stars, eyes of the universe, millions of cold, unblinking eyes, gazed down at us. I made of that starry night a fine shawl for the two of us. *It was enough*. Enough that he lay curled in the crook of my arm, warm weight and butter-soft skin, breath delicately flickering in and out as he learned to breathe the air I breathed. Enough that I could run my fingers through his thick curls, marvel that the toes and fingers were as they should be. No more, no less. A nose and two perfect nostrils. Two eyes, shut for now, in contented sleep, but I had seen them: soot black, soft and glistening, as though an earlier life still lingered in his dreams. Two ears—

Two earrings and a baby's vest. Made of burnished gold. A father's present. The promise of immortality. A gift from a god.

The night dreamed on, but I was suddenly awake. He did not stir as I slipped the vest over his head, pulled it down over his rib cage. It fitted perfectly. He did not cry as the kundala pierced his shell-like earlobes. Instead, he smiled. A rooster crowed, scratching through the darkness, letting in the milky light of pre-dawn. I placed him in the cane cradle. Despite its size it was light enough for me to lift it. I stepped out of the chamber. He slept on, the child god, his face sweet, serene, fragile. Trusting. Nothing moved, not even a breath of air. Was the world dead? Or was it that the day had arrived, too early, at a dead end? No way forward, nowhere to go. I tread the path to the ghat. A fine shadowy mist crept along the river bank, as though conniving with me. Except for a family of ducks paddling in the water there was no one about. I climbed down the cold, uneven stone steps till I reached the last one, the frontier that separated me from the unfamiliar. Towards what were these waters rushing? What was the song they were singing—a lament or a lullaby? The wavelets brushed gaily against the last step, receiving my son with fervour. The cradle rocked as it settled into the new rhythm. It rode the waters, moving away quickly. Too swiftly the current carried him away, too soon.

O child! May good befall you at the hands of all that inhabit the land, the sky and the celestial regions.

May all your paths be auspicious!

May no one obstruct your way!

10

Kuntibhoja was jubilant. 'Every eligible raja in Aryavarta has accepted the invitation to Kunti's *swayamvar*,' he said.

The rajmata made a sour face. 'Didn't I always say that getting this girl off our hands would be a problem? Three years since she matured and not a single offer.'

'She will choose her husband from an assembly of the finest suitors,' Kuntibhoja said with a kindly nod at me.

The rajmata shot him a knowing look. 'As usual, you are exploiting the situation. But this time I agree with you. Bringing everyone together in a celebratory atmosphere is a good idea. God knows, we've had nothing but bad news ever since that catastrophe at Mathura.'

The event she referred to had occurred eighteen months ago at my brother Vasudeva's wedding to Devaki. Kansa, the ruler of Mathura, had spared no expense for his favourite sister's wedding. As the host, he had been on his best behaviour. The atmosphere had been cordial right up to the end when it was time for the bridal couple to depart. While the *bidaai* ceremonies were going on, a guest had arrived, uninvited and unexpected, the sage Narada. Kansa had welcomed him with due respect and invited him to bless the newlyweds.

Narada had greeted this request with an enigmatic smile. And then, right there before all the Yadava clansmen, he had said, 'In your time till now, you have done nothing but adharma, Kansa. You have become the embodiment of evil. The stage has come for dharma to be restored.'

Kansa was unperturbed. 'Is that a promise or a prophecy, O Munivar?' he had asked, politely enough, but with a slight curl of the lip.

'Don't challenge the gods, foolish man!'

'Why not?' Kansa had sounded genuinely puzzled. 'Has even one of them ever been able to stop me from doing what I want? The gods are powerful only because we men are afraid of them. One *must* challenge the gods, Munivar. A man who has nothing to fear can conquer the whole world.'

'A man who has done adharma on the scale that *you* have has plenty to fear,' said the sage. 'Your days of conquest are coming to an end, and the final victory will be that of dharma.'

'And exactly who will ensure this victory?'

They said that the sage did not reply at once. When he did so, his tone was measured, each word resounding in the pin-drop silence, like a blazing meteor travelling through a dark night. 'Devaki's eighth son will slay you. *He* will re-establish dharma.'

They said that Kansa laughed so much that he could barely stand. 'Devaki's son?' he spluttered. 'A babe that hasn't even entered his mother's womb will slay *me*? They say ascetics like you have special vision that allows you to see the future, but you seem to be hallucinating.'

Everyone trembled at his temerity, but the sage was quite composed. 'It *will* happen.'

Kansa was known for his mercurial temper, and now his mood suddenly changed. He grabbed hold of Devaki's arm, drew out his sword and put it to her slender neck. Ignoring her terrified shriek, he snarled. 'Now will you recant, Munivar?'

The sage gave a pitying smile. Without another word, eye witnesses later swore, he disappeared into thin air. Devaki fainted. Kansa stared at her, clearly taken aback and debating silently about what to do next. He was about to plunge the sword through her, when Vasudeva cried, 'No!' It was a signal for other men who had been dumbstruck by the spectacle to recover their wits and intervene. Devaka, the father of the bride, Ugrasena, the deposed monarch, Akrura, the Yadava chief, all rushed to stay Kansa's hand.

'She is your younger sister,' Vasudeva pleaded. 'You can't kill her merely because of a passing sage's words. It will only convince the world that you take this prophecy, or whatever, seriously.'

Kansa viewed him through narrowed eyes. 'So you don't believe it will come true?'

'Narada rishi has a terrible reputation in all three lokas for making trouble. The words of such a man can, in my opinion, be ignored.'

Kansa frowned in thought. Akrura saw that he was wavering and quickly added, 'We are your kinsmen and wish you well. Listen to our advice, it is meant for your good. Killing your sister Devaki will create more talk than you can handle.'

Kansa quelled them with a glare. 'You are both wily fellows. Don't think I cannot see through your ploy. But you do have a point. I should not kill Devaki. I have a better idea. I will take care of her children.' To Vasudeva he added with a great show of politeness, 'Honour me, dear brother-in-law, by enjoying my humble hospitality a little longer.'

The guards were summoned and ordered to escort the newly-weds to their new quarters—in the Mathura prison. A year later, the rumour went that Devaki had given birth to her first child in captivity, a boy. Stillborn, they said.

❖

On the day of the swayamvar, my toilette took hours. I was up very early so that the maids could start on the elaborate rituals that would make my hair and skin glow. While they went about their tasks, they talked freely. It was all anyone had spoken about for days: the preparations for the swayamvar and the names of those who would attend it.

Rubbing oil into my scalp, Shanta said, 'I think Raja Damaghosha of Chhedi would be a good choice for our rajkumari.'

Kapila looked up from her task of spreading a handful of sandalwood and lentil scrub on my feet. 'What's so special about him?'

'Nothing that I know of,' admitted Shanta. 'But the patrani Srutakirti is the rajkumari's own sister.'

'That means nothing,' Kapila said with a sniff. 'A rival wife, even if it is your own sister, is still a rival. Rajkumari Kunti should marry someone who will give *her* the status of chief queen.'

'In that case she has hardly any choice. The rajas of Aryavarta are mostly old men. Married many times over.'

'Old men want young wives,' Kapila giggled. 'It makes them feel virile. And even if they aren't, it makes them *look* virile.'

'It is the prospect of a contest that makes them feel virile,' Shanta said drily. 'Why do you think they have come here in such numbers for the swayamvar?'

'But there is no test of strength for anyone to pass.' Kapila made a little moue of disappointment. 'It would have been exciting if there had been an archery or a wrestling contest.'

'Our rajkumari is not a prize to be won in a wrestling match,' Shanta said severely. 'Besides, she is the one who is going to do the choosing.'

Kapila shifted her attention to my ankles. 'I've heard that, years ago, the king of Kashi had organized an elaborate swayamvar for his three daughters, but it turned into such a disaster that every raja in Aryavarta has been chary of holding one since. Do you know the whole story?'

'Nobody knows the whole story except Bhishma of Hastinapur. He abducted the princesses on behalf of his younger brother, Maharaja Vichitravirya.'

'What happened to them?'

Shanta shrugged. 'They married the maharaja. End of story.'

'They say Bhishma is the finest warrior in Aryavarta,' Kapila said. 'If that is true, he must be extraordinary.'

Shanta wrapped a damp warm cloth around my hair. 'Well, he certainly chooses extraordinary means of picking out wives for the men of his family,' she said. 'Just last year he marched an army across the desert to lay siege on the kingdom of Gandhara because he sought the hand of its princess for his nephew Dhritarashtra, the blind prince.'

'And now it is the turn of Dhritarashtra's half-brother to seek a wife,' Kapila said. 'Well, this time round, Bhishma won't have a say. It will be Maharaja Pandu himself. I've heard that he has accepted our invitation...Isn't he reputed to be the best archer in Aryavarta? Maybe he'll shoot an arrow of love straight into our rajkumari's heart.' She smiled impudently at me and lowered her voice a notch. 'Rajkumari, shall I suggest something?' Without waiting for my nod, she went on, 'When you are holding the *jayamala* in your hands, take a good look at Maharaja Pandu...They say he is *very* fair. Definitely better looking than Sahadeva who is dark and squat—so what if he is Emperor Jarasandha's son?—and everyone knows that an alliance with Magadha is truly advantageous.' She added ingenuously, 'Of course, Hastinapur is much older and is still regarded as powerful. And Maharaja Pandu *is* its ruler.' She put her hand to her bosom and gave a sigh. 'So many qualities in one man! In your place, I would be tempted.'

Shanta had become very still. Her eyes were trained on me, the look in them speculative, questioning. I kept my expression carefully neutral.

The hours tarried along. I was dressed slowly, scrupulously, as a bride is decked. Ready at last I stood before the mirror. The image that gazed back looked solemn, but a little lost. *It will have to do*, I decided. I would never be a raving beauty, but the past year had done me good. My body had lost its gawkiness, grown more shapely, and gained a few inches in height. My face had acquired gravitas. The scrubs, oils and unguents had also worked their magic, leaving me with clear, glowing skin. The bridal lehenga was of a colour that suited me, butter yellow silk with a fine muslin veil, a cloth of gold. Marisha, my birth mother, had sent a wedding present, a pair of heavy gold *kangan* that I wore on my wrists. But the piece of jewellery that I liked best was what the patrani had given me, a gold girdle for my waist.

Her words, spoken a short while ago when I went to seek her blessing, had been sombre. 'Women in our society generally do not have the freedom to choose their husband,' she said. 'Some would say that you are lucky, but I believe that it is going to be a difficult test for you. Choose with your heart, but also listen to your head. Remember one thing: no matter what you choose, at some point it will become a burden.'

I turned sideways to study my profile. There was more composure in this view. It gave me confidence. But when I turned back and met my haunted eyes in the mirror the doubts returned, my heart caved in. How would it turn out?

❖

As I entered the hall it was humming with male conversation interspersed with outbursts of laughter. My knees began to tremble. The herald made an announcement and gradually the buzz gave way to silence. Everyone turned expectantly towards the head of the hall where Kuntibhoja waited to make a speech.

'Noblemen of Aryavarta,' he began, launching into an oration that I barely paid heed to, even though I stood right beside him. It opened with salutations to the gathering and a special mention of some of the august personages, Jarasandha for instance, who had graced the occasion. Kuntibhoja then did a quick round-up of all the revels of the past few days, who had won which dicing game and who had thrashed his opponents in wrestling. And now, he said, we had arrived at the finale—the swayamvar of his foster daughter, the virtuous Kunti, also known as Pritha. He harped a fair amount on my virtue and enumerated my qualities in very general terms: good pedigree, sweet-tempered, mature, skilled in housework. He dwelled on the good luck I had brought him and repeated the high praise that Durvasa rishi had bestowed on me. At this there was a murmur in the hall and several nods of approval; Durvasa's word obviously counted. It felt a bit strange to be thus evaluated. I thought there was something quite hollow about his speech. At last, Kuntibhoja went to his throne and sat down; beside him was my birth father Shura. Along the length of the hall were two rows of suitors, seated on ornately-carved chairs. They were in all shapes and sizes, the noblemen of Aryavarta, decked in their finery, even if several of them looked slightly dishevelled and hung over. The celebrations had been on for about four days, friendly matches of hand-to-hand combat, sword fights, archery contests, chariot races, dice games, followed by nights of entertainment, eating and drinking.

Why had they come? Was it for the spectacle alone? It was true that a swayamvar was a rare event, an anomaly. The more acceptable way in our society was for the prospective bridegroom's family to advance a proposal which the girl's family could accept, or reject with a plausible enough excuse. Sometimes, when a king had too many daughters of marriageable age, or even one daughter who had not received a single proposal—as was the case with me—he resorted to hosting a swayamvar to which everyone of royal birth was invited. Had all these men made an appearance because refusing the invitation would have been seen as an insult? Kuntibhoja had claimed that the tale of my year in Durvasa's service had been doing the rounds of Aryavarta. No other recommendation was needed, he had implied. The ability to please the most demanding man in the world was considered a rare asset in a woman. Was I some kind of freak? Was it curiosity that had brought them here, as would be the case with those who travel to see a calf born with two heads? The Woman Who Pleased the Angriest Man in the World. What would they say if they knew that I was also The Woman Who Gave Birth to the Sun God's—*No, don't think of that.*

As I began my slow walk down the wide aisle separating the two rows of suitors, I felt as though I was in a trance. No longer in my body, no longer in control. Was I even capable of choosing? I clutched the heavy garland of fresh pink lotuses and tulsi leaves, half afraid that it would fly out of my hands and encircle the wrong neck. Purujit walked beside me, supporting my elbow to prevent me from tripping on the edge of my lehenga if my knees buckled. I was glad of the veil even though all it offered was flimsy protection against the gamut of male stares: bold, ogling, assessing, curious, intent, expectant, speculative, sleepy, or just plain jaded.

The herald called out the names and titles of each aspirant for my hand. There was some excitement in the air as I stood before some of the more renowned suitors. I had heard that bets had been placed in the gathering; gambling was in the blood of kshatriyas. There was a collective sigh as I moved away to the next man, even a joke or two, but all this changed to apprehension as I passed an entire row of suitors and reached Jarasandha. I could make out that Purujit was a bundle of nerves. He hadn't quite lost his boyish admiration for the monarch.

Fortunately the emperor was fast asleep. As I slowly came to stand before him, he gave a loud snore. There was a nervous titter among his neighbours, almost of relief. I started on the other side. Damaghosha of Chhedi, a heavy-set, short-legged man with pockmarks on his face, leered at me and I felt a twinge of pity for my sister Srutakirti even though I had never met her. As I came to Sahadeva of Magadha, Jarasandha's son and heir apparent, Purujit squeezed my arm. But I ignored the pressure and moved on. Reaching somewhere in the middle of that line, I felt the sweat beads forming on my brow. My heart was pounding so hard I thought everyone would hear it. Kshatriyas, though disciplined on the battlefield, could be an unruly bunch elsewhere, quick to draw arms. If I passed this row, too, without selecting anyone, it would be perceived as a slight by the entire gathering. Kuntibhoja would never be allowed to live down the shame. And I would remain a spinster all my life.

The herald, too, seemed to be growing increasingly desperate. His voice carried a note of urgency. 'Maharaja Pandu of Hastinapur,' he proclaimed. 'Born into the ancient illustrious clan of Bharata. Noble son of Maharaja Vichitravirya, grandson of Maharaja Shantanu, great grandson of Maharaja Pratipa...'

It was only when I heard the cascade of trumpets, drums beating, the conch blowing that I snapped out of my daze. My arms were empty. The garland had moved almost magically from me to him. Purujit looked relieved, Kuntibhoja beamed his approval, even Shura looked pleased. Were they approving of my decision, or just thankful that I had, at last, made it?

It was done, it was over.

PART TWO

Pandu

1

Marriage, for a woman, begins with a journey. She leaves her father's house to spend the rest of her life among unfamiliar people. Which place does *she* call home—the one she is expected to give up or the one she is required to embrace and serve? What part of herself does she discard? What does she take forward? After seventeen years in Kuntibhoja's house, I had only a handful of happy memories, the rest was either pitiful or painful, frequently both. Thus, when the time came for me to leave my foster home, I did so without regret. I left behind nothing, I took nothing with me. Not even a personal maid, as was the custom.

Purujit accompanied me to the edge of Kuntibhoja's lands. It was early morning. The countryside was quilted in lime yellow and parrot green, the colours of Basant. We stopped at the border to say our goodbyes under an azure canopy that unfurled in all directions. It looked untouched, that heaven, filled with diamantine clarity, pure and bright as the future upon whose verge I stood. The sun was mild, the air silvered with the sound of harness bells and the creak of wheel axles from the long cavalcade that would follow us on our journey. Kuntibhoja had not been miserly in his wedding gifts, bestowing cattle, cloth, gold and gems to enrich the coffers of Hastinapur.

The journey took three days. My vehicle was a covered cart pulled by a team of strong bullocks. Pandu rode a lighter open chariot driven by two black horses. He brought it alongside my cart.

'Tell me something about yourself,' he said.

'I was born Pritha,' I said. 'I am called Kunti.'

'What would you like to be known as?'

'I don't know who Pritha was, so it will have to be Kunti.'

He smiled, as though he appreciated my answer. He had nice teeth, white and even. His skin was the colour of sandalwood paste. He had the high forehead and narrow face of a scholar, but his mouth, with the lower lip fuller than the upper, hinted at sensuality. His jaw was square, with a faint dent in the chin.

'It will have to be Maharani Kunti,' he said.

A shiver of anticipation ran through me. He was watching me. Beneath half-closed eyelids, his eyes were tawny gold, smudged with something dark and untamed. 'As my consort you will have the status of patrani, but that position should have gone to my half-brother's wife,' he said. 'It would be prudent if you display the respect due to her.'

'Oh.' I felt deflated. *Strictures already?*

Maharani by accident, the rajmata had said when she heard that I had picked Pandu at the swayamvar. She said it with a pitying smile and a certain gloomy satisfaction, as though it was just the kind of flawed choice that could be expected from me. 'Everyone believed that the crown would go to the elder son Dhritarashtra, although he is blind. They even declared him *yuvaraja*. But when it came to the actual coronation ceremony the *mahamantri* had an objection—and the younger boy Pandu was quickly made king.' She had looked at me askance. 'One has heard that all is not well with him either. His father Vichitravirya didn't live a long life.'

'Nonsense, Daadi,' Purujit had said in robust defence of my choice. 'Maharaja Pandu is in good health, able-bodied and fit. He is the finest archer in all Aryavarta. I saw it for myself in the archery competition. He determines the exact position of his target simply by the sound it makes.'

The rajmata was unimpressed. 'Hunh! *Sound* is all the Kuruvanshis can make. To flash and flaunt is all they know. They have not forgiven us Vrishnis for breaking away all those centuries ago. They look down on us. Take it from me, girl, the Kurus will never let you forget what a big favour they've done by tolerating you in their fold.'

Just as you tolerated me in yours.

Her words had raised some apprehension in me, but on that immaculate morning, I banished all qualms about the future. I would make an effort, I told myself, to win the haughty Kuruvanshis over.

Keeping my tone friendly and interested, I said to Pandu, 'Please tell me a bit about your family.'

'You'll meet them soon enough.' My face fell at his reply. He must have noticed, for he said in a more kindly way, 'What do you want to know?'

'What is she called, your elder brother's wife?'

'Maharani Gandhari.' After a moment he added, 'Bade Bhaiyya likes being called maharaja. After the coronation, I insisted upon sharing the title with him.'

'Do you let him wear the crown too?'

He gave me a look of surprise. 'How did you guess?'

I smiled but remained silent. Lowering his voice as if we were conspirators, he said, 'When we are alone, he tries it on. Vidur, the mahamantri, is a stickler for rules and doesn't approve, but we don't worry about that, Bade Bhaiyya and I. The crown is his as much as it is mine.'

'And the throne of Hastinapur?' I couldn't resist asking. 'Do you and your elder brother take turns to sit on it?'

He shot me a wary look. 'No, of course not.' Staring at me uneasily, he said, 'I hope you will not ask such improper questions. It will upset people.'

'I'm sorry…I don't want to upset anyone.'

He seemed placated. 'It will take you a little while to settle in the ways of our family,' he said. 'You may find one or two people slightly intimidating. Bhishma Pitamaha, for instance, and Daadi Satyavati, but that's only their demeanour. They are both wonderful.'

'What about your mother?'

'Mothers,' he corrected drily. 'I have two.'

'I was given away in adoption,' I said. 'I've never known what it is like to have even one.'

'*One* mother would probably be fine. Two can be—' he paused, searching for the precise word, 'overpowering.' I raised my eyebrows. He looked sheepish. 'They are sisters and were widowed quite early,' he said. 'They haven't had much of a life.'

'Did your father die in battle?'

'No,' he said curtly. 'In his bed.'

The tight set of his mouth warned me not to pursue the

subject of his family any more. I turned away to study the landscape.

Our procession was winding through the countryside between the two great rivers, Ganga and Yamuna. This was the heartland of the Kuru kingdom. A fertile, level terrain, folded here and there by hills covered with forests. The fields, ripening with wheat and barley, glowed like a mantle of gold. Lulled by the cart's rhythm, fanned by the spring breeze, I dozed off intermittently on the cushions, and the finer details of that journey seemed like scenes from a vision: grazing grounds where young men tending the cattle slept under the trees; grey, dry bush where herds of chinkara, leaping gracefully into the air, sped away in alarm at our approach; dark groves housing votive altars dedicated to the spirits of the countryside, stone deities daubed in red and ochre, grinning fiercely at passersby. Lamps burned before them, and offerings—flowers, milk, fruit and grain—placed earlier in the day by the worshippers were now being eaten by marauding monkeys and twittering sparrows.

At dusk we stopped near a rivulet. The animals were unyoked. The sound of their jangling bells was a new note in the evening cacophony of bird cries. As the day wound itself down and the orange glow of sunset faded, fires lit up in a string along the length of the caravan. I was grateful for a chance to stretch my legs. Watching the distant stars radiate their luminescence in the night sky, I wondered if they were silently plotting out my future.

In the late afternoon of the second day we came back to the river, the Yamuna, broad and placidly smiling. On its bank was a deep, tangled and strangely forbidding forest.

We skirted along its edge. An uncanny hush prevailed over the place; even the wind seemed to hold its breath and the creak of our carts tore through the silence in a way that made everyone nervous. In between the trees, barely visible in the murky light of the jungle, I caught a glimpse of an abandoned city, secretive, sinister, a place of broken columns, shattered brick walls, gaping windows and doors that led nowhere.

'What are those ruins?' I asked.

'Khandavaprastha,' Pandu said tersely. 'Don't look that way—the place is cursed.'

And yet I could not help but look. Khandavaprastha, I knew from Kuntibhoja's tales, was where the ancestors of the Kurus had first established their kingdom. Why was it abandoned? The stillness seemed to be accusing the world for ignoring what had happened there. I shivered and closed my eyes, falling again into a doze. With every *yojana* that we travelled, the past seemed to drop away. Was it, I wonder, really a new beginning, and if so, for whom?

'Wake up,' he said, shaking my shoulder. 'I want you to see something.'

The sun had begun to go down. Silhouetted against its blood-orange glow, his face looked like an image fashioned from gold, a supernatural being, half-human half-god, unfathomable, out of reach. The wind played with his hair, raising it, pushing it back; a vein throbbed delicately in his temple. He looked so striking that I felt awash with a fierce passion. *My husband. He will give me children. I will never call upon a god again.*

'This is the spot from where you get the first glimpse of Hastinapur,' he said. 'I wanted us to see it together.'

Together. For me that one word melded our destinies even more securely than the seven circles around the sacred fire that had joined us in marriage. Love between a man and a woman seems a mystery, intimate yet subtle, its nebulous shape a rush in the blood, an imprint on the soul; its essence to be divined in songs, stories, secret yearnings and dreams, but never to be evaluated, examined or weighed in words. It is unknowable, until the moment one is struck by it. And then it is as if the world is lit up from within. He had touched some coil deep inside me and, as it sprang to life, I was filled with an urgent desire to cover the desert of my existence with something meaningful and lasting that I could create for him alone. But even as the desire was born I felt its death. *He is a man. He will break my heart one day. Only a man can do that.*

'Look!' he said. 'Can you see it?'

In the far distance stood the high brick ramparts of the city. The light of the cow dust hour was a gossamer-fine ruby haze that dissolved the landscape, softened its edges so that everything seemed imprecise in its contours, like a dream resting upon air. Beyond the walls, I caught a glimpse of flat white roofs rising as though built upon a gradual slope, surmounted finally by the glinting, gilded domes of the palace. I knew it was a bustling city, but from that viewpoint the impression was of immobility and unchangeableness. Nothing that happened here was lost or insignificant. There was never a time when it did not exist, never be a future when it would not be. We were merely passing through. Hastinapur would outlast us all.

The evening was filled with the strident cries of birds

coming home. Even so, we clearly heard the squeak and scrape of something approaching us. At first I could not make out what it was, but as it drew near, I saw that it was a massive *ratha* in the shape of a swan. Pulled by a pair of caparisoned elephants, it was fifteen feet high, half as wide, with two decks. The upper deck was covered with a canopy of red silk. Below it was a *gaddi,* the size of a double bed. On the lower deck was space for several attendants. Behind this strange contraption was a procession with soldiers, white-turbaned dignitaries from the city council, and musicians clashing cymbals, beating kettle drums, blowing conches and strumming on stringed instruments.

'Prepare yourself, Kunti,' Pandu said, his tone conveyed displeasure at the sight. 'That weird object is the grandest ratha in Hastinapur. Grandest as well as the oldest—it belonged to my great grandfather Maharaja Pratipa's chief queen, Maharani Sunanda.'

'Who is the *sarathi*?' I asked, watching with interest as a trim, agile man of medium height got off the charioteer's seat, handed the reins to a groom and came towards us, breaking off from the sedate walk into a little run, his face changing from grave to smiling as he approached us. There was decorum in his manner, but familiarity too.

'Vidur,' Pandu replied.

'The mahamantri?'

'Vidur, my younger brother.'

I can never forget that night, its witchery. It was as if I was finally reaching some place to which I'd been journeying all my life. The gates of Hastinapur were flanked on either side by a pair of giant stone elephants. Soldiers stood on the ramparts holding up flaming torches. The air was like the finest muslin, soft, delicate, shimmering. *Alive.* Saturated with light. Hastinapur, first among cities, was a golden bubble. Oil lamps burned along the labyrinthine streets, they trembled in corners where lanes met and parted ways, they peeped out from doorways and windows, they were arrayed on the colossal flower arches that had been erected all along the route to the palace—I counted six. The countless dancing flames, the radiance from the lamps, the wavering edges of shadows made everything look ethereal. From temples across the city bells pealed in wave after wave. There were people everywhere, lining the roads, peering out of windows, looking down from the rooftops, hanging out of doors whose lintels were decorated with strings of fresh mango leaves. The shining round faces of children wordless with wonder, the faces of men and women, young and unlined, mature and wrinkled, all seemed bathed in a shared joy. They were cheering, they were chanting. I listened.

Maharaja Pandu ki jai.

Maharani Kunti ki jai.

He was their king; they were welcoming me, his queen. I saw then, bright and vivid, a vision of the life I wanted to lead.

2

The night surged on like a powerful river. The instant I entered the great lighted hall, I felt the undertow of history's current tug at me. Dominating its length were the stone idols of illustrious ancestors: Bharata, Samvarana, Kuru, Hastin, Pratipa, Shantanu. Below them, in flesh and blood, was the family to which I had been given. The welcome rituals for the bride seemed endless, but they allowed me time to observe my new relatives. Led by Vidur, with Pandu by my side, in strict order of protocol, I touched several pairs of feet while their owners murmured the traditional blessings of a long married life and the flowering from my womb of a hundred sons.

The rajmata was first. Satyavati was in her mid-sixties, but her face was youthful, narrow and artfully made-up. It was not an attractive face, it lacked warmth, was too fixed in expression, the chin was too pointed, but it was still a fascinating one. Her eyes were dark and smoky, their gaze distant but compelling. Her mouth, red and sensuous, was no longer pliant but tight-lipped, as though, over the years she had become accustomed to frequently conveying censure by merely moving a tiny muscle, raising an eyebrow or pursing her lips. She was not tall, but she held herself erect in a way that made her seem so. The dove-grey silk, a colour sober enough for a widow, looked both cool and exotic on her. She smelled of something warm, moist and mildly exciting.

'*Chiranjeevi bhava*,' she said, blessing Pandu first. Her voice was husky. A smile of genuine affection transformed her face. The glow was there just for an instant. Then her gaze shifted to me, and grew cool and sceptical as she sized me up. Her mouth twitched ever so slightly. '*Sowbhagyavati bhava*,' she said, with the utter disinterest of an attractive woman viewing an ordinary one.

Pitamaha next. He was almost as old as Satyavati, but unlike her he had that rare and timeless quality called charisma. An untamed, animal-like magnetism that was a combination of alertness and arrogance, a vigour evident in the lithe grace of his long limbs, a will visible in the square stubborn jaw, and an intelligence that radiated in the bright, amused, almost challenging look on his face. Standing with his legs apart, elbows slightly out, head held high, he had the air of a man who was fully aware of the enormous power he commanded, yet sure enough of it to appear unpretentious. His lush mane, liberally silvered, came up to his shoulders, lending him both dignity and charm. His eyes were deep set and expressive. *You would do well to trust me,* they said. *But you had better not cross me.*

'Welcome, daughter-in-law.' His voice was both powerful and pompous. The look he gave me was kind and, indeed, welcoming, even if it did seem to gloss over me. I was, after all, only another female.

Moving on, I found myself opposite the former princesses

of Kashi, Ambika and Ambalika. Though the scandal of their abduction by Bhishma from their own swayamvar and the subsequent forced marriage to the yuvaraja of Hastinapur had occurred long ago, it was still talked about—as an example of kshatriya derring-do. At least two years separated the Kashi siblings in age, but they looked like two peas in a pod. Beautiful they undoubtedly were—in the lush style that sculptors use to endow carvings of apsaras, the heavenly nymphs, and that, to men, epitomize feminine beauty. Skin like freshly-churned butter, thick, curly hair tinted brown, curves lovingly landscaped—from the bee-stung pout of their red lips to the pop-out twin gourds of their breasts to the pinch of the narrow waists widening into broad hips and shapely thighs. Even the drab, loose, ochre-coloured widow's garments could not quite conceal the lusciousness of their bodies. Pandu's terse reply to my query, earlier in the day, about how his father had died flashed through my mind. In his bed...*obviously with these two*. I lowered my head to hide my expression and dutifully touched their feet.

'Sowbhagyavati bhava,' Ambika murmured in a breathy voice and, lifting me up, pulled my head to nest in her soft, cushiony bosom. Seemingly overwrought by emotion she burst into noisy sobs. After a moment or two, I gently disengaged from her heaving, tumult-ridden embrace. The younger sister Ambalika, Pandu's birth mother, was more composed. She raised her right hand, palm outwards and calmly repeated the blessing, but her eyes, large and hazel brown, were clouded with anxiety. She studied her son's face, quickly but carefully, and the stitch on her own forehead deepened.

We moved on. Did I imagine it or was there a ripple of apprehension in the gathering? Vidur's tone was carefully calibrated as he made the introductions, respectful and formal.

So this is Dhritarashtra.

Strangely, given their similar heredity, there was no obvious resemblance between Pandu and his elder brother. They were opposites in the way that the burning blaze of the mid-day sun makes the cool light of dawn appear weak—less than what it is. If Pandu had appeared wiry at first glance, he now seemed puny. Dhritarashtra's physical proportions, his sheer vitality, drew every gaze to himself, making other men in the room look like pale cadavers. He was tall, taller even than Pitamaha, and built like a bull, broad-shouldered, bulging muscles, immensely strong. His forehead, high and rounded, had the smoothness of a rockface weathered by the wind. But it was his gaze that was terrible. His eyes pinned me under the weight of that heavy-lidded, emotionless gaze. He could not see me, yet I felt as if he could. His lips curled in a tight, catlike smile.

'Welcome, Maharani,' he said, in a flat drawl. 'Please accept our salutations...It is a day of good fortune for Hastinapur now that its maharani has arrived.'

'Maharaj,' I said, as calmly as my dry mouth and pounding heart would allow. 'I am so much younger in age than yourself. Please do not belittle me. I have a name. It is—'

'*Of course*, you have a name,' he said silkily. There was a look of sly amusement on his face. 'What is it now? Pritha?' He swivelled his head to the right and left, addressing the gathering as if he were discussing the name to be given to a new cow. 'Shall we call her Pritha?'

There was stunned silence in the room. I glanced at the man beside me, my husband, but he looked straight ahead, a meaningless smile frozen on his lips.

'*I* am going to call you Kunti,' said a soft voice, well-bred yet firm. 'Not maharani, but my younger sister Kunti.'

The blindfolded woman on Dhritarashtra's right held out her arms to me, inadvertently brushing him aside. His face was, for a brief moment, contorted in fury, but it no longer mattered. Nothing mattered. All that counted was that I had a friend. Knees buckling with relief, I clung to her.

'And you will call me didi,' Gandhari concluded.

'Thank you,' I whispered.

For an instant her embrace tightened as if to reassure me, then she let me go.

I do not remember much more of that night. I was led away by maids down lengthy corridors lit by torches to my own wing in the palace. The hands of strangers undressed me, washed and dried my body, helped me into a fresh set of clothes, offered me food and drink. I was shown into my bedchamber, a room with arches and pillars and high ceilings, full of gloomy shadows cast by the light from tall stone lamps. The air was scented with pine incense. Bone-tired, I climbed into the bed, surrendered my head to the pillows, and was immediately swallowed by the deep river that was the dreamless, voiceless night.

3

I had travelled to Hastinapur not merely to begin a new chapter, but also to seek refuge from a painful past: I had entered it as its queen. At times, it seemed like a hallucination. When in those early bewildering days did the realization sink that all this was really happening? Was it when I found that I had to do no more than look around and people came forward to wait on me? Not only were they attentive to my smallest need, they seemed eager to satisfy my wildest fancy, as though a smile or a nod of approval from me was all they craved. Was this how queens really lived—from one whim to the next? Or was it just a ploy to keep the armies of dasis occupied? Did I really need four women to wake me up or help me with my ablutions? Was it necessary to have my hair done every day by a *sairandhri* who favoured an elaborate, time-consuming style and insisted that I wear a gold and gem-studded *chudamani* on my head? Did I need so many clothes? Couldn't I dress myself?

No, I was told. I may not have secured the world's gaze, but that of Hastinapur was firmly fixed on me. What colours I favoured, what jewels I wore, what I said—everything about me was duly noted, not always by admiring eyes. I felt, at times, a twinge of regret for my former life. I had been of no consequence, but that meant I had also enjoyed a certain freedom. The ruling family of Hastinapur imposed an iron discipline on its women: again and again, I was reminded that to be a queen, I must be *seen* as one.

Pandu had tactfully suggested that my first task every morning, after the bath and dress ritual, should be to present myself before my two mothers-in-law and seek their blessing. It would ease their loneliness, he said, to chat with me. In reality, however, it was an opportunity for the two Kashi sisters to assess my appearance.

There was something unreal about Ambika and Ambalika. There had been a third sister, Amba, the eldest of the trio who, too, had been abducted from the swayamvar long ago, but her name was never openly mentioned. That ensured her a permanent place in the dimness where illusions are formed; like any self-respecting wraith she had gained breath through the whispered stories. So much so that the remaining two siblings, although flesh-and-blood, seemed like pale understudies, the residue of another fuller persona. In Ambika and Ambalika the form was all too present, but in their eyes there was a lack of purpose, a missing lambency that made them seem not inaccessible, just impervious.

'Don't pull your hair back so,' Ambalika would say to me in her taut voice. 'Your forehead is too broad.'

'The sairandhri wanted me to have five ringlets on my forehead, but it looked silly.'

The crease in her brow would deepen. 'Maybe she knows what she's talking about.'

Enter Ambika with a small smile of sympathy cast in my

direction. 'Give her time,' she would say, her tone equally placatory towards both her younger sister and me. 'She'll learn.' After a pause she'd add softly, 'Of course, one can't compare with a *real* princess like Gandhari...Even the rajmata says that Dhritarashtra's wife has a wonderful sense of dressing.'

Ambalika's mouth would twist in irritation. 'Much good it does her! All anybody ever notices is the ridiculous blindfold she insists on tying.'

A chill would settle over Ambika's features. 'My daughter-in-law is a devoted wife.'

'She's nothing but a drama queen.'

Ambika's face would turn pink; she'd throw a reproachful glance at her sister and retire with a wounded air to the open balcony. For a while, she'd determinedly ignore everyone, pretending to teach her parrot, a foul-tempered bird, to sing a song that her late husband had composed as a paean to her considerable charms. It started innocently enough with *O lotus-eyed one* and quickly jumped to the *twin worlds of your breasts* before leapfrogging on to *hips that are the house of lust.*

'Stop it,' Ambalika would plead at this point, looking at me uneasily. 'Can't you see that you are embarrassing poor Kunti?'

'It's all right,' I'd murmur. 'Please let her sing—if it makes her happy.'

Ambika would break off and stare into space. She'd turn to me and say: 'Oh, he was *such* a romantic man, my lord, so virile. As his patrani, I should know...Dhritarashtra has the same sort of vigour. He, too, is a real tiger among men.' A beady look would enter her eyes. 'Did you see the love bites on Gandhari?' She would point at the fleshy upper reaches of her bosom and say. 'There was one just here.'

By now I would, indeed, begin to feel embarrassed. For a moment or two there would be complete silence in the room. Ambalika would shoot a look at me from under her long eyelashes before pointedly changing the topic to something that made for more appropriate conversation. After several minutes of aimless chitchat I would make my escape.

❖

I knew they were whispering. Not just the mothers-in-law but the maids as well. Nothing was ever private in a palace, certainly not the conjugal relations between the maharaja and maharani. I wasn't imagining the pitying looks on the faces of the dasis who came in every morning to wake me up after Pandu had spent a night in my chamber. They would look at me, purse their mouths, and look away. But who could I go to about this strange quandary that I found myself in?

I decided to speak to the sole person who could do something about it—my husband. It was early morning, the only hour of the day when we would be alone together; the rest of his time would be taken up by the sabha, in meetings with officials, in consultations with Vidur and Pitamaha, or in the company of Dhritarashtra. That morning, as we walked through the palace gardens, he was describing to me a hunt that involved a rather long-winded pursuit of a wild boar. Like his Kuru ancestors, Pandu was inordinately enthusiastic about hunting. He was in mid-flow when I interrupted.

'This isn't easy for me.'

He looked at me with concern. 'Am I boring you? Shall we talk of something else?'

'Let's do that, Maharaj,' I said with a forced chirpiness. 'Let's talk, for a change, about what the whole palace is speculating about.'

To give him credit, he didn't pretend to misunderstand. A guarded expression entered his eyes. After a moment, he said, 'We are one, Kunti. The marriage rites have made us stakeholders in each other's lives.'

Such prosaic words! 'But not in each other's bed.'

'There is nothing to be discussed,' he said coldly.

There was a lot to be discussed: I was hurt by his indifference to me. My yearning for him had been tamped down, over the days, into a dull but persistent ache. He'd slept a few nights in my chamber. I'd tried with hesitant caresses to convey my ardour to him. His hands had moved over me. I had felt him tremble with desire, sensed an urgency. But it would end abruptly with him pulling away, murmuring that he was tired; he'd fall asleep, or pretend to.

For the first few nights I lay still, reassuring myself that it was enough: with him beside me I was safe, nothing bad would ever happen to me. But, as the hours stretched and the lamps dimmed, as he turned away and dropped deeper into his own separate dream, I lay awake, strange thoughts rising in my head like spectres from lives past. Foreboding would fill me, a paralyzing fear that the shadows on the ancient walls were inching closer. Despite his proximity and his part in my life, I would never have a complete understanding of him, of his strange nature. Below his characteristic poise, I sensed murkiness in the depths. He was my husband, but that was one of his many roles, a mask that he could put on and exchange for another, at will. Slowly, seamlessly, our relationship—that seemed to exist only in daylight, in full view—was making a mask of me as well. I was losing myself. His queen but not his wife—what was I becoming? Finally, the inky darkness of those silent nights would engulf me, as though I, too, was another forgotten chapter that had entered Hastinapur's long sinister tale. What happened, or did not happen in this bedchamber, would become, as dawn approached, one of those things that were not to be discussed.

I stared at him. Despite my distrust, I felt the hot melt of desire; it swamped my senses so that his mere presence made me lightheaded. Why could he not feel some part of what I felt? *Is it me? Is there something about me?*

Seemingly unaware of my feelings, he resumed his former conversational tone. 'Pitamaha is going away for a few days to inspect the borders of the Kuru country. I will be busy with him and the rajmata till late evening. What are you planning to do with your day?'

'I'll find something,' I said, making it clear that I didn't particularly care whether I did or not. 'One of your mothers teaches her parrot how to sing. I could give dance lessons to the swans in the lake.'

A twinkle entered his eyes. 'I wouldn't put it past you, Maharani Kunti. There's an iron will in there. I get the feeling that when you set your mind on something you don't rest till you get it.'

'Nothing could be further from the truth, Maharaj,' I said, bitterly.

To my surprise, he smiled. There was sweetness in it,

and affection. He reached out for my hand and, pulling it gently, brought me close to him. 'Let us be friends, Kunti,' he said, looking deep into my eyes. 'Let's get to know and understand one another…It isn't possible here in Hastinapur where there is so much to claim my attention, and you, too, have onerous duties to fulfil. If only we could get away for a few days to some quiet place. What do you think? We could go away to the forests in the foothills of Himavat. Solitude is what we both need.'

Does he really mean it? Does he want to spend time with me? My heart leapt at the thought. And yet, that watchfulness, now a second nature to me, made me say, 'A king should never be away from his kingdom without a good reason. It gives the wrong message.'

He dropped my hand as if it had bitten him. 'In my case it would be the right message!' he said sharply. 'I did not want this kingdom. It belongs to my half-brother, do you understand? I was happy to be its *senapati*, take charge of its army, extend and secure its borders.'

I listened to him in silence. Deep down, hadn't I begun to sense his repugnance to his role as king?

He eyed me angrily. 'Do you even know what it feels to be born in a palace like this one? It's suffocating. You are a puppet dancing to many strings. Who pulls them—fate, family, society—it does not matter. You are doomed to dance till it kills you!'

I was shocked by his reaction, but I had some idea of what he was feeling. The House of Hastinapur was proud of its antiquity and held it up for display. Every piece of furniture stood exactly where it had stood for centuries; when it fell finally, another exactly like it was placed in the same spot. It also meant that every human had his or her own proper place in the hierarchy—a way of behaving, a manner of speaking—and was expected to keep to it. No one spoke out of turn, neither did anyone speak their mind. We were all puppets, but who or what was manipulating us? Was destiny just a glorified name for tradition that had turned repressive?

He said: 'The outdoor life, pure, clean and free, is all I have ever wanted. In the open, with my bow and arrows, I feel truly alive. Instead, I have to spend hours closeted in the council hall, pretending to listen to the myriads of problems of my subjects, nodding my head solemnly and opening my mouth to give direction and ruling on legal and administrative matters that are of absolutely no interest to me. Vidur sees to everything, anyway. I just have to put my seal on it...That is what this crown is all about. I have got it by default! It should have gone to my brother. He grew up believing that it was his. He was destroyed when it was taken away from him. I *begged* him to take it, but he would not...Perched on my head it isn't anything but an unbearable weight! I want nothing more than to shed it.'

All those hours in Dhritarashtra's company have given him a deep sense of guilt.

Choosing my words, I said, 'My foster father's kingdom was nothing in comparison with Hastinapur, but even we had heard of your wonderful reputation, Maharaj.'

'Not mine,' he said, his face closed. 'Pitamaha's reputation is what has upheld Hastinapur and kept our enemies at bay. He is the giant banyan of dharma under whose umbrella we tiny creatures survive. As long as he lives—and it may well be forever—no harm can come to Hastinapur. It doesn't matter who is planted on the throne, Kunti. Pitamaha is there to protect us.'

'From without, yes, but from within?'

He looked at me with suspicion. 'What do you mean?'

I took a deep breath and tried to marshal my thoughts. 'I am told, day in and day out, that I must be *seen* as the queen. By extension, does that not mean that you, the king, who is the protector of dharma in his kingdom, must be seen as strong, just and farsighted? You understand warfare, my lord, you know that a commander of an army needs to be focused only on victory in the battlefield, but in the day-to-day governing of his kingdom, what must the king look for? The bigger picture and all it entails. In other words, the king should be seen as a man of vision.' I paused. He was listening intently to every word. 'A blind king on the throne, Maharaj? What would your subjects make of that?'

'What are you trying to say?'

'Only what the shastra says. The king protects his country, not the other way round. *He* serves the country and not the other way round. You are a scion of the great Bharata who established this dictum, your forebears upheld it time and again in the past. Going by it today, *you* are the right person to sit on the throne of Hastinapur. The right to rule is not a laddu to be divided and enjoyed between siblings. It is a duty to be accomplished.'

'These can't be *your* views!' he said, with an edge to his voice. 'Who has been talking to you?'

'No one.'

He looked disbelieving. 'For a moment just now you sounded exactly like Vidur.'

I sighed. 'Maharaj, I have barely met the mahamantri, and always in your presence. We don't communicate in sign language with each other.'

He had the grace to look sheepish, but only for a second. Then he adroitly changed the subject. 'Yesterday, when I had lunch with Bade Bhaiyya, Gandhari Bhabhi inquired about you,' he said. 'Do call on her.' It was worded as a request, but it was clearly what he required of me.

I nodded. My life had changed irrevocably, but it seemed to me that not much was different.

4

'You never visit me, Kunti,' she said, gently reproachful.

'I hesitated only because I thought you were busy.'

Gandhari looked rueful. 'My music lessons do take up a lot of time.'

'You're studying music!'

'Why not?' She sounded amused. 'One doesn't need eyes for it, only a good ear.'

'Yes, of course,' I said in confusion. 'I happen to be tone deaf, which is why I was impressed.'

'Gandhara has a rich tradition in sculpture, music and dance,' she said. 'Dance would be difficult for me, wouldn't it? Have you noticed how many pillars they have here? There are twelve in my apartment alone. When I first arrived, I kept bumping into them.'

I stared at her, speechless. We were sitting in a spacious and airy pavilion overlooking an enclosed garden with a lily pool. Gandhari was wearing pale yellow, and looked cool and graceful as a water lily herself. Though she was just a few months older and had shown friendliness from the start, I have to admit I was ambivalent about her. She was, reputedly, the most beautiful woman in all Aryavarta. She was also, they said, uniquely blessed by a boon from Shiva. Her womb was prolific—it would bring forth a hundred sons—which made her the most sought-after woman in all Aryavarta. And now, because of the blindfold, she was being acclaimed as the most *virtuous* woman in all Aryavarta.

Staring at her openly, I couldn't make up my mind. Beautiful she undoubtedly was. Blessed, probably—though how any woman could give birth to a hundred babies was beyond me. But virtuous? Is choosing to be blind so that you are not better off than your handicapped husband a sign of virtue, or just plain show-off? The blindfold was impossible to ignore, it had made her the cynosure of all eyes. It was common knowledge that her father had acquiesced to the match under a threat of his kingdom's annihilation. A new thought came to me: *Maybe the vow to wear it lifelong is a subtle revenge against the people who have forced her to marry a blind man. Maybe even against the man himself.*

It was late Vaisakh. A pale ghost of a breeze sighed tiredly through the ashoka trees at the garden's edge. There was no one else with us but Gandhari's maid, a sturdy, slant-eyed woman with an impassive look. She had accompanied Gandhari from the kingdom in the mountains, and never left her unattended. Indeed, she seemed an extra limb of her mistress, in the way she anticipated her every wish even before it was articulated.

'Will you have some pomegranate juice?' Gandhari inquired with charming solicitousness.

The maid silently reached for the jug and was about to pour when Gandhari said, 'Let me do that, Saubali.'

The maid hesitated, then handed over the jug to Gandhari,

placing a tumbler before her. The ruby red stream flowed out of the jug till the tumbler was full. Not a drop spilt.

'You're amazing,' I said.

Gandhari kept the jug aside, trying to, but not quite succeeding in hiding the look of triumph. 'It takes a bit of practice, but it's easy.'

I sipped the drink and remarked on its sweet, refreshing taste.

'The pomegranates of Gandhara are the best in the world,' she said. 'My brother Shakuni ensures that we get a regular supply.'

'With so much from Gandhara in your life here you probably don't miss it,' I said politely.

'No.' Her tone was distinctly cool. 'I don't miss what I cannot see.'

I was stricken. 'Didi, please forgive me if—'

'You haven't said anything wrong, Kunti. I am learning to adapt to my new life in Hastinapur, as no doubt, you, too, are learning...How will I do that if I keep harking back to Gandhara?'

'Didi, I didn't mean that!'

She gave a brittle laugh. 'It's just that it's—taking me longer to adjust than I had expected.' Her mouth trembled. The maid glanced sideways at me and murmured something quickly in a strange dialect. It sounded like a warning. Gandhari steadied herself, assumed her earlier composure, the slightly superior air that the black band across her eyes somehow heightened. After a while, Saubali said something again, just a short phrase. Gandhari stiffened and turned her head towards the door leading into her rooms. Dhritarashtra was approaching us with his large confident stride. Though he was accompanied by an attendant, he seemed to have no trouble finding his way towards the pavilion.

'So this is where you hide,' he said.

A strange look passed over Gandhari's face, like the shadow of a cloud skimming over a lake's still surface. Then she smiled. A teasing, playful smile that somehow, I felt, did not reach her eyes. 'Ah, so you *have* discovered my secret place,' she said in a tone that sounded artificially bright.

He stood still. 'You're not alone,' he said harshly. 'Who is there with you?'

I stirred. Gandhari gestured to me to be quiet. 'No one, my lord. Just my maid.'

He smiled, a slow, lewd smirk. I glanced at the maid and saw that she had turned pale. Her eyes had a hunted look. I cleared my throat. He turned his head to face me, nostrils flaring with suspicion.

'You're bluffing! There is someone else here.'

'Only me, Jeth ji,' I said quietly. 'Didi was just playing a joke on you.'

The transformation was immediate, like a chameleon changing its colour. A snide, sly look passed over his face. 'Ahh! *Pritha*—my dear sister-in-law,' he said smoothly. 'To what do we owe this good fortune?'

'The good fortune is mine, Maharaj.'

'No, no, please don't say that,' he went on in the same velvety tone. 'Gandhari, you must look after our guest. I hope you have invited her to eat today's lunch with us.'

'She's *not* a guest, my lord,' Gandhari said. 'She's my—'

He cut her short by raising his voice over hers and

insisting, 'But she is, Gandhari...It isn't every day that the maharani of Hastinapur thinks of honouring us with a visit.'

There was an awkward silence. Then Gandhari calmly said, 'Do have some pomegranate juice.'

'Thank you,' he said, and took a seat, making it clear that it was his intention to stay.

Saubali came forward with the jug. As she stretched her hand to pour the drink, he reached out and casually squeezed her breast. Hard. Saubali shut her eyes for an instant, then opened them and stared straight at me. There was a strange, animal-like expression in her eyes, a mixture of helplessness, shame and resentment. Its message was clear: *Now, do you understand? What is the maharani going to do about it?*

Shocked and sickened by what I had witnessed, I averted my gaze.

The morning dragged on, but its charm had fled. Gandhari and I chatted in a forced manner. Dhritarashtra did not comment, but the smirk on his face was so unsettling that I could only envy Gandhari the protection of her blindfold. Did she feel as I felt, that beneath all the empty things we were saying, the platitudes and the polite responses, there was now something else—a crouching silence, sharp-edged and dangerous—listening to every word? A short while later, much to my relief, the servants came to lay out lunch for us. Gandhari was the perfect hostess, urging me to try the different dishes, but everything was ashes in my mouth. After the betel nuts had been served, I stood up to take leave.

Gandhari held my hand and squeezed it. 'I didn't know how quickly time fled,' she said. 'I enjoyed your company so much that I'm going to invite you again. You will have to make time for me, Kunti.'

Dhritarashtra gave a kindly nod. 'Better invite her soon, Gandhari,' he said, his tone jovial. 'Pritha is going to have no time for you. Shortly, she will have company of her own, or maybe one should say *competition*, hmm?'

I had a nauseous sensation.

'What do you mean, my lord?' Gandhari asked.

He placed an arm possessively around her shoulders and drew her close, but his unblinking gaze and the predatory grin were directed at me alone.

How can a blind man's empty gaze hold so much malice?

'Oh, am I to be the one to break the good news?' he said with a fake self-conscious air. He shrugged as if to show his helplessness. 'Well, then…The rajmata has decided that Pandu needs another wife and Pitamaha has succeeded in securing one for him. That, too, after paying a hefty bride price.' He paused and added slowly as though savouring every word, 'Madri, the sister of Raja Shalya of Madra-desh, will soon be a *sapatni* to the patrani.'

At the precise moment that the death-blow lands, you don't feel a thing but the heavy force of it. Perhaps at the moment you are dying your senses become sharper and you become intensely aware of the world, or some tiny, insignificant aspect of it. Gandhari's ramrod-straight posture. Dhritarashtra's large hand around her narrow waist, his fingers splayed to rest possessively on the swell of her breast. The persistent buzzing of a bumble bee. The thunderous noise of something crashing inside me. It evaporated in me at that moment—the prospect of happiness.

5

The room was cool, its air scented with vetiver. I found her standing by the window, looking out at the day. At that hour the sun's rays ricocheted off the earth's surface with blinding force. In the distance was the river Ganga, diminished in this season to a silver thread, frayed in parts. Closer was the sweep of the sandy bed where local cultivators had laid out carpets of green by planting vines of musk melon and cucumber.

'I don't like ornamental gardens,' Satyavati said. 'They are an extravagance.'

This was the first time I was in her apartment. The contrast between these rooms and the wing I inhabited was stark. With none of the rich furnishings and ornate furniture, it was the space of an anchorite: a low platform bed in the centre and, by the window, a reed mat on which stood a short-legged silver stool and a few cushions. An earthen water pot sat in the corner.

'Sit down,' Satyavati said, directing me towards the mat with a nod of her head. I obeyed, tucked my legs under me and waited. The right side of my head was throbbing with a dull pain. She studied me in silence. After a few moments of holding her inscrutable gaze, I felt uncomfortable and looked away. Though I had dressed carefully and done up my face, I knew that the kohl around my eyes, however well-applied, did not hide their puffiness.

'For some women tears are an indulgence,' she said.

I returned her look stonily. *What would* you *know about tears?*

She gazed past me, as if addressing someone else. 'Tears are nothing but your will turned to water…and when that happens the battle is as good as lost.'

My resentment bubbled over. 'Why are you telling me this when you are the one who has brought this humiliation upon me?'

Her eyes widened. 'Is that what you think?'

'Yes!' Despite my effort to control them, the tears started afresh, hot and choking.

'You *love* him?' she said, on a rising note of incredulity.

Is she laughing at me? I wiped my eyes and stared at her defiantly. She raised an eyebrow to remind me that she was waiting for a reply.

'Yes—yes, I do.'

She looked thoughtful, then made a moue of regret. 'Lust is needed to build a dynasty, but *love*? It is too tenuous an emotion. He is a king. His duty is to provide heirs.'

'What makes you believe that I can't give him an heir?'

'He cannot wait forever.'

I felt the heat rise in my face. Was she suggesting that *I* was the one at fault? 'You mean *you* cannot wait. You and Pitamaha. Are you two bent upon leaving a legacy of suffering and sorrow?'

A look of distaste passed over her face. 'Spare me the melodrama.'

'It is not drama. It is an ordinary human emotion called suffering. But what would you know about that?'

She tilted her head to one side as if giving serious consideration to my words. 'I am not heartless,' she said, her tone mild. I looked at her silently. 'You've eaten nothing for three days.' She shook her head as though reproving a five-year-old child. 'Nothing to eat and nothing to drink…Why?'

'I am not about to die of starvation or thirst. Don't worry, Rajmata, you won't have another woman's death to account for.'

She puckered her brow. 'What do you mean?'

'I am neither blind, nor deaf, nor a fool,' I said. 'I don't know exactly what happened all those many years ago, but the story of Rajkumari Amba's humiliation is still told in Aryavarta—she killed herself, didn't she?'

Her face became stern. 'I don't quite see what relevance that has to what we're discussing today,' she said coldly.

'She blamed Pitamaha for her plight, and she wasn't wrong. Who enters a swayamvar, uninvited, and abducts not one but *three* princesses? Only Bhishma, on behalf of the House of Hastinapur. Who marches all the way to Gandhara and threatens to wage a war unless the princess is given in marriage? Who pays an exorbitant price to purchase a *second* bride for a king who has been married barely two months? Only the Hastinapur royal family—and you say you are *not* humiliating me?'

She was unperturbed. 'Marriages between noble families are arranged for reasons that are obviously beyond *your* understanding. What would you, with your Nagavanshi blood, know about that?' She paused, as if choosing her next barb. 'You were adopted by the Bhojas, I'm told. Are *these* the manners that they taught you, or did you get them from the Vrishnis who gave you away?'

'Please don't bring my family into this,' I retorted. 'This is only between you and me.'

Her mouth curled. 'Between me and you—and who exactly do you think you are, girl?'

Inwardly I cringed, seeing myself, for a moment, through her eyes. *An upstart! A girl who has married above her station and cannot adjust to her new life.* I was nothing more than a nuisance; a needy, sulking, ill-mannered girl. I was suddenly angry with myself and with her. With everyone. As the rage mounted, a part in my brain began to cool and the emotions congealed into words. 'Not just a womb, Rajmata, but a little more than that. I—I am the maharani of Hastinapur.'

Not a muscle moved in her face. 'That you are,' she said, with such calmness that it took the wind out of my sails.

She clapped her hands. Maids came in with covered plates and placed them on the low table. After they'd gone, Satyavati went to the water pot and poured out two tumblers of water. She removed the cloth covering the plate before me. I looked down and was surprised. It was not made of silver but of ordinary clay. Neither did the food look as if it had been prepared in a palace's kitchen. A small heap of cooked rice, dal with ridge gourd, a portion of greens, a smidgen of ghee. There was also a bowl of spiced buttermilk.

'You know what they call me in Hastinapur, don't you?'

she said with a hint of irony. 'The Fisherwoman…The food from my kitchen is simple, but I hope you will enjoy it.'

I gaped at her. Was she a shape-shifter? As the aromas from the dishes curled up my nostrils, I swallowed hard to keep the saliva from flooding my mouth, but I made no effort to touch the plate. She waited, then reached out with a deep sigh, mixed the rice and dal into a bolus as one would do for a small child, and held it to my mouth. What else could I do but accept and swallow the morsel? We ate in silence. The meal was over all too quickly. My plate was clean, not a grain on it.

She waited till the maids had removed the dishes and placed a platter of bananas before us. When they'd gone, the rajmata spoke. 'Even after forty years as their queen, they hate me. Hastinapur has not ceased to blame me for depriving it of its rightful ruler—Gangaputra.' She used the name by which she always called Pitamaha. 'If only my sons had lived…' She stopped and looked at me as if uncertain about how to proceed. 'Samrat Shantanu never forgave me either. Can we truly say why we act the way we do? Can we blame it on Kama deva, who knows how to arouse our senses? All the samrat felt for me was lust.' She shrugged. 'Maybe lust is all a king can feel for a fisherman's daughter. Maybe it was all *I* ever felt—when you are young, your emotions are influenced by the awakening needs of your body as much as by the rosy visions that fill your head.'

I shifted uncomfortably. *Why is she telling me all this?*

'My father was Uparichara Vasu, the king of Chhedi,' she said. 'I never saw him, neither did I see my mother, a fisherwoman. When I was born, I had a twin beside me. A boy. My father gave me away to Dasharaj, the chieftain of the fisherfolk, but he kept my brother and made him the king of Matsya.' She smiled sadly. 'Our stories are not so dissimilar, after all...If I had remained a fisherman's foster daughter, time would have flowed over me the way the river passes over a tiny pebble. But, owing to a king's desire, and my own dreams, I became a queen. Now I will forever be judged. What verdict does the future hold for me? Will it be sympathetic, or will it ask uncomfortable questions about me?' She threw her hands up. 'My foster father Dasharaj insisted on an outrageous condition to my marriage. As a result, Gangaputra, then crown prince, had to give up the throne for *all* time. He took a vow of celibacy, became Bhishma. Why did I allow myself to become the instrument of such a huge injustice?' She sighed. 'I have had forty years to answer that, yet I have no ready answer. I tell myself that I was young and had no say in shaping my life. But you may then ask, wasn't it flattering for a girl like me to be wanted by a king even though he was older than my father? And didn't I, deep down, want *this*, all this, for myself?' She leaned forward and searched my face. 'Tell me, what would you have done in my place?'

I tell myself that I was young and had no say in shaping my life. 'I don't know,' I said uncertainly.

'I like to blame it on my foster father Dasharaj,' she said. 'He was a cunning fisherman. Once he discovered that I had caught the eye of the Kuru samrat, he used the fisherman's tactic for bringing in a big fish: let the bait sink in, play it along till it is deeply embedded in the creature's flesh, and only then start pulling in. As for me, I had grown up believing the tale of my royal birth. At one time it had made me feel different from the other girls I grew up with. I was convinced that I was meant for a better life.' She hesitated as if she was about to tell me a shameful secret. 'They used to call me Matsyagandha.'

I was astonished at the cruelty of the name. Fishy Smell.

'It hurt at that time,' she admitted. 'But now, quite frankly, I don't care. I know who I am and what I have done for the people of Hastinapur. Let them call me Fisherwoman or any name they choose. So what?' Her tone was cool, the sardonic glint back in her eyes. She continued: 'However, Gangaputra had a good reason to hate me. He deserved to be king. He ought to have been the father of sons who would have grown to be strong like him. *I* was the reason all that was snatched away from him. But if ever he saw it that way, he did not show it to me. He gave me the respect due to a mother, never disobeyed my wishes, treated his two young half-brothers with affection. He was the perfect son in all respects but one…When the circumstances changed, he, too, should have made an adjustment. It was nothing more…But he did not agree.'

I waited, but she did not elaborate further. She looked out, lost in her reverie for several minutes. The sun had crossed its zenith. Shadows appeared outside the window, slowly lengthening, like a dream scene that begins sweetly enough, but foreshadows a nightmare.

'We had a few good years,' she said. 'Everything seemed to go well. There was peace on the borders, prosperity within. The gods were kind. It even seemed as if my "crime" might have been forgiven. But I wanted more than the grudging acceptance, the reluctant respect of Hastinapur—I wanted wholehearted admiration.' As if chiding herself, she continued, 'That was my mistake: I asked for too much. *Birth* is the defining circumstance of our life, even though all women's lives are the same.'

When Shantanu had known that his time on earth was coming to an end, she said, he had been haunted by remorse for what he had done to his eldest son. 'At times, he said that it was the lust that ran in his blood. His ancestor Yayati, too, had exchanged his old age for his youngest son's youth so that he could continue to enjoy the pleasures of life. At other times, he would rant about how he had betrayed the trust his forefathers had placed in him, that a king must choose his heir based on merit alone...He said that he should never have revealed his passion for me, because, after all, Gangaputra did only what was expected of a dutiful son; he, Shantanu, had left him no choice but to make a terrible sacrifice. He, Shantanu, had failed as a king...This went on and on, the self-judging, self-loathing and self-flagellation.' Her eyes were misty with rekindled pain. 'I wasn't spared either. He would look at me with *such disgust*. Worse, he couldn't bring himself to even look at my two young boys. They weren't his sons, he said, but his sins...As he lay dying, I promised Maharaja Shantanu that nothing, *nothing* would endanger his noble line. Kuru blood ran in me and my sons, too, I said. His grandsons would rule from the throne of Hastinapur, they would remember him with respect among the names of his illustrious ancestors.'

Shantanu died and Chitrangad, the elder of Satyavati's two sons, was crowned king. As he was still too young to rule, Gangaputra stepped in as protector of Hastinapur. He took charge of his half-brothers. 'He would have made men out of them,' Satyavati said. 'But I made it difficult for him. I was a bad mother to Chitrangad and Vichitravirya; I spoilt them with my love. It was only after Chitrangad died that I grew desperate. Vichitravirya was the sole heir. We'd made him yuvaraja, but what if something happened to him? He was not mature enough for marriage, but I was terrified that some calamity would befall him too. Then we heard that the raja of Kashi had invited the eligible young men from all the ruling houses of Aryavarta, but he had not invited the crown prince of Hastinapur...It was a deliberate slight, of course. Traditionally, the House of Koshala has always offered their marriageable daughters to us.' Her voice grew pained. 'But the raja had some idiotic notion about holding a swayamvar! I hounded Gangaputra to do *something* to avenge it. And he did what he thought was best.'

At her behest, the story went, Bhishma had abducted the princesses of Kashi. She gave me a curious look. 'I've heard that you are well-educated...I have a question for you. Among kshatriyas, it is acceptable, isn't it, to abduct a marriageable girl?'

I nodded, feeling vaguely uneasy about the conversation. She was talking about the *rakshasa* form of marriage. The capture and abduction of a girl of marriageable age is one of the eight forms permitted by the shastras. Not just permitted but, in the olden days, even encouraged. Yes, it would have appealed to Bhishma's strong sense of pride. By abducting the princesses, he had not only avenged the slight to the House of Hastinapur, but also established his supremacy before a gathering of his peers *and* won brides for his half-brother.

'Since you brought up Amba's name, I have this to tell you,' Satyavati said. 'As soon as she told us that she was secretly betrothed to Shaalva, king of Saubha, we understood that there had been a blunder, albeit unintended. We tried to make amends by sending her to Shaalva, who, she claimed, loved her and would accept her. She was sent with all due honour, as we would have a daughter of this house, but you know what happened...She was just unlucky, that girl Amba. Shaalva should not have rejected her, poor thing! It was not honourable of him, was it?'

I was astounded. Was she really so naïve? Had she *no* idea of what it meant to be born a kshatriya? Manliness is *everything* to a kshatriya. Honour is the armour he wears to protect it. It has to be solid and shining. How can he respect himself unless his peers respect him?

'When Pitamaha defeated him in battle after the abduction, he left Shaalva with no other option,' I said. 'For him, Amba was now another man's wife. How could he take her back? If he hadn't rejected her, Shaalva would have been the laughing stock of all Aryavarta. It was hard on Amba, but he did what was obligatory for him.'

She looked at me with something like admiration, but behind it there was a glint of—was it *triumph*? Nodding her head, she said, 'Shaalva did what was necessary for him, but what of her? She had nowhere to go. Her reputation was destroyed forever. If he had truly *loved* her wouldn't he have understood her terrible plight?'

'No kshatriya will love a woman so much that he will risk being disgraced,' I said wryly. 'Duty and honour are the two limbs that make a kshatriya able-bodied—in his own eyes.'

Her gaze was level with mine. I saw naked steel in it. 'If you understand this, you understand everything,' she said. 'Pandu, *too*, is bound by his dharma. He will have to do his duty by his ancestors and by his kingdom. And, no doubt, you, who know so much about kshatriya dharma, are also aware of what *you* should do.'

The mask was down. I recognized her for what she was, the hidden hunger in her. She was a predator, patient and wily, but also focused and ruthless. In her eyes was the clear message to me: while fertile wombs were absolutely essential to the Kurus, hearts as fragile as mine were dispensable. I was outclassed, I had sense enough to realize it. The fight went out of me. *Now there is only pain.*

She leaned forward and plucked my hands out of my lap, spread the palms out gently and studied the scar. Then she looked at me. There was genuine compassion in the soft curve of her mouth, but her eyes remained unrelenting. She had said whatever she had called me to hear. We stood up. It was time for me to leave. At the door I stopped and turned. She looked up with some irritation. *What now?* As though having finished this rather annoying little business with me she had firmly put me where I belonged, outside the circle of her attention.

'Love…' I stopped as my voice shook. Steadying it, I continued, 'Love is a choice *I* made. I chose him from a gathering of the most powerful men in all Aryavarta. Not because *he* was the most powerful man—you and I know that there are more powerful than he. Not because he would make me a queen—we both know there are other men who would have done the same. And not because he alone would give me sons—we both know that it may not happen. Your spies are everywhere, aren't they? Are you certain that they have told you the truth about what goes on in my bed?'

'I need no proof of my grandson's manliness,' she said, sounding amused. 'Desire is a strange thing, but even more strange is the lack of it—especially in a scion of kings like Nahusha, Yayati and Dushyanta. They were all virile men. It runs in their blood.' She smiled in a kindly way and delivered the blow. 'No, the trouble lies elsewhere.'

I flushed. 'There's *nothing*—'

'These things happen,' she said firmly. As though counselling me, she added, 'In time you will accept it.'

I tried to grapple with what she had just said, the finality of it. *This is not my home. These are not my people. Even if I live my whole life in their midst, I will remain an outsider.* Tears, treacherous tears, rose to my eyes. *It's true, then. He doesn't find me attractive...It is me he has a problem with. Everyone knows this!*

Her face, wiped of all emotion, seemed like a death mask. Only the eyes flashed briefly. '*You* are the maharani,' she said with slow deliberation. 'Whatever you do, don't let anyone see you cry.'

She turned back to the window and resumed studying the view.

6

That day the sairandhri came in early. Towelling my hair dry she started to work on it, giving her full concentration to the task. On my part there was none of the usual fidgeting or grumbling while she slaved over my coiffeur; instead, I was as still as a corpse. My hair, lustrous and fragrant after the wash, was brushed, braided, looped and pinned into place at the back of my head, high but not right on top. Finally, she fixed a lotus-shaped chudamani on my head and handed me a mirror.

I studied her effort and asked with exaggerated politeness, 'To which era does this hairstyle date?'

Pat came the reply, equally formal: 'Maharaja Pandu's great grandmother used to wear her hair like this.'

I smiled sweetly. 'So now when Maharaj introduces me to his new wife, he can say, *Meet my great grandmother*... Well done!'

The sairandhri pursed her mouth in disapproval. 'Maharani Sunanda was a discerning woman with a good sense of style.'

'Times change, and so do styles.'

'You have the same bone structure that she had. She, too, was taller than average, broad-shouldered and—'

'Plain?'

She shot me an exasperated look. 'This style brings out your best features, plays down the heaviness of your jawline, makes your neck look long and graceful, and takes the attention away from the broadness of your shoulders.'

Studying my image again, I pulled out a pin and let down a strand on one side, curling it around my finger. 'It's too formal.'

'True,' she agreed. 'Only a maharani would have the confidence and ability to carry it off.'

I narrowed my gaze. *Are you being insolent?* Our relationship had been cool, but I had begun to recognize that she was an artist in her own way, passionate about her work and good at it. Why shouldn't she take pride in it? It wasn't her fault that she had *me* to work with; I'd never had time for anything but a simple, unfussy single braid. Indeed, her skills were wasted on me. I smiled in capitulation. 'All right. Let's show them what a real maharani looks like.'

She accepted the unspoken apology with a slight tilt of her head. 'We could loosen it a bit,' she said, plucking out another pin. 'It will still look classy but contemporary, more befitting your youth.'

A dasi came to help me with my clothes. As I dressed, the sairandhri watched with an odd expression. 'What?' I asked. 'Don't you like the dress?'

'That colour?'

It was the green of tender mango leaves. 'Why not? It's a colour that I happen to like. It symbolizes, I've been told, renewal and fertility...The right message to those who are speculating about me.'

'It is also the colour of jealousy.'

I glared at her. 'Is *that* what they are saying?'

'No, but they are asking questions.'

'Such as?'

'What drove Pitamaha to agree to pay a hefty *kanyashulka*? Gold, gems, elephants, horses, cattle, chariots, slaves. Was it, indeed, necessary to pay bride price for a *second queen* when the first one is barely two months old? Is Maharaja Shantanu's line in danger again?'

'*Again?*'

Her gaze slid away. 'I don't know,' she muttered. 'It's just what some people are saying.'

I had a feeling that she *did* know, but I was not going to get it out of her. I removed the clothes. 'Take them away.'

'What shall I bring instead?' the dasi asked nervously. 'What will you wear for the wedding feast?'

A guest at my own husband's wedding—what should I wear? 'Fetch the dress that came last week,' I told the dasi. It was a colour that Pandu's mother Ambalika had picked out when the cloth merchants from Kashi had brought samples to the palace. The exact shade of the sindoor in the parting of my hair. The colour of rage, torment and murder, but also the colour of life and desire. The colour of marriage.

An hour later, when I presented myself before them, the two mothers-in-law looked me over in silence. Ambika raised an eyebrow, Ambalika gave a thin smile. They both looked away. *Good!*

'They must be waiting for you to start the ceremony,' Ambalika said. 'You had better hurry.'

'Why should she?' Ambika asked with a sniff. 'It's like

telling a lamb to skip along to the slaughterhouse because the butcher is waiting.' She looked at me and her face crumpled. '*Poor child!*'

Ambalika was annoyed. 'As usual you're making a mountain out of nothing. Kings do take second wives, you know, it is very common. Kunti understands that.' She turned to me, kindly concern flowing from her eyes. 'Don't you, Kunti?'

'It's not easy, but I'm trying to,' I said. *Why pretend otherwise?*

Ambika closed her eyes. 'The more you try the less it makes sense,' she said. She opened them and gazed fondly at the parrot in its cage. 'True or not, dearest heart?'

The bird hopped from one foot to another and cocked a beady eye at her. *O lotus-eyed one*, he squawked in his ugly voice. Delight broke over Ambika's features. 'Did you hear that?' she asked excitedly.

Your generous thighs...

Ambalika's face turned purple. 'Shut that idiot up!'

Ambika ignored her and picked up a piece of raw mango from a bowl of chopped fruit that she always kept ready just in case the parrot looked as if he could do with a treat. She pushed in her thumb and forefinger through the cage's bars and held it out. 'This is for you, my prince,' she said. The bird leaned its neck forward and took a vicious bite at her thumb. She yelped and made a crying face before bursting into a loud wail.

Ambalika looked in my direction with a dry smile. 'The more you try the less it makes sense,' she said.

❖

Just before leaving for the temple in the palace where the wedding rites would be held, Pandu came to me. 'Don't think that I am happy with this arrangement,' he said in a low voice. 'I know it is unfair to you, but I am helpless. I have to think beyond myself.'

I sent him a bleak look. Despite his lack of happiness over the wedding, he had dressed for it with care. Hair groomed and shining *mukut* in place, bare upper torso to show off the well-developed biceps adorned with gold armlets, a new silk dhoti to cover his lower limbs, a gold belt around his narrow waist. Every inch the royal bridegroom. *How can I ever trust him again?*

He tugged at the gold kundala in his right ear. 'Pitamaha, in his wisdom, thought it was best.'

'Pitamaha, in his wisdom, wants you to have sons as soon as possible,' I said sharply. 'Are you sure you're going to be able to oblige, Maharaj?'

His glance was reproachful. 'Don't make this harder than it already is. You are the maharani of Hastinapur. No one can change that.' Was he offering me a consolation prize? Still, it was reassuring to know that he felt the need to do so. *Maybe somewhere deep inside he does care about me.* 'It's going to be a simple ceremony,' he said. 'I insisted on that.'

Liar, I thought, even though he hadn't, strictly speaking, told a lie. The council of ministers, headed by the mahamantri, had decided that the wedding should be kept low-key to avoid further talk. There had, indeed, been murmurs about the expenditure involved in securing this match—the Bahlikas of Madra-desh had set a new standard in the bride price they had demanded. There was even speculation that it was so because they had hoped to turn away Pitamaha by citing this unusual custom of their family. However, Pitamaha had insisted that tradition must be respected. He would, he declared, be happy to pay whatever the bride price.

Looking at my face, Pandu sighed. 'Think of her as your younger sister,' he said. I knew what was on his mind. Hadn't his father married two sisters? Hadn't they lived amicably? Kings had more than one queen. As many as were required to give them heirs. Marriage for a king was all about securing the throne in perpetuity. How else could he do that but by continuing the dynasty? In the process, if he acquired rich and powerful relatives like the Bahlikas, there was no harm. 'Kunti,' he said, his expression so tender that it made me want to throw myself into his arms and beg him to change his mind. 'You will always be dear to me. *Please*, for my sake, make an effort.'

What he was really saying, of course, was Be Nice To Her.

7

Sapatni. As it turned out, the first time I set eyes on her, the co-wife, I was no longer angry, I was afraid. She was only fifteen, on the cusp of womanhood, but the combination of exuberance, artlessness and kittenish coquetry made her seem younger. She was everything that I was not: slim, straight as a reed, dainty, her face as fresh and unsullied as a spring dawn. She smiled frequently, and when she did, her dimples showed. Her eyes were an unusual blue-grey, cool and sharp. She made me feel lacklustre and old-fashioned. *Are we going to be paired as binary opposites for the rest of our lives? The Plain Wife and the Pretty Wife.*

She was clearly enamoured with her new husband, darting small, keen glances at him whenever she thought that no one was looking. It would have been unbearable to watch, were it not for the fact that Pandu seemed completely oblivious of her; he was almost brutal in his indifference. He looked directly at me once or twice, holding my gaze till I was forced to look away. For some reason that intense stare, more intimate than anything we had shared so far, made me ill-at-ease, as though it was somehow inappropriate.

The long journey from the north-western corner of Aryavarta had worn Madri out, but she tried to put on her brightest face. It would slip every now and then, revealing a glimpse of a bewildered, exhausted child, missing and searching for the contours of her familiar world. To my deep annoyance, she attached herself to me. At the lunch after the wedding ceremony, she sat beside me, directly opposite Gandhari. It was obvious that the blindfold fascinated her. She stared openly, but was well-mannered enough not to do it for long. On the other side of me, the two mothers-in-law sat together.

'Madri makes a pretty bride,' I heard Ambika say. 'Not as perfect as Gandhari, of course, too short for that, but not bad.'

'All brides look beautiful on their wedding day.' Ambalika's tone was dismissive.

'You're right.' Ambika nodded. 'We, too, were beautiful brides—'

'Till life scarred us,' Ambalika said. Acid words, burning a hole in the careful façade of our lives. I turned to look at her. Her moods were not as changeable as Ambika's. She was more phlegmatic, and this degree of bitterness was unusual. I realised how little I knew about these two women even though I saw them every day.

Meanwhile, Madri had barely touched her food. 'Eat something,' I told her in an undertone. 'It will look bad if you don't.' She nodded, but made no move to eat. Instead, she watched with complete fascination as Gandhari delicately picked at her food and put it into her mouth, morsel after morsel.

'Didi, tell me something,' she whispered in my ear. 'There are at least fifteen bowls around her thali. How does she know what she's eating?'

'See that nose of hers?' I whispered back. 'It's longer than yours.'

She looked at me, puzzled. 'So?'

'All the better to smell with.'

Her mouth formed an O, eyes rounded to match it. Then, as she realized it was a joke, she exploded in a fit of giggles. 'Are her ears, too, broader than mine?' she asked, in clear bell-like tones. The rajmata glanced in our direction, frowning disapproval. But it was difficult to make Madri stop giggling once she had started off. I understood another thing then: it would be difficult to *not* like her. For some reason the thought did not make me feel any better. Even if I joined the splinters and made it look whole again, it would hurt—this shattered heart of mine. Pain was inbuilt in the new topography.

The meal was coming to an end. Satyavati rose and we all followed. Ambika shoved a last piece of fried brinjal into her mouth and hastily chewed it. There were a number of women's rituals still to be carried out, but nothing that involved my active participation. I watched quietly as the songs were sung, the gifts presented. It felt strange, as though I was both inside and outside the scene that was unfolding. Was it just nine weeks ago that I, too, had undergone the exact same experience? As dusk set and the temple bells began to chime, the palace was illuminated by thousands of tiny lamps. The bride was led by the women to her nuptial chamber.

I stepped into the quiet gloom of my own room, the silence, my lonely bed. Everything had changed, then why did I feel that nothing had?

8

Dundhubi. The sound of war. How can a mere instrument, cowhide stretched over a wood frame, convey so much belligerence? They say that it is the fist of Indra; when it comes crashing down, the call to arms reverberates through the universe creating trepidation in every living heart. A call like the lion's first roar—a maw opens wide and swallows the enemy's morale before the blow is struck. A cry that spreads spine-chilling fear. Villages empty in a frenzy: panic-stricken mothers rush to grab their babies, men hurriedly drive the cattle herds into the comparative safety of the woodland. Run, run, everyone. Save yourself! Dundhubi: a battle cry that wins battles.

'Pandu has never lost a battle,' Dhritarashtra remarked with a smirk. 'But then, one must remember that he has never really fought one either—isn't that so, mahamantri?' Vidur shifted uncomfortably. Pandu, always overshadowed in his elder brother's presence, gave his usual response of a noncommittal smile. Pitamaha's eyes twinkled with the secret amusement that he got out of watching the display of sibling rivalry. Rajmata Satyavati, though, was displeased.

'Hastinapur does not fight needless battles,' she said. 'We are not power-hungry.'

'Nevertheless, we could do with a little more, isn't it, Daadi?' Dhritarashtra asked in a smarmy tone. 'A few more slaves, more heads of cattle, horses and elephants in our stables, gems and gold in our treasury. Nor would we say no to a little more land.'

Vidur cleared his throat. 'It was Kuru land to begin with,' he said in his mild, pedantic manner. 'We are only taking it back from those who grabbed it.' His face took on the grave look that always presaged a quote from the shastras. '*If a king did not inflict punishment untiringly on evil-doers, the strong would roast the weaker, like fish upon a spit.*'

Satyavati nodded. 'Don't forget that, for twenty-four years, Hastinapur was without a king. The Dasharnas are unruly robber tribes who need to be brought under the rule of law.'

Dhritarashtra, wrinkling his brow with mock concern, asked, 'But where was our *pujya* Pitamaha, the protector of Hastinapur, when the robber tribes were running amok?'

Before anyone could respond, Kripacharya, the *kula guru* said, 'Mentoring you and your brothers, Maharaj.' His reproving tone carried the message, and Dhritarashtra put an end to the baiting.

'Your point is well taken, Kula Guru,' Pandu said, with smooth charm. 'We need to be reminded of how much we owe Pitamaha. It is now time for us to prove that his effort has not been wasted.' Turning to Pitamaha he said, '*You* are the father, mother and first guru. Bless me, Pujyyavar, so that I may wrest back what our enemies have taken from us.'

'I have no doubt of that, Maharaj,' Bhishma's orotund voice seemed tuned for a long speech, but emotion got the better of him. 'You will return Hastinapur to its old glory…*I* have full confidence in you.' He grasped Pandu by the shoulder and gave him a deep long look before letting him go.

By turns Satyavati, Ambika and Ambalika blessed Pandu. *Vijayee bhava.*

Finally, he stood before me. The husband I shared with another woman. I blamed her for what was happening: among the rumours doing the rounds was that the bride price paid for her was so big that the state's coffers were empty. And now that I was sending my husband off to a war to recover the family fortune, *she* stood by my side! As I raised the silver thali with the five ghee lamps to perform the ritual *aarti*, her hands joined mine in holding it. They were shaking. I stole a look at her. Tears swam in her blue eyes, threatening to spill over. *Stupid girl. Doesn't she know that a* virapatni *should not cry while sending off her husband into battle—it is inauspicious.* I was relieved that Pandu did not look at her. Over the flickering flame of the diya, his gaze was trained on me.

What should I read in this look? Doesn't he know how completely he has shattered my heart? How can he even hope for absolution from it? What do you want me from me? Everything, except my forgiveness. I will not forgive you. Thirty days have passed since the wedding. Thirty nights that you have spent with her. What did you share? What does she mean to you? And what of us, you and I?

I dipped my thumb in the vermilion paste and drew a tilak between his eyebrows. 'I am starting out on a *vijay yatra*, Kunti,' he said. 'Won't you wish me luck?'

My resentment disintegrated. My eyes grew moist.

'Vijayee bhava, Maharaj.' Apprehension flickered across his face. 'What is it, Aryaputra?'

'You are the patrani, Kunti,' he said, humbly. 'I leave everything in your care.' His glance wavered for an instant. 'Including her.'

Her. The sapatni.

What had I ever meant to him other than an ally? I felt nothing—a stab of sadness is all. It would pass.

By then he, too, was gone.

Love depletes you. It restores you. Love is regeneration. It gives rise to a new receptivity. Love transforms. It is the lone spark that drives away the darkness in the depths of our hearts. It is all we need, but it can also reduce us to nothing. Love is the dancing flame that burns the lamp's soft wick to blackness. Love can, on occasions, bring pleasure, but it always, *always* brings pain.

❖

It was now a question of counting. Days multiplied into weeks, weeks stacked into months. The rains came. Leaks appeared in the palace's roof and dasis placed bowls beneath them. Outside my window, the sky was a grey mantle. The ground along the river had turned into an ocean and the far bank existed only in memory. The last downpour had contracted to a soft but persistent drizzle. I lay on a couch by the open window, my hair left loose. The sairandhri sat on the floor and drizzled a few drops of warm oil into it.

'Hastinapur has had a long line of queens, but the oddest was that one,' she said, glancing at the river. 'A mother who drowns her own son.'

My heart tripped on the secret rhythm that had never left me. *He is alive. He is. Somewhere, he is.*

'Not one, but seven sons,' the sairandhri continued. 'However, she is still a mother. And her heart is that of any mortal mother.'

'What do you mean?'

'Gangaputra—she flows in his veins. She is the torrent that churns inside him. Her energy, her ruthlessness, her fury. She is his mother after all, and she will not allow Hastinapur to forget the wrong it did him. This is her way of reminding us.'

'You mean there were no floods before Pitamaha took the oath?'

She shook her head. 'I've heard it from my grandmother. She was a child then. She said that the first flood came the year Maharaja Shantanu brought home a second wife.'

'Strange, isn't it?' I observed idly. 'The gods withhold the rains or send us a deluge, but it is the ruler who gets blamed for both.'

The sky had grown darker. There was a deep rumble. The drizzle thickened into a heavy shower. 'The river is rising again,' she said.

I sighed. 'My life, in contrast, has ebbed to a trickle.'

'Could it be that one has too little to do?'

'And what would you have one do?' I asked, bristling at her temerity.

'Only what a maharani *should*—watch over the welfare of her husband's people.'

'I've done my duty visits,' I said, deliberately choosing to misunderstand her.

'You've visited your mothers-in-law and that's your duty done?'

I maintained a pointed silence.

She said, 'The people who live by the water have suffered. Crops drowned, huts reduced to muddy mounds, possessions washed away—by the same river to which they pray every day.'

From my window I had seen their fishing boats gliding up and down the river in fair weather. On those long moonlit nights that I had spent awake, the graceful white sails and the coppery glow from the lamps on the boats had been my company. I had listened to the plaintive songs that threaded the waves and drifted on the breeze. Songs of yearning, a sad lament or a bittersweet love song. For days now there had been no moonlight and no songs.

'Where are they?' I asked, turning my head to look at her.

'They are safe but homeless. The rajmata has given them sanctuary, but the administration, which should take care of their needs, is busy in other ways.' She paused, then said, as though provoking me, 'There is a war on, they say.'

❖

Happiness is a composite emotion, a distillation of bliss, delight, joy, ecstasy and ease. Misery, on the other hand, is unsubtle. Opaque as the unseeing eye, hard of hearing, thick-headed with its own anguish. Like an abyss, it offers nothing but darkness. Yet the acknowledgement of a condition more miserable than one's own can be an eye-opener.

They had been housed in the empty stables behind the palace. It kept them dry. The stables had big wooden doors, but no windows. They were airless and foul-smelling. The stench of horses' urine had seeped into the earthen floor that was covered with bits of straw. One end of the building served as a shelter for livestock. At the other was a communal kitchen. Fuelled with dried cow dung cakes, fires blazed, curries bubbled in clay pots, acrid smoke and the aroma of rotis rose in a dense fug. Naked babies crawled, children squabbled, chickens squawked. Only the men were still. With the boats gone, they did not know how to fill the hours. They sat in a huddle with sealed, sullen faces staring at nothing. The women, however, were on their feet, their chores giving shape to the day, making it similar to other days of their lives. The rains had brought the usual assortment of diseases: fever, cough and cold, dysentery. The sick, listless on beds of dry grass, had to be tended and coaxed to eat, the livestock had to be cared for. No, the women had no time to sit.

'What do you want?' I asked, without thinking. No one responded. The silence stretched like an accusing finger. 'I mean...what can we offer you?'

The women looked at each other. 'Firewood,' said one.

'Milk for the babies—we lost many milch cows in the flood.'

'Medicines and blankets.'

'Cane wood, tools and twine.' The feisty old woman who said this was the wife of the mukhiya. Her hair was salt and pepper, face florid, but her body, used to hard work, was robust. 'The men need to build their boats and make their fishing nets,' she explained. 'The rains will not last forever.'

A palace official had accompanied me. I nodded to him to make a note. He pursed his lips and looked sceptical. 'There is a shortage of wood,' he said to the mukhiya's wife. 'There is a war on.'

She snorted. 'Don't we know it? Your tax collectors honoured us with a visit yesterday. We asked them why we should pay our taxes and they said exactly what you just said. "There's a war on." What of the taxes we paid all these years? Is there no obligation to us?'

The official stared back wooden-faced.

Later, the mahamantri scanned the list and pressed his lips close. 'There is a war on…' he began.

'These people are clear that they have paid their dues and are therefore entitled to the state's protection,' I countered. 'Secondly, the flood may not have evil designs on Kuru land, but it is no less an enemy than a foreign invader. It has left them bereft of their homes and livelihood. Their villages are under water. Where do they belong?'

The beginnings of a smile entered his eyes. 'I could pull out the account books and check out the first,' he said. 'But against the second point I have no argument. In self-defence, I promise that I will do what I can.' He hesitated, then added, 'You should also speak with the rajmata. Perhaps you are aware that she has, over the years, supported several welfare initiatives.'

'You mean building temples and giving away cows? Royalty everywhere does that—it is ostentation, nothing more.'

'It is more than that,' he said, reproachfully. For the next several minutes he lectured me on the rajmata's good works: many cisterns had been dug in the land so that women did not have to trudge far to fetch water; homes had been built for widows and elderly women who had no one to take care of them; fruit and vegetables from the palace gardens, and milk from the royal dairy were sold twice a week at very cheap rates so that the poorer families were assured of nutrition. He ended by saying, 'I'm telling you all this for a reason. Speak with her, Maharani, for the sake of these people.'

I listened without comment, but took his advice. A few days later I was informed that the rajmata had ordered that every requirement of the flood-affected populace be supplied.

9

Winter came early to Hastinapur. The ground was covered with frost every morning. Fog crept into the ancient palace, seeped into the light so that murkiness overlaid everything. It congealed in corners, creating phantoms. It shifted shape so that the mind was never at ease, but full of new ghosts. Though fires burned in huge braziers, and smoke from scented wood drifted lazily through rooms, it seemed that, wherever I was, there was a chilly gloom left by the departure of the sun.

The river had receded. The villages on the far bank had been rebuilt. When I looked out I could see signs of daily human activity. It warmed me in a quiet way to hear the songs that floated again on the night air. I would wait for the sails to appear against the setting sun, for the glow from kitchen fires on the land. At the mahamantri's request I had agreed to be the patron for some of Satyavati's welfare projects. It provided me with a reason to get out of the palace, meet men and women from different communities and learn about their lives, customs and concerns. I found it preferable to sitting in the Kuru sabha every day—as was expected of me.

Meanwhile, life in the palace went on as usual, but how different it was from the world I had left! In this, the first winter away from Kuntibhoja's house, I found myself missing the vibrancy and liveliness of it. I had been alone there too, but it was merely the separation of the outsider. Hastinapur was my home now, but I loathed it—the constant preoccupation with form and formality on the one hand, on the other the emptiness within me. I hated waiting for news of him, but I waited all the same.

We didn't hear anything for a long time. Then, as the season edged towards spring, news began to arrive in daily bulletins. The vijay yatra had achieved all that Pandu had set out to do. The robber tribes had been punished. Mithila was subjugated. The army of the Kurus was invincible, a scourge to its enemies, spreading through the countryside, pushing the eastern borders further and further away. Kashi, Suhma, Anga-desh, Pundra, Banga-desh and Kalinga were now vassal states. Their treasuries had been emptied to enrich the Kurus. Across the sweep of Aryavarta, trains of camels travelled west, laden with fine cloth, furs and beautiful hides. All bound for Hastinapur. Gold, silver, rubies, emeralds, corals and pearls; war elephants, horses, cattle; chariots, weapons and slaves.

The mood was euphoric. Pandu had strengthened the crumbling Kuru empire and turned the declining fortunes of the royal family. In anticipation of the good times, delegations of powerful merchants crowded the passages outside the sabha, waiting to submit proposals for business and trade to the council of ministers. Guilds petitioned for funds. Goldsmiths, weavers, masons, carpenters, metal workers, swordsmiths and even soothsayers thronged—all drawn by the new prosperity of Hastinapur.

And the camel trains continued to appear.

❖

'It isn't only war booty,' Madri said. 'Even the territories Maharaj has *not* conquered are sending us tributes.'

We were alone, standing on the palace terrace, looking out at the city stretching its limbs in the gentle sunshine. A chilly breeze made me draw my shawl close.

'Why would they do that?' I asked.

'So that he doesn't burn them to ashes…Maharaja Pandu has razed entire kingdoms to the ground.'

For days now, dust-covered armies had been trudging in through the main gates of Hastinapur, passing below the palace walls. Armies that were made up, not of soldiers returning home, but of the displaced and the dispossessed. Whole communities had been rendered destitute. To be adrift must be the cruellest fate for a human in this world. No place to call their own. No one to welcome them. With all that remained of their worldly belongings piled in bundles on the head, they plodded past in a daze. The women, some pregnant, others with babes saddled on the hip, men leading children by the hand. Something about their faces, bewilderment, red-eyed fatigue, an air of bereavement, had touched a chord in me.

'So much misery,' I murmured.

Madri looked surprised. '*You* should be happy. We have gained so much.' She threw her hands wide apart in a sweeping gesture. It was child-like. I could not help but smile, then I caught a fleeting shadow in her eyes. *She's envious of me? How strange!* The curtain dropped. Her gaze was veiled again. 'When do you think he'll be back?' she asked.

'Soon,' I said, looking away to hide my confusion.

After a while, she asked in a barely audible whisper, 'And then?'

I felt a prickle run along my spine. 'And then?'

Her eyes were on me, alert. 'Another bride for our maharaja, do you think?'

'Why—why do you say that?' I asked uneasily.

'He needs sons,' she said on a sharp note. 'Now. More than ever.'

'What do you mean?'

She made a gesture of impatience. 'You see it all clearly, yet you pretend to be unaware. Dhritarashtra is blind, but he is not stupid. Didn't you notice how delighted he was when the king went off to wage a war? Deep down, didn't he hope that the maharaja would not return?'

My breath caught sharply in my throat. *This one is no fool.* 'I find this conversation completely inappropriate,' I said. 'They are brothers and—'

'Rivals,' she completed crisply. The word hung in the air, a noose. 'Not very different from you and I,' she said, continuing to eye me steadily. 'I have his heart and you are jealous.'

My cheeks were burning at the truth in her accusation. 'Enough!'

But, as though spurred by my warning, she went on. 'You see me as a rival, but *I* am no danger to you. We are in the same boat—and it's going to sink.'

I stared at her. 'What do you mean?'

'The others are beginning to suspect it,' she said. 'But you and I *know* that he cannot have children with either of us. Something is needed before that and he cannot—'

A fierce swell of satisfaction rose in my heart. *It was no better with you either.* 'I don't think we should be discussing this,' I said.

She flushed. 'Don't treat me like a child. You may be the first queen in the sabha, but in the royal bed chamber, I am no less than you.'

I said nothing; there was nothing to say.

'You think I stole him from you?' Her eyes bore into me. 'Had everything been normal with him, I would have fought you for the power you have—and won it too! He respects you, but it's *me* he wants. It is my body he lusts for.'

'Madri, control your tongue!' My head was throbbing. *How dare she!* I forced myself to look at her again, studying her face carefully. She had become pale, lost weight. There were hollows under her eyes, and drooping lines around her mouth—they hadn't been there before. *She's genuinely worried.* 'What is the matter with you?' I snapped, with sudden irritation. 'Are you homesick?'

She lowered her head, the slender, fair nape exposed. How young and vulnerable she looked! 'This is your home now,' I soothed her. 'Has anyone been nasty to you? Said something?' She raised her head and stared at me, silently pleading. I felt a sudden sense of danger.

'*Baanjh*.' Her voice was very low. 'They were calling you that before I came here. Now they are calling us that—you and me. They talk of the sowing ritual that the king must perform when the fields are ready. How can his chief queen be by his side if she is barren? It is inauspicious.'

My stomach lurched. *When there are no more kingdoms left to crush, what will he have to do to prove his virility to the world? Will he throw me out? And her too? It is always a woman's failure, if she cannot conceive.*

Perhaps Madri saw something in my expression that made her feel that I was now more receptive. Her face grew animated again. She began to talk in an urgent monotone. 'Dhritarashtra and Gandhari have been quietly consulting all sorts of people. Astrologers, vaidyas, midwives and even courtesans.' At the last word she giggled, but quickly suppressed it. 'They've had a havan done on certain days, always before sunset...Haven't you seen how much attention he pays her? Always finding an excuse to touch her. Just because he and she cannot see, it doesn't mean that his plan is invisible too.'

'What plan?'

'To get back the crown that was taken away from him by making Gandhari pregnant as quickly as possible.'

I raised my hand to my cheek in dismay. 'But—how will that—?'

'It is possible,' she said, with a cynical twist to her mouth. 'The crown would have gone to Dhritarashtra if the mahamantri had kept his mouth shut at the coronation.'

'But the mahamantri was right,' I said. 'The Kurus have a law that a disabled or diseased man *cannot* rule the kingdom. The king has to be physically fit. Why, their own grandfather Shantanu became king because his elder brother Devapi renounced kingship as he had a skin disease. The law must be obeyed.'

'The law!' she echoed hollowly. 'When the stakes are high, laws have been changed before.'

'Not when Vidur is the mahamantri.'

She gave me a slow, sly smile. 'You spend too much time in the mahamantri's company and now you've begun to parrot his words.' I looked away. My meetings with Vidur had always been about official matters, yet even that had become fodder for gossip. 'Words are a mask we make to hide the truth,' she said.

It struck me that coming from a mouth so tender these words were all the more outrageous. But there was something else, a fear that was slowly sliding along my spine, rising and expanding, till it seemed as if every single one of my senses was on alert. *She is right. No, she is wrong—it's nonsense, don't trust her. What happens if Pandu fails to produce an heir?*

'The mahamantri can quote the rule book forever,' she went on. 'If Gandhari manages to produce a son first, the Kurus will have their next successor. Dhritarashtra will see to it that his son gets what was taken away from him. Our husband has never been able to get over the guilt of getting the crown by default. The rajmata will give in because she doesn't care where and how the succession comes from as long as it is ensured, and Pitamaha, well, even though he loves the brothers equally, everyone knows the reason why he arm-twisted Gandhari's parents into an alliance with Dhritarashtra—for the hundred sons her womb will produce. The hundred sons who will strengthen Dhritarashtra. *If born at the right time*, the first one will win him the throne. If Gandhari has a son before either of us, we are sunk. Have you thought about that?'

I was struck once again by her sharpness. She was right about Pitamaha. He was equally affectionate towards both brothers, but did he have a secret sympathy for Dhritarashtra who, like him, had been forced to give up the throne of Hastinapur?

'In these past months, while our husband was away, several things have changed, but the change is so innocuous that one would think nothing of it,' Madri said. 'Gandhari's brother, Shakuni, is now a permanent feature in Hastinapur. They say he is a tantrik who practises black magic. Have you seen his eyes?' She gave a delicate shudder.

Despite myself, I was amused. Shakuni had unusual eyes: one the grey-green of a mountain river, the other a sludge brown. In addition, he had a pronounced limp in one leg from a hunting accident. I felt sorry for Shakuni. While he viewed everything in Hastinapur with open-mouthed awe of the hillbilly, the snooty Kurus didn't think much of him. To imagine him as a powerful tantrik was laughable.

'Why is he here?' went on Madri. 'Ostensibly, the reason is to visit his beloved sister. But do visiting brothers linger for months in a sister's marital home? It defies all norms of propriety. Yet no one has raised a murmur. And now Shakuni sits in the sabha every time it meets. People are wondering why the crown prince of Gandhara minds Hastinapur's business rather than that of Gandhara, but who dares to question it?'

I frowned. 'I didn't know this.'

She sent me a reproachful look. 'Unlike you, I've been keeping my ears to the ground...In the king's absence, Shakuni has become Dhritarashtra's confidante. Another thing: Dhritarashtra has attended the sabha every single day. He listens carefully to what goes on and asks questions on matters of law and ordinance, he also gives his opinion. Though he does not sit on the throne, he is edging closer to it.' Her expression turned openly accusatory. 'I am saying all this because you are so indifferent. You don't even come to the sabha anymore.'

I felt a stab of guilt. Despite repeated requests from the mahamantri, my presence in the Kuru sabha had been negligible. It was not indifference as much as pique. I was still sore about the unseemly rush Pitamaha and Satyavati had shown in getting a second wife for Pandu, and this was simply my way of getting back.

'Have you spoken to anyone else about the...erm...the maharaja's condition?' I asked.

Madri shook her head.

'Good.' My mind had begun to race. *It is a condition, no more...Maybe there is a cure...Who can help me?* The glimmer of an answer came to me a few days later, although I did not realize it then.

❖

That morning I had gone, as usual, to my mother-in-law's chamber. Ambalika was alone. This happened rarely, as the two sisters, despite their regular sport of sniping at each other, clung together as though conjoined. As so much was happening in the sabha everyday, they had taken to sitting in the queens' gallery. Judging by the rather low interest they took even as spectators, it seemed that this was just another way to pass the time. Though she paid little heed to his words, whenever Dhritarashtra spoke, Ambika's eyes would be fixed adoringly on him. Ambalika, on the other hand, yawned her way through the events.

She was, unusually for her, lying in bed. 'I have a headache.'

'Would you like me to rub the balm?'

'Would you?' she asked gratefully. 'The maid brought it in a while ago, but—'

I drew the curtains partially so that the light in the room was muted. The pain in her head, she explained, was dull but persistent. I ran my fingers along her neck and shoulders. The muscles around her shoulder blades were knotted. I smeared the balm on the affected area and rubbed it in before working at the knots, gently kneading the flesh.

She sighed. 'That feels good,' she said with a little laugh. 'I might even fall asleep.'

'You've not been sleeping well?'

'I've never been a sound sleeper,' she admitted. 'After Pandu was born, it became even more difficult, the slightest cry would startle me out of my sleep even though he had a wet nurse, because I could not…' Her voice dropped to a whisper. 'I had no milk.'

'Surely there are remedies for that. Didn't the midwife suggest any to you?'

'There was no dearth of suggestions. I ate bottle gourd for months because they said it was good for the milk. Result: no milk and a permanent loathing for bottle gourd.'

'What was he like as a baby?'

'Who?'

'Pandu—who else?'

'I thought you might be asking about Dhritarashtra. *He* was the baby everyone fussed over, though it was Pandu who was the more delicate child, a weakling with a birth weight so low that the midwife thought he wouldn't live beyond a month.'

'And you?'

'I?'

'What did you feel when you first saw him?' I asked, welcoming this chance to talk about my husband. She shivered and was silent. She was quiet for so long that I thought she had fallen asleep. I covered her with a light sheet and was about to tiptoe out of the room when I saw her face. It was wet with tears. 'Ma?' I said softly.

A deep shudder ran through her. Her eyes were closed. 'God forgive me,' she said, pressing her mouth with her hand. 'I could not bear to look at him…His hair, that face, those blank eyes—when his hands reached for my body they felt like claws. He was a beast. *That stink*. I—I—' Fresh rivulets ran down her cheeks.

I stared at her. What was she going on about? The memory of her newborn son? Her husband? Minutes slipped by. She opened her eyes wide. Her tone changed suddenly. There was defiance in it. 'Well, it happened. At least, I did not faint like *she* did. Pandu was puny when he was born, but look at him now. Can anyone say that he is not normal?' She turned on her side so that her back was now towards me. I understood that she wanted to be left alone.

10

I stared at the bust of Vichitravirya. It was a silly face, with nothing distinguished about it. He did not have his father Shantanu's strong jaw or his half-brother Bhishma's impressive physique. A weak chin, loose-lipped mouth, sensuous and faintly pouting. *When his hands touched me, they felt like claws. He was a beast. That stink*. What had she meant?

'He loved the arts,' a voice behind me said. I whirled around. Pitamaha. I took a step back. 'Music, dance, poetry. That sort of stuff.' His tone was dismissive. 'Fancied himself as a poet, too, I believe, though songster would perhaps be a better word...Different from his brother over there.' He pointed to the next bust. 'But not all that different either.'

'And what was he like?'

'Chitrangad was a wrestler. Quite a good one, but not good enough to thrash a gandharva.' He gave a thin smile, but his eyes were cool and assessing. 'Why this sudden interest in history?'

The question was clearly meant to unnerve me. 'Family history, Pitamaha,' I replied demurely. 'This is *my* family now.'

'I'm happy to know that you've come around to that view.'

'Gandhari Didi mentioned that a famous sculptor from Gandhara has just completed a bust of Maharaja Dhritarashtra.'

'The best sculptors in Aryavarta are right here in Hastinapur,' he said frostily.

'Yes, of course,' I agreed. 'But I find our family's history more interesting than sculpture. Do tell me more about them,' I said pointing to Vichitravirya's bust but including Chitrangad as well.

'There isn't anything to say. Neither of them lived long enough to achieve anything.' He turned away and moved towards the other statues. 'Now Pratipa is an ancestor you can be proud of. I must tell you about him sometime.'

'Thank you,' I said.

'No, not at all...I'm pleased we could have this chat. I've heard of the case you made for the flood-affected villagers. The rajmata mentioned that you were taking an interest in her projects—that's very good!'

The commander-in-chief giving a pat on the back to a subordinate. Yet I could not help feeling gratified. 'I'm glad I could do something.'

He nodded, as if satisfied with my response. 'I have a piece of good news to share. I have arranged Vidur's marriage with a kinswoman of yours—the Vrishni chief Devaka's daughter Parashavi.'

'Parashavi?' I said. 'I'm afraid I don't—'

'Her mother was a dasi,' he said smoothly. 'Just like Vidur's mother.'

Oh! So this bride, like me, isn't worth abducting or buying.

Pitamaha concluded, 'It is best if a man marries one of his own kind.'

❖

If she was surprised by my visit, she did not show it. I had noticed her, a small bird-like woman with a quiet dignity, at the wedding feast for Pandu and Madri. She was Vidur's mother. Before his birth she had been Maharani Ambika's dasi, this I had heard. Now she had a set of rooms in the palace—a sign that she was no longer a slave.

In the little garden outside her home there was a profusion of marigold bushes. A couple of sparrows and a peahen, delicately picking her way through the grass, pecked at the grain sprinkled on the ground. The room faced east and the morning rays slanting in through the door made the old walls look cheerful. The furnishings were simple. We sat on a reed mat. On the low table before us was a platter of seasonal fruits that she urged me to eat, with rough kindness. She shook with silent laughter, as though she found the question I had come to ask absurd.

'It's not a secret, Putri,' she said. 'Can anything ever be a secret in a palace like this one?'

'Well, if they are not Maharaja Vichitravirya's sons, then whose sons are they?'

'But they are his sons. Their mothers were his queens.'

'But he did not father their sons. The dates don't tally. The maharaja was dead when—'

'They are, unquestionably, his sons.'

I changed tack. 'Well then, who was *your* son's father?'

A cautious look entered her face. 'Why do you want to know, Putri, if I may ask?'

'There's a reason,' I answered evasively.

She nodded as if she'd expected the reply. 'Even though I don't leave these rooms, I get to hear things…You are new here, but you can see what's going on and it frightens you.'

'I am concerned, yes.'

'For yourself?' There was a shrewd look in her eyes.

I thought of the first time I had entered the city—as its maharani. That magical evening when I fell in love. 'For Hastinapur,' I replied. 'But also for the maharaja, myself… and Madri.'

Her smile was full of sympathy. '*You* are the chief queen, Putri, and Maharaja Pandu is a good king. With you by his side he will be a great ruler. Just what Hastinapur has needed for a long time.' She was silent for a while. 'My son Vidur—they blame him, even though they don't say it aloud. But let me tell you, he was thinking of Hastinapur. *He alone*. If he had kept his mouth shut, the coronation would have taken place as planned. The blind prince would have been made king. They wanted that, the two of them, but what would it have meant for Hastinapur?'

'The two—Rajmata and Pitamaha?'

'Who else?' she shot back. 'It made no difference to Bhishma. Nothing matters to him except his oath of celibacy. As for *her*! She never had any scruples. Look at the way she treated the Kashi princesses. Bhishma was their brother-in-law so she commanded him first, saying that the Kuru line was in danger of dying out if he refused. He said no. She told him that he could be king, but he still said no.'

'Commanded him to do what? He said no to what?'

She looked at me for the longest moment. The meaning of her words dawned. 'Oh!' I spluttered in shock. 'But—but he had taken a vow of celibacy.'

'The very vow he took for her sake, that's the beauty of it,' she said with a tight smile. 'How furious she was with him when he refused to do the needful!'

'What happened then?'

'He told her to call in a noble brahmin for the job. Whenever a kshatriya line was endangered before, it was rescued in this way.' Not trusting myself to speak, I nodded at her to continue. 'She's a sharp one, the Fisherwoman. She called *him* in.'

'Called who in?'

'The sage Krishna Dwaipayana. He compiles the sacred texts, they say. Veda Vyasa, that is what he is called.'

I recognized the name. Everyone knew of the rishi for his scholarly achievement of splitting and categorizing the four Vedas. 'What does he have to do with all this?'

She took a while to reply. 'He told me he was her son.'

'He told *you*?' I repeated stupidly. 'Her son? Whose son?'

She frowned at my slowness. 'Don't you get it? Satyavati's son. *Born when she was yet a kanya.*'

I took a deep breath to slow my whirling head. 'Let me get this right,' I said. 'Satyavati had a son before she married Maharaja Shantanu. He grew up to be Rishi Veda Vyasa. And one fine day, soon after Vichitravirya's death, when the Kuru line was in danger of extinction, she called him to make her elder daughter-in-law pregnant—*is that what you are telling me?*'

She nodded grimly. 'That's right.'

'*No*,' I cried. 'It's *not* right—it is wrong.'

'Try telling her that.' She twisted her mouth. 'Royalty lives by more flexible rules than the rest of us. Ask Vidur, he will tell you the exact one. It even has a name. They call it *niyoga* in the shastras. In special cases, if a kshatriya cannot give his wife children, he can ask a kinsman or an illustrious brahmin to do it.'

'I have heard of it,' I said. 'I thought it was the husband who asks—'

'Satyavati didn't care for all that! And she didn't ask, she demanded. Later, she explained it away by saying that just as Bhishma was Maharaja Vichitravirya's brother, her kanina, illegitimate son, too, was similarly related. Therefore, it was all right to order her daughters-in-law to welcome him. Who was *she* to command the widowed princesses to sleep with a stranger? The witch! They were royal princesses of an ancient house. She respects nothing, that woman. *Tchah!* The unspeakable things she has done, all in the name of Hastinapur—*she* will be the cause of its ruin!'

Silence fell while we wrestled with our separate thoughts. After a while, I asked, 'What was the rishi like?'

She dragged her thoughts back to the question. 'Decent. The very soul of dharma.'

I could not bear to look at him. His hair, that face, those blank eyes.

'Not repulsive? But the princess—'

'*They* were princesses.' Her tone made it clear that princesses occupied a different world from hers. 'Although they had spent several years warming their husband's bed, they had no idea of what it can be like when a man and a woman really—' She permitted herself a tiny smile. 'Besides, he had just come from the forest. He came only because Satyavati called him. When he heard what she wanted, he agreed, but he pleaded for more time. He wanted the princess to keep a vow for a year, but that fisherwoman didn't agree to a word he said. *Now! Immediately. Tonight*. She insisted on getting it over with, even though he said that Ambika would not be able to receive him. His hair was matted, beard unkempt, body unwashed…He was right. The princess was not ready. How could she be? All that Satyavati told her was: "*Be prepared to receive your brother-in-law tonight.*" She thought it was Bhishma—poor girl. Who knew about that sinner's kanina son? Hadn't she carefully kept it a secret all these years?'

I trembled. She saw my discomfiture and took it for revulsion. 'It's important that you should know what happened, Maharani,' she said fiercely. 'Everything that is happening today, and will occur tomorrow, is a result of what took place on those two nights when the Kashi princesses were forced to sleep with a stranger so that they would produce sons—it was their duty, they were told.' She leaned closer. 'Those were the two darkest nights in the history of this godforsaken palace…Nothing like that ever happened before. *Anarth!* Such evil!'

A peacock cried. The peahen tiptoeing across the grass looked up. There was a flurry of wings and the male bird flew over the low hedge and landed close to her on the grass. The jewelled colours on his tail glowed in the sunshine.

Vidur's mother sighed. 'My poor innocent princess…

When I went into her room early the next morning, she was still unconscious. Curled up on the floor with her knees drawn to her chin. Naked as the day she was born. Never said a word about that night, but she has never been the same after it passed. Outside the door was Satyavati. She had waited all through that night. When rishivar came out, I heard her ask, "It's going to be a boy, isn't it?" He must have said something bad to her because she sat down as if felled like a tree in a storm. *No*, she kept saying. But then she recovered her wits and said, "This one is a fool. You must do it again." Fool? That was *my* princess she was talking about! God knows what she told Ambalika, what threats she delivered...She and Bhishma, together they ruined the lives of all three sisters—Amba, Ambika, Ambalika.'

'Tell me what happened with Maharani Ambalika.'

'Things went wrong with her too,' she said. 'She was always the stronger of the two sisters, but even—' After a moment she said in a slower, sadder voice, 'The next morning when her maid went in, she found Ambalika in her bed, eyes wide open, but blank. She was as white as death. We couldn't get her to speak for days.'

'What did Satyavati do?'

'The rishi had told her that the second child, too, would not be healthy. His words came true...She went back to Ambika and told her, "You are going to do it again and this time you are going to do it right".'

That night, however, it was Ambika's maid who received the sage. She said, 'The princess begged me. Her exact words to me were, "I'll kill myself if you don't agree. Blow out the lamps, stay in the dark, wear my perfume".'

'Did you?'

'When a man and a woman come together with desire, why should there be darkness around them?' she asked. 'With the princesses of Kashi, he hadn't liked it any more than they did. With me it was different. He saw that I was no dainty creature and he smiled. Such a charming smile, it was. That night, it was good between us. I made him happy, he said.' She sighed and was silent for a long time. 'He, too, gave me pleasure. He gave me a son who will be remembered. He gave me my freedom. What more can a woman hope for?'

'What happened after the babies came?'

'To be fair to Satyavati, she is a good grandmother—to all three grandsons. She has never discriminated, but has always been equally affectionate and generous towards Vidur.'

'And the two princesses?' I murmured hesitantly, not sure of the question itself.

Vidur's mother nodded. 'Satyavati has not forgiven them, but it is Ambika she really blames…Strangely, Ambika is a good mother, but Dhritarashtra, her own son, cannot forgive her. *He* blames her for his misfortune. That is how Satyavati has brainwashed both the princes—by implying that their mothers are to blame.'

We were silent for a while. I struggled to understand what she had revealed. 'Tell me about Pandu,' I said.

She looked at me with pity. 'When he was born, he looked so strange, not like a human child, but a sickly-pale mewling creature. He was underweight. Worse, his mother refused to nurse him. When he needed her, she could not bear the sight of him, and later—it was too late.'

'*Late?*'

She grew pensive and spoke haltingly, as if searching for the words. 'Here, within Hastinapur's walls, Pandu is still trapped in his frightened mother's womb. He can only hear the frantic thudding of her heart, feel the rush of terror in her blood. He can only curl up and hide from view.' Perhaps she saw something in my face, a growing trepidation, for she stopped speaking. After a few seconds she said quietly, 'Guilt is a subtle emotion. It has many forms…There is also Dhritarashtra, who does not allow him to forget.'

Below the marigold bushes crouched a spectre, a grey cat. It watched the birds. It inched forward.

'Pandu was a sweet-tempered, thoughtful and sensitive child,' she said. 'Everyone made a huge fuss over Dhritarashtra and the younger brother was neglected. But he never showed resentment. He always put his blind half-brother before him. And now he has become a shadow of Dhritarashtra.' Her voice turned harsh. 'Dhritarashtra knows exactly how to control his younger brother.'

I felt a tight knot in my chest.

Suddenly she stood up and went to the door. At her approach, the birds flew away. The cat looked up, yellow eyes gleaming with something unnameable.

'Pandu is, in every way, healthy,' she said, looking at me squarely in the face. 'He is a fine archer. He has skill, judgment and focus.' She paused, then spoke at a slower pace. 'When Vidur quoted the shastras, he did it for the right reason, but I do sometimes wonder—did he end up doing the wrong thing? Would it have mattered if Dhritarashtra had become king?' I looked at her silently. She sighed. 'You and I don't have the answer to that…Only time will tell.'

Narrowing her eyes, she continued, 'But *you* could shape the answer, Maharani.' Her voice took on an urgent note. 'Take him away from here. Go to some other place. There must be tranquillity somewhere in this world…Take him where he can be the man you want him to be.'

11

Rishi Kindama. Who was he? Why did he come into our lives? The first question is now irrelevant, but the second could perhaps be answered by another question: what would our lives have been if he had not appeared on the threshold that day? It is as if that day, that brief meeting in which all our separate destinies were intertwined, had been poised in time and space, like a stage set for a scene that was inevitable.

Upon Pandu's return, Pitamaha declared that the king needed a period of rest after the arduous campaign. 'The weather is just right for you to go to the royal park in the foothills,' he said, adding meaningfully, 'You need to spend time with the two queens.' The park was Pitamaha's personal property. One went there by invitation only. It was a great honour to be invited, and Pandu stressed this as we made the twelve-hour journey by chariot from Hastinapur.

He chose to share the chariot with me. Madri rode a young mare, milk white with black ears. It was a gift to her from Pandu, after she had confided in him that she missed the horses of her native country. Apparently, the horses of Madra-desh were as famous as the women of that land were for their equestrian skills. Seated on the steed, Madri looked impressive in an elemental, disturbing way. Pandu, I noticed, was mesmerized by the sight of her riding at a canter. Oddly enough, I did not mind this as much as I would have done earlier. After that conversation with Madri on the palace's terrace, my rancour had reduced somewhat. We were, as she had said, in the same leaky boat—not friends but allies. I had also noticed Pandu's relief when he saw that I was no longer aloof and cold towards her. He was grateful. And so, seemingly, was she.

As we travelled to the park, he talked about the game for which it was famous. It was here that his grandfather Shantanu had killed his first tiger, as had Pitamaha when just a lad of sixteen. He gave a blow-by-blow account of both incidents, ending with how the dead animal had been felled by a 'single arrow straight through the heart' and then strung on a pole and paraded through the streets of Hastinapur.

'What a bloodthirsty lot you Kurus are!' I joked.

His expression clouded. 'Yes.'

The months of campaigning had changed him. He had always been reserved, but now there was a ruthless air about him. An arrogance that made him, in my eyes, even more attractive than before. I recalled the manner in which he entered Hastinapur, taking his time to acknowledge the cheering crowds with a smile, a wave and even a word or two. Every inch the victorious battlefield commander, but also, unquestionably, the king as he strode into the sabha and up the steps to the throne.

Did anyone else notice this new confidence or were they all too busy marvelling at the treasure that he had amassed? That same day, he gave it all away—to the rajmata, Pitamaha,

Dhritarashtra, the two mothers and Vidur. As if he could hardly wait to get rid of it. He enriched them many times over, but it was to Dhritarashtra that he gave the larger share. When the donations were being announced in the sabha, Dhritarashtra could barely conceal his excitement. He had immediately declared that a substantial part of *his* share would go in yajnas to thank the gods.

'If Maharaj had meant all along to give it away, why did he go to such lengths to win this wealth?' Madri had wondered aloud. The same thought had been in my head.

The sun was directly above us when we reached the royal park. It lay in an amphitheatre of low, densely-wooded hills. The narrow valley was nourished by a forest stream. We crossed the shingly bed of the stream and travelled along a rough track overhung by the feathery canopy of the tamarind, jamun and wild mango trees among whose branches sat grey apes, watching our progress with interest. Around us Nature lay shrouded in the deep blue shade cast by the midday sun. Somewhere deep inside the sleepy jungle, a solitary woodpecker hammered away, *tok-tok-tok*. The foliage thinned and we found ourselves in a small clearing at the heart of which stood the royal lodge. The chariot came to a stop. The servants ran out to greet us. There was, I noted with a sense of relief, just a handful of them.

Our life in the hunting lodge sketched out its own easy pattern. Pandu and I were, by habit, early risers, starting our day as soon as the impenetrable dark began to thin. It was deliciously cool at that hour. Pandu chose this time to go out for a ride—solitary only because Madri, who had been invited to accompany him, liked to sleep late. I would sit outside my room and watch the wildlife make its way to the stream. A family of chital, a lone barking deer, and twice I saw a tiger. Partridges filed demurely through the tall grass, peafowl paraded on a large rock by the water. The forest hummed like the home of a competent housewife going about her daily tasks. As the sun's rays made their cautious advance into our glade, Pandu would return, skin gleaming with perspiration, demanding food and drink. By now there would be a smattering of people waiting to meet him: the headmen of the hamlets in the forest, officials who had ridden out from Hastinapur with briefs and messages, hunters who would offer to guide him to the best hunting. In all that time, Kindama rishi was the only hermit who came to meet the king.

I was alone when he appeared. What I remembered later was that, just a moment earlier, I had been staring at that precise spot under the deep green shade of the jamun tree, watching a sambhar stag. The creature had never before appeared at the stream. His ears spread to catch the slightest sound, he surveyed the clearing with a lordly air. The antlers rising above the great head had the grandeur of a semul tree in winter. He had looked straight at me for an instant, then lowered his head and scratched the tree's trunk with his horns.

A maid came in just at that moment to seek my instructions on a small matter. After dealing with her, when I turned to look at the stag, he had disappeared. In his place stood a man, lean and bronzed, wearing nothing except a loin cloth. Black, waist-length hair twisted into thin ropes, a long beard and a lush moustache trimmed downwards, revealing a full lower lip. There was something odd about the way he blended and yet stood apart from his surroundings, as though he had been conjured by the play of light and shade that was the secret language of the forest. Where had he come from? Was he a hunter? He carried no bow and arrows. A sanyasi? But there was no wooden staff or water pot to mark him as a wandering sadhu. His gaze, I noticed, was trained on me. He gave a slight nod and began to cross the stream with barely a splash. He padded, without hurry, across the stretch of open garden. The breeze, I noticed, had died down. A deep stillness prevailed. When he was just a few steps away, I saw the sacred thread. A brahmin. I went forward, hands joined in greeting.

'*Putravati bhava*,' he said. His voice, deep and raspy, gave the blessing weight and solemnity.

Two words. Would they create the future?

'It will happen,' he said, eyes narrowed into slits, looking and yet not looking at me. 'Now tell the king that I have come to meet him.'

Pandu's welcome was more effusive. He insisted on washing the brahmin's feet himself and requested him to honour us by having a meal at our house. He had, it appeared, heard of Kindama, a sadhu who had a *dhuni*, the sacred hearth he tended, deep in the forest, though no one knew precisely where. He was rumoured to have special powers. Some said he understood the language of birds and, therefore, knew everything that was happening in the world. Others said that he could take the form of any animal in the forest, a tiger one day, a deer the next.

That day, he was a poor eater.

'No grains,' he said, as I went to the kitchen. 'Nothing cooked...Fruits of the forest and unspiced buttermilk is all.'

Pandu protested. 'Rishivar, allow us to serve you a little kheer, at least.'

The sadhu sent him an amused look. 'You have come to the forest, Rajan, and yet you cannot stifle the desire for luxury?'

Pandu flushed. Before he could apologize, I spoke: 'He is a householder, Rishivar, and a bowl of kheer is not a luxury to tempt you, but an offering made to you as our *atithi devata*. An offering befitting your status—and ours.'

Pandu and Madri exchanged horrified glances, but our guest seemed not to mind. 'Nonetheless, humour me today, and just serve me what I ask for.'

When I returned with the fruit, I found him engaged in a deep conversation with Pandu. 'This body should be used as means to transcend materiality,' he was saying. 'It is nothing but a vessel through which we seek and perceive reality.'

Ah, sage speak.

He finished the buttermilk, but barely touched the fruit. After a few minutes, he stood up abruptly. Later, I remembered only his parting words. 'Your sons will be heroes, Rajan.'

It did not sound like a blessing so much as the punchline of a private joke, the meaning known only to him. I was reminded suddenly of Durvasa. *You will be the mother of heroes.* A nameless dread filled me. But Pandu was looking gratified. He smiled at Madri. She blushed. 'We will both have sons,' she whispered to me.

'If only life was as simple as that,' I said.

❖

Later, Madri and I were asked to give our accounts of the events that led to the killing of Kindama rishi. The truth is that there was no version other than Pandu's. I was not there when the deer appeared again. Was it the same animal I had seen earlier? All Madri told us was that it was an unusually large stag. She was alone with Pandu and she was the first to see it, she insisted.

Fate and Time are relentless, but they do not work alone. They work with human nature: the choice one makes and the chance one takes. Together they wrought the changes in our lives, thrust us forward on life's journey. Does that mean that everything that happens to us happens for a reason? One's desire may be the cause, but who devises the conclusion? Are we, despite our individual responsibility, powerless in the shaping of our own fortunes?

I was helpless to prevent it, I saw that even then. I could not stop myself from loving him. I could not stop him loving her more than me. Nor could I stop her from using this knowledge to score her little victories over me. A white steed with black ears, she had asked for and got. On that golden morning, when she sighted the stag, she demanded a deerskin. 'Maharaj, you have to kill him for me. The skin will make a fine covering for my chamber in the palace when we go back.'

Yes, we were about to return. The queries had been coming to us for weeks. I had urged him to return, argued with him till I sensed that he was weakening. 'I know,' he'd said, tiredly. 'I know I should go back. I just wish I did not have to.'

'A king cannot spend all his life hunting,' I said. He did

not respond, but his face told me that the reminder had soured his idyll. For a long while afterwards I was taunted by the thought: *Would we have gone back to our old life if Madri hadn't asked for the deerskin?* It was nothing more than the whim of a pretty woman who knew she had her man in thrall. When a pretty woman asks prettily, it's enough to fire a man's ardour. To make him feel that he is worth something. To make *her* feel she's worth it. There was an attachment between them, an affinity that kept me out. I was alone in my yearning for him. But that, too, is love.

He returned later than usual that day, hours later, when Madri, having got bored with waiting, had gone for a ride. There was something about his walk, unsteady and dragging, that first warned me. He held the bow, but the quiver of golden-feathered arrows slung on his shoulder was empty. My heart began to hammer in my chest. Something dreadful had happened. I ran to meet him. He seemed to back away as I came close.

'You must be tired. Shall I get you a cool drink?'

He shook his head then lowered it. 'I—I've done something terrible,' he said.

'What?' When he began to talk, it made no sense. I tried to piece it together by repeating the details. 'You shot five arrows?' I asked, careful not to raise my voice. 'But why, Aryaputra, when there is no archer in the world better than you? Why five when one would have been good enough to kill a deer?'

'Because I am the scum of this earth,' he said, in a voice filled with self-loathing. 'Lust runs in my blood. It is *inside* me.'

'Please don't talk in riddles,' I said. 'You have the hunter's instinct, but you also have the eye of an archer. Then how did you not see?'

He shook his head wordlessly.

'And the deer spoke to you? Are you sure?'

'I'm not lying,' he said.

'What did the deer say?'

His gaze changed, slid away, like something glimpsed in the grass. 'He said, "You must bear the blame".'

'Blame? What blame?' I asked, my mind reeling. 'Is it a sin for a hunter to kill a deer?'

'It is to kill a brahmin.'

'*Brahmin?*'

'Kindama Rishi...He had taken the form of a deer.'

I stared at him in shock. He gave a bitter smile. 'It's clear from your face that you don't believe me, but let me tell you that it only gets worse.'

'Tell me.'

And he did. The wounded brahmin had asked him, 'Would any hunter kill an animal that is in the act of mating? What sort of an archer are you who shoots without thinking? What manner of king are you who does not recognize that his foremost duty is to protect the weakest of creatures?'

Pandu had immediately understood: as a protector, a king cannot be unarmed, but violence was not the same as cruelty. A king capable of such brutality that he had shot at a deer in the act of mating with his doe had no moral right to rule.

Please forgive me, Rishivar, he said.

Then Pandu repeated the dying man's last words to me. 'The fruit of this act must be yours...You brought me grief when I was happy. For this, O pitiless man, I curse you. You, too, will feel fervent desire for the woman you love, and you too will die before appeasing it.'

The woman you love.

12

A thousand cows for killing a kshatriya; a hundred cows for the death of a vaishya and just ten cows if the victim was a shudra or a woman. These are the fines imposed as punishment when the crime is murder.

'For brahmahatya, the murder of a brahmin, there is no fine big enough,' declared Kripacharya. 'No way to make amends either. No convenient ritual like a *japa, tapa, homa,* yajna, *tarpan* or *shraadh kriya.* No purifying bath in a holy river or lake. No redemption for the soul. No *mukti* and no *moksha.*' He held up a finger to reinforce the point. 'However, in a special case like this one, when there are mitigating circumstances—'

'You may say what you like, Kula Guru,' interrupted Pitamaha, his deep voice ringing through the sabha. 'This was not murder. It was a mishap. Murders are intended, mishaps occur unintentionally. *They happen.*' There were several nods of agreement from the audience. Pitamaha continued, 'We have to bear in mind that there was only one witness to the death of rishi Kindama—the king himself.'

Everyone turned to look at the king. His face was expressionless.

'He could well have hidden this incident from us.' Pitamaha shot Pandu an annoyed look. 'There was no need for you to share this information, Maharaj.' Turning back to the sabha, he added in a louder tone, 'But he made a clean breast of it. Isn't that enough to convince you all of his innocence?'

Several heads nodded in assent.

'*I* am convinced,' Pitamaha announced. 'In fact, I would even go so far to say that he was the victim of a deception. There are other questions we should be asking. For instance, why was that brahmin masquerading as a deer? Why was he copulating with a deer? Isn't that a bestial act? Why is there no punishment for *him*?'

A murmur went around the audience. Everyone turned to Kripacharya. The question seemed to confound the kula guru. He stared at the floor, frowning hard. After a moment, as though making a humble submission, he said, 'Rishi Kindama is dead, Gangaputra.'

Pitamaha brushed away this inconvenient fact with a wave of the hand. 'How does that answer my question?'

There was a titter in the audience. Kripacharya looked beseechingly at the mahamantri. Vidur stood up and cleared his throat. 'Kula Guru, you spoke about mitigating circumstances. Surely, the detail that when Maharaja Pandu aimed the arrow, when he let it fly from the bow and when it struck its mark, the target was, *in fact,* a large deer, can be called a mitigating circumstance.' He turned to Pandu. 'Didn't it happen that way, Maharaj?'

Pandu, who had been, all this while, sitting with his head lowered, a picture of dejection, now straightened up. 'Yes,' he said with quiet dignity. 'That is exactly what happened, but what does it matter, Vidur? I thought I had killed a deer, but these hands that aimed the arrow have the blood of a brahmin on them.' He held out his hands as though he was the plaintiff and they the culprit. 'It is *my* karma. Whatever be the punishment, I am ready to suffer it.'

A chorus of dismay ran through the sabha. Sitting with me in the queens' gallery, Madri dug her nails deeper into my arm and drew blood. 'It's not true,' she whispered, her eyes wide with distress. 'It is my karma, too. *I* wanted that deerskin, I sent him after it. Why doesn't he tell them that? He is not to blame. It was all *my* fault.'

I quelled my irritation and said softly, 'Listen, the kula guru is speaking now.'

'Mahamantri is right,' Kripacharya said. 'If it was indeed murder, the punishment is clear, Maharaj. You would have to award yourself the death penalty.' He waited for the pandemonium to subside before quietly delivering the blow. 'But while this was not murder, it was, nonetheless, a sin.'

Before anyone could react, Pitamaha stood up. 'Stop splitting hairs!' he roared. 'Murder it is not, sin it may be—well then, tell us what is needed to expiate the sin? Vidur, come out with the solution!'

'If it is a sin, atonement is the only way,' said Vidur, distractedly. 'I cannot be more specific. There *is* no precedent. It is up to the maharaja, as the ultimate arbitrator of justice, to decide on the nature of the penance for this…sin.'

All heads turned to look at the king, no longer the accused, but the judge. Seeming to realize it, he sat up straight. 'Thank you, Vidur,' he said with composure. 'I have made up my mind. The only appropriate thing for me to do is accept the way of *tyaga*. I must renounce the kingship and go into the forest to take up *sanyasa ashrama*. Without blessings, without salutations, without choices, without possessions. This will be both my penance and my punishment.'

Vidur looked down. Pitamaha's shoulders drooped. Dhritarashtra cleared his throat. 'Maharaj! That is too severe, both as punishment and penance,' he said, his voice breaking. 'Please reconsider.'

I thought the plea sounded false. Perhaps Pandu thought so too. Without so much as a glance at his elder brother, Pandu said in a detached voice, 'My decision is final.'

The words hung in balance, were weighed and assessed. One by one, several of the ministers stood up and spoke, lauding the king's noble intention to ensure that dharma was upheld, but urging him, all the same, to withdraw his decision to abdicate. Then it was the turn of the elder citizens, who pleaded with one voice that the king change his decision; it was too drastic. Couldn't the king award a simpler punishment to himself? Did he have the right to renounce a responsibility that had been placed on him? Was it fair to the populace that there should be no king on the throne *again*? Did he not understand that a kingdom without a king was destined for severe misfortune?

Pandu listened courteously to these appeals. 'I am a descendant of a noble line,' he said. 'My forefathers have always known what is ethical and what is true; they have had the courage to make difficult choices. I ask you to remember my ancestor Devapi whom Hastinapur chose as its ruler despite his skin ailment...What did he say? That he would not be king because he feared that his personal affliction would not allow him to fulfil his responsibility to his people. I draw my inspiration from him. *A king must be without blemish*. This unfortunate incident is a blot on my noble line. I must work through tapas to remove it. Till that is done, *I* do not consider myself fit to rule.'

One of the citizen elders spoke up. 'Rajan, as you have chosen to cite the example of your venerable ancestor, please recall what happened after he left the kingdom. There were no rains for two years. The wells and ponds dried up. There was a severe drought. Rajan, we sympathize with the personal burden of brahmahatya that you have to bear. We understand your individual desire to atone. But why are we, your people, also being penalized?'

'It does not matter who sits on the throne,' Pandu said. 'With Bhishma Pitamaha as the caretaker, Hastinapur will remain safe from threat for all eternity.'

It went on in this way for a while, the eloquent arguments and the sincere pleas, the gentle but firm refusals. I noticed there were those who had begun to nod quietly and say that justice had been served—they expected no less a gesture from a scion of Bharata. Strangely, I felt nothing. Beside me, Madri was snivelling. The rajmata looked too upset to speak. She left her seat and did not return. Ambalika was staring at the floor. Ambika looked expectant. 'What is going to happen now?' she asked, of no one in particular.

'You are going to be the next rajmata,' Ambalika said drily. 'Congratulations!'

'Oh!' A look of self-importance settled on Ambika's face. She glanced at Gandhari. We all did. Behind the black silk blindfold, Gandhari had the still grace of a swan floating on a dark lake. Her hands were locked in a tense grip, lips pressed tight as though she did not trust herself to speak.

Below in the sabha, Vidur was in a huddle conferring with Pandu. Pitamaha was talking quietly to Dhritarashtra. Everyone seemed to be waiting for someone else to make the next move. Silence fell and Vidur spoke: 'Maharaja Pandu, who will rule in your name while you are in the forest?'

'I appoint Dhritarashtra as my regent. He will be answerable to Pitamaha and Rajmata Satyavati, and will be guided by your wisdom, Mahamantri.'

'We have heard you, O Rajan.' Vidur bowed his head. 'We respect your wishes.'

Dhritarashtra stood up and climbed the few stairs to the throne. For a moment he stood there, head lowered in thought. It seemed as if he wanted to say something, but was unsure of how to word it. Whatever it was, the moment came and went. Pandu removed his crown and gave it to Pitamaha, who looked at it silently for a long moment, then placed it on Dhritarashtra's head.

Madri was puzzled. 'Is that all it takes? Moving the crown from one head to another?'

'Shh,' I said, looking around furtively to see if anyone else had heard her. 'This is all we need concern ourselves with.'

A cry went up. '*Maharaja Pandu ki jai.*' It rang repeatedly through the sabha. And then someone remembered to say, 'Maharaja Dhritarashtra ki jai.' But the response to that was tepid.

❖

I had spent barely eighteen months in Hastinapur, yet friendships had come into bud and a few had even flowered. Perhaps that is why, though I tried to be dispassionate, there were so many teary farewells. The maids wept, the two mothers-in-law shed copious tears and Gandhari, who could not weep because of the blindfold, nevertheless clung to me as if she could not bear to let go. Even the rajmata was teary-eyed as we made our farewell. Though I told myself that tears meant nothing but a social courtesy that I was exchanging, like the embraces, mine, too, flowed with abandon.

'Why wear these strange clothes?' the sairandhri asked with a frown. 'Has Maharaj renounced the life of a householder as well?'

'Yes,' I replied, fingering the cloth of bark that the dasi had laid out. It was rougher than what I was used to wearing, but the dyer had dyed it a pleasant ochre shade.

'Well, if he is taking to the mountains to atone for *his* sin, why are you not staying back?' she asked truculently. 'Why does a renunciant need to take his wives with him?'

'He would have liked us to stay back, but Madri and I have convinced him our place is with him.'

She looked at me and raised an eyebrow to signal her disbelief.

'This is the appropriate dress code for my new life,' I said.

'Is it also appropriate that you, a married woman, are not going to wear any jewellery at all? Not even the bangles and toe-rings that are auspicious for you?'

I laughed. 'Don't look so stern. It is a relief not to be covered from head to toe in metal. I feel so much lighter.' She eyed me briefly in silence, then began to work on my hair. 'Keep it simple,' I told her. 'From tomorrow, I'll have to do it on my own.'

Her look became fierce. 'Whatever else you may or may not have picked up from the Kurus, you've certainly picked up their penchant for milking every situation for what it is worth.' When she'd finished fashioning my hair into a bun, she picked the chudamani to fasten it on the top.

I shook my head. 'Not that. I should not wear that anymore.'

'*Now* is when you need to wear it, Maharani,' she said, in a tone that brooked no arguments.

When the moment came to leave, it was surprisingly devoid of drama. In fact, it was a bit of an anti-climax. Pandu had planned to walk out through the city gates—maybe there was more than a grain of truth in the sairandhri's observation that the Kurus had a penchant for theatrics. But word reached the palace that the citizens were planning to beg him to return, or else they intended to accompany him into the forest. To avoid discomfiture for all concerned, Pitamaha ordered that his chariot drop us all to the edge of the Kuru lands. So it was that only Pitamaha and Vidur saw us depart. When I turned back for a last glimpse, Vidur was still standing on the palace's steps, looking at us.

13

Shatashringa. That was what we named the forest. It had taken us many weeks to reach this spot, our journey drawing us deeper into the Himalayas towards the peak Gandhamadana, onward to the glacial lake of Indradyumna, and even further to this place that was so elevated that the clouds lingered all day in a fine mist. The hundred crags that inspired us to create the name also lent it a magical aspect. Several cascades threaded the forested hill slopes, the spray from the mighty torrents added body to the thin air and refracted the light, sifting and shifting it, so that the colours were born and died from moment to moment. It felt as if we were living inside a pulsating rainbow. The many sounds of water: roaring, gushing, whooshing, pushing, frothing in hidden pools, dripping quietly off moss-covered rock faces, gliding secretly through the dense undergrowth, made it appear as if Nature was offering a libation to the gods. The air tasted fresh and cool, of sap coursing through the veins of green things.

Though we were far away from Hastinapur, we were not alone. There were ashramas in the forest where sages and adepts lived a quiet life. And there were the rules: the killing of animals and birds was forbidden, as was fishing in the pools; there were plants and berries one could not pluck, flowers that were noxious not just to touch, but even to smell, for that alone could make you lose your senses.

'When are we going to eat proper food again?' asked Madri, staring glumly at the earthen bowl of purple-pink berries whose tartness had been offset with a sprinkling of rock salt.

Pandu looked up sharply from his plate. 'Kunti has offered it to you with good grace,' he said. 'Accept it in a similar spirit.'

For an instant Madri looked surprised that he had even spoken to her. Since we'd reached the forest, he'd had little to say to either of us; sometimes several days would pass before he uttered a word. As the reprimand sank in, she wilted. But she finished her portion without fuss.

Later, I told Pandu, 'You shouldn't be so hard. This is difficult for her.'

'She'll have to get used to it.'

'Is it only about yourself? Aren't we also in this?' He eyed me without replying, then turned away. 'Are you going out again?' I asked, riled by his lack of response. 'Where do you go? What do you do? Why don't you talk to us anymore, Aryaputra?'

'Look around you, Kunti…In this world I am not "aryaputra", we are not king and queen.'

I forced myself to be calm. 'We are still man and wife.'

'In name only.'

There was a knock on the door. Pandu did not bother to hide his relief. A small band of bark-clad ascetics waited outside. Without a backward glance at me he joined them as they walked away. Madri came to the threshold and stood beside me.

'He isn't the man we married,' she said tonelessly. 'He has become someone else...I relinquished my earlier life because my lord chose to do so, and I did not want to live without him, but I cannot recognize my husband in him anymore.' She turned to me with a look of sadness and bafflement. 'Who is he now, Didi?'

'I don't know.'

Her gaze shifted to the chudamani in my hair, and a trace of amusement entered her face. 'But you are still Maharani Kunti.'

'Yes,' I said.

There was a twinkle in her eyes, the first in a long time. 'Then I am still your despised sapatni Madri.'

It was hard not to smile back. 'Yes. You are exactly that.'

❖

Pandu's new companions were *siddhas*, spiritual masters, who shunned human company and lived in mountain caves. It had taken him many months to gain entry into their closed universe, but it now seemed as if he had always been one of them. He had embraced their lifestyle with the passion of someone who was exorcising an evil spirit within him.

Lust runs in my blood, he had said. Does it all boil down to the blood that courses in one's veins? What happens when there are cross-currents in that stream? Does a human drown in the whirlpool of conflicting desires? What can he do to rise above it? What must he do? These were the questions circling in my head, like scavengers hovering over a dying animal, as I watched Pandu subject himself to every discomfort possible. He practised long hours of meditation in difficult postures, balancing on the edge of a precipice or standing under an icy waterfall; he starved for days, and when he ate at all, it was a frugal meal, always raw, with no grain; he barely slept, but sat through the night in meditation. He, a man who had once led an active outdoor life, brimming with restless energy, learned to sit so still that ants would crawl all over his body and he would not be aware. He guarded his speech as if it was Kubera's treasure. In fact, he had so utterly discarded his former life that there was, indeed, nothing left to say.

'What do the rishis live on?' I asked him once, because it remained about the only subject on which we could still talk.

'Fresh air,' he replied. After a moment, he added, 'And water.'

'There's plenty of that here.'

'It has properties that enhance one's life span,' he said. 'Some of the rishis here are a thousand years old.'

'How long does it take for the body to get used to living on fresh air alone?'

'As long as it takes.'

'You are nearly as thin as the air. One of these days, we'll breathe you in.' It was a weak joke, but he didn't even accord it the politeness of a smile. His sense of humour had gone the same way as all the other things that he had renounced: a love of fine clothes. superior horses, a lively discussion, his passion for archery. Nor did his eyes follow Madri any more, not even in surreptitious sidelong glances. On some days, I got the feeling that we, his women, were invisible to him, shut off even in dreams, as past lives are. Yes, the man had changed, the husband in him had moved out, and like a sleeper who wakes up and leaves his shape on the bed, what remained was an imprint, a vestigial reminder of what had once connected him to us. Onto this, Madri and I pinned our relationship with him.

'What do they actually do, these siddhas?' I asked him. 'Why *are* they—what are they for?'

'Because *we* need them,' he replied. 'Not just for their deep knowledge of the medicinal plants that grow here and nowhere else, but for their purity. They are pure energy, tapas makes them so. The light—haven't you noticed the light here?'

'It is different.'

'The vibrations in this place are generated by the combined tapas of the rishis. They have health-giving properties, like the water and the air.'

'Have the vibrations worked on you?' I asked. 'Are you well now?'

He didn't reply immediately. 'For the first time in my life, I am free of pain.'

'That must be a relief,' I said. He gave me a look that, for some reason, reminded me of our earlier rapport.

There were times when he would be gone for days in the company of the adepts. I gathered that there were arcane rituals performed deep inside the caves. He always returned revitalized. It seemed to me that he looked younger and that light that he talked about was now *in* him. Strangely, I felt no desire for him. It was, I understood, possible to live like this and even be happy. This happiness seemed more plausible. It demanded little of you because there was less to demand from life. Austerity towards oneself, I learnt in Shatashringa, is always a good thing. Especially, austerity of speech. Silence was a solvent that, in the end, left one with nothing to think about, not even secrets. Mine. His. Shatashringa had set us free.

Madri, who had no secrets, found it a prison. She was full of fears. Fear of how the mist in Shatashringa forest would suddenly thicken, so that your next step might well be your last. Fear of the cloud bursts, flash floods, the sudden shaking of the ground beneath our feet. I had to accompany her when she wanted to answer the call of nature, which, in the beginning, was the only reason she left our simple dwelling. In those early days she wanted to talk of the past. Of what had happened and why, of what had not and what should have. I tried to be patient, but occasionally I did get cross with her. 'Stop making yourself the centrepiece of this tragedy,' I told her.

'At least you accept that it is a tragedy. A bigger one for you than for others—since you had the most to lose. Don't you miss anything? No regrets at all? No hidden longings?'

There is no loneliness as dark as the one that encloses a secret. *He must be five now.*

'Look!' I said pointing to the indigo sky. 'There is a new moon tonight.'

14

I no longer asked Pandu where he went when he left with the sages. But I waited for his return. On that night of the new moon I waited till dawn. As the red gold ball crested the mountains and started spinning out the first shining threads of daylight over the pale snows, he came home. There was something different about him, a brightness in his eyes as if a sheath had been removed and a new resolve unfurled.

'They did not take me with them,' he said.

'Where have they gone?'

The morning breeze soughed through the deodars. The question I had asked swam further and further away. At last, he said, 'To Brahmaloka.'

'And where is it?'

'Northward.' He pointed to the highest peak, Himavat.

'The siddhas said that the journey was too difficult for you and Madri.'

I was surprised. 'You mean, you asked them if we could accompany you? But you've never done that before!'

His mouth worked for a moment before the words emerged. 'It was a rare chance to see something ordinary mortals don't get to see, and certainly not women. Last night, there was a gathering of the gods and sages in the court of Brahma, the self-created One. I was very keen to witness it. I did not know how long I'd be gone—or even if I might return.' He waited for me to say something. I answered with a polite silence. 'They described the journey,' he continued, without missing a beat. 'On the way is the lake Manasarovar. Beyond it lies the retreat of the gods, a place of beautiful gardens, mighty rivers, golden-domed palaces. There live the gandharvas and the sound of their celestial music fills the air, veined by the soft chimes of anklets as the apsaras swirl in dance. There are deep underground caves filled with gold and precious stones. Wealth beyond human imagination.'

Something about his tone suggested that he was leading me, not up the mountain trail, but down the garden path. 'Is *that* what you wanted us to see?' I asked.

He tugged at his ear. 'Beyond all that lie vast windswept spaces, rock and barren soil, rivers of ice. Nothing grows there, not a blade of grass. There are no animals, not even a rat and certainly no birds, the air is too thin even for them.'

'But how would we have travelled through such hard terrain?'

'That is what the siddhas pointed out…You both would not survive the journey.' His mouth drooped. 'It was an excuse, of course,' he said dispiritedly. 'They knew, as I know, that the gates of heaven cannot open for me because I am sonless.' He looked at me. 'Do you know what it means for a man to be sonless?'

The roar from the rapids filled my ears. 'No, my lord,' I admitted. 'I do not.'

He talked then of the debts, four in number, that every

man must discharge before the end of his life: to his ancestors, the gods, the sages and his fellow men. He had, he said, cleared all but the most important one, the debt to his *pitris*.

'If I don't have a son,' he said, 'how will my ancestors be reborn? I need a son, Kunti.' It was not an entreaty but an assertion. 'The sages said to me last night that I will have not just one but many sons. The sages cannot lie. When I asked them what they meant, they said, 'You are an intelligent man. Think about it.'

'And have you thought about it?'

'You alone can rescue me.'

'How?'

'There are at least a dozen ways by which a man can get himself a son,' he began. 'The best kind is of course the son a man and his wife have together, but unfortunately the truth of my situation is such that I cannot follow that path.'

I said nothing. He was referring to Rishi Kindama's curse; we had never spoken of it after that fateful day. The silence had created a convincing narrative that allowed us to live together without raising the usual doubts that surface when a woman's body remains unfruitful for too long. Moreover, it was a story that Madri completely believed, and heaped further blame on herself for it. There was such a tendency toward melodrama in that girl! As for me, what did I believe? Had the dying rishi, indeed, cursed Pandu? Would just a single move from his side towards Madri or me really lead to his death? There was no way I was going to test a rishi's word. Not again.

'The next option is the son born of a man's wife,' he said, 'as a result of a generous contribution from a brahmin rishi.'

A cold finger slid up my spine.

'Then there is the son he can get by *paying* another man a fee to plant a seed in his wife.'

'I will not permit this kind of talk,' I said curtly.

After a moment, he said, 'There is also the son the wife can obtain for her husband by sleeping around indiscriminately for the sheer pleasure of it—but that, too, is a disgusting idea, don't you think?'

'I think that this entire conversation is disgusting.'

He spun his hand, fingers splayed to show his lack of options. 'We have to choose from one of these solutions. There are other ways, of course. For instance, if you'd had a child with another man before your marriage, that child would bear my name.'

Where are you? Can I get you back? The next instant I realized how impossible it was. Where was I even to start my search? And how would I explain it to Pandu? Truth is, so often, not a simple thing. A lie is so much simpler. Maybe that is why husbands tell lies and wives refrain from speaking the truth. It didn't matter so much that I did not trust him. What mattered was that he should trust me. I stood up abruptly. 'Enough, my lord!'

He looked at me in surprise. 'Why are you so distressed, Kunti?' I pressed my lips tight, aware that he was watching me. After a while, he said, 'Well, what do you think?' When I still did not reply, he cleared his throat and emphatically declared, 'It is the only way! There are young men in the ashrama, noble rishis who could…help us out, if only you'd agree.'

'I will never agree,' I said angrily. 'And you shouldn't

be saying such things to me. I am *your* wife. I can think of only you in that way. Even the mere thought of another man touching me makes my skin crawl.'

He looked put out. 'Aren't you being selfish?'

'Perhaps you should ask that question of yourself.'

His voice hardened. 'You are not the first woman who has been asked to do this. I could give you several examples. Why, I, too, was born of the seed of another man in the field of Vichitravirya. There was no blame attached to my mother.'

'I am not a field,' I said. 'Just as you are not a king. Have you forgotten? *What* patrimony will you leave your son? How will he grow up?'

His face grew pale and taut with anger. *So much for penance.* 'We'll worry about that later, he said. 'First you must do as I command you.'

'Impossible...I will not sleep with another man.'

'A woman is not considered immoral for doing whatever her husband asks of her—if she does it out of love for him.'

'Love has nothing to do with what you want from me. You care nothing for my feelings, only for the fruit of my womb—that is all you are interested in.'

He sighed, but did not bother to deny it. 'Kunti, I'm not asking anything wrong of you. On the contrary, it is your duty to obey your husband.'

'Why do you men always say that when you want to force your writ?' My voice rose. 'I recognize only you as my husband, but there is a limit to what you can ask of me. If you had the sensitivity you would understand.'

He held up his hand, silencing me. 'A branch of our family, the northern Kurus, a tribal people who live not far from here, still follow the practice where one woman *can* have several husbands.'

'But in the plains where we both come from, my lord, it is different. It has to be one husband for every woman in her lifetime.'

'Whether in the plains or in the hills, it is a sin for a woman to refuse her husband when he makes a request for a son of her.'

'How can a refusal be a sin? What sin?'

'The sin of killing an embryo,' he pronounced grandly. 'I can't give you a son, but *you* can certainly give me one. It is a sin for you to deny me that son.'

'Just one will do?' I asked, sarcastically.

'For a kshatriya, one son is as good as having no son at all.'

'And how many will you want?'

He groaned. 'These questions of yours, Kunti!' Then, seeing the set of my face, he said quietly, 'He is going to need brothers.'

There was a moment of absolute stillness. 'Is Maharani Gandhari expecting a child?'

'Yes.' His face was unreadable.

'But that is good news!' I said.

'Good and bad.'

'Why bad?'

'It is turning out to be an unusually long pregnancy. Eleven months now…They are worried, but not overly so. That boon she is said to possess is on everyone's minds. A hundred sons.'

Boons and curses. What would our lives be without them?

The time had finally come; the words, however, came slower. 'When I was a young girl,' I said, 'Rishi Durvasa visited my foster father's house and I was placed in his service. Pleased with me, the temperamental rishi gave me an incantation that, he claimed, would beckon any male god.'

He heard me out without interruption. After a while he said, 'Use the mantra to call the celestial, Kunti.'

'Which one?'

He became thoughtful. 'The most prized quality in a king is a sense of justice. And the most virtuous of gods is also the god of judgement, Dharma. A king who is just and virtuous can never commit a sin. Call Dharma.'

'So be it.'

❖

He was born in the month of Kartika when the pale pink blooms of rhododendron covered the hillsides and the red kaaphal berries had ripened on the trees. Entering the world with the minimum of fuss, he gave a lusty cry to herald his arrival and then fell silent. I watched as Madri bathed him in lukewarm water, wrapped him in soft linen and tenderly handed him to me to suckle. It took him a few seconds to get used to the squishy embrace of my breast, then I felt the warm, sweet tug on my nipple and our relationship was sealed. He was asleep in the crook of my arm when Pandu came into the birthing room.

As my pregnancy had advanced, there had been a discernible change in Pandu. Though he still spoke very little, he seemed more approachable. He had even started helping around the house, collecting firewood and fetching water, tasks which had grown difficult for me in the last weeks. Just a few days prior to the birth, he had brought home a milch cow and her calf, a gift, he said, from the ashrama.

'I have a list of names,' he said to me now, as I lay resting. 'Bharata, after my great ancestor is one, Pratipa is another. Or we could call him Dharmaraja after—'

'No,' I said quickly. 'Let's not name him *after* anyone.'

'How about Ajatashatru? It means "one without enemies".'

I looked down at the sleeping infant, the petal soft lips. In time, as the contours of his face became more distinct, chin, mouth, eyes became attuned to his thoughts and emotions, I, like everyone else, would have to learn to read him. Whose features had he come with? Whose nature? What destiny? The god who had fathered him had been pokerfaced as he had gone about his business. But this time around, I, too, had been detached, turning over on the side and falling asleep when it was over.

Pandu continued to mull over names. 'How about Yudhisthira?' he asked. 'It means "one who is still in battle".'

I frowned. 'Is that a good quality?'

He smiled in a superior way. 'Coolness in the face of an adversary is a rare quality. Only the best soldiers have it.'

'Poise, self-confidence, a steady head,' I murmured.

He nodded eagerly. 'Yes, all of that.'

I smiled. 'It is a good name, my lord, for your first-born.'

'Yours too,' he added, tenderly. 'He will also be known as the first Kaunteya. It has a ring to it.'

'He is a Pandava,' I said, adding, just to make it crystal clear, 'That is how he will be known. No other name is needed.'

'Pandava,' he repeated, trying the new sound on his tongue. His face shone with joy. 'Let me announce it to the world.' He went out. A few minutes later, I heard him blowing the conch shell. Three long blasts. The sound rang through the forest. Later, some people said that a voice had boomed down from the sky: *This child will grow up to be the best among men, the most virtuous, the most truthful. He will be a king whose fame will spread in all three worlds.*

The very next day a messenger was sent to Hastinapur with the news of the royal birth. When the man returned, Vidur was with him. I felt a surge of joy so sharp that it surprised me. I had not expected that among all the people I had left behind, he was the one I would miss the most. The long climb into the mountains had left him out of breath. He got off the shaggy pony with some difficulty. Watching him approach with slow, careful steps, Pandu's mouth twitched.

'Marriage suits you rather too well,' he called out.

'Plains folk like me would need an extra pair of lungs to survive here,' grumbled Vidur.

'Welcome!' Pandu reached out to wrap his half-brother in a deep embrace.

After Vidur had been made comfortable with food and drink, he asked to see the new prince of Hastinapur.

'You mean your nephew.' There was an edge to Pandu's voice.

'Yes, he is that too,' said Vidur, equably.

When I brought the baby to him, his face broke into a smile of pure delight. Cradling the infant in his arms, he said, 'I have prayed for this very moment to come to pass.' So quickly had we grown unused to displays of emotion that his words and his moist eyes left us feeling slightly embarrassed. 'When I go back, I'm going to be asked about him in minute detail, so tell me whom does he resemble? Does he have the rajmata's nose? His grandmother Ambalika's colour? She has sent some things for him. Maharani Gandhari, too, has sent a shawl made of very fine wool.'

Pandu's eyes grew flinty. 'He needs no comforts from the palace. My son was born in a mountain hut and must learn to live the life he was born to.'

Vidur drew a sharp breath. 'Nevertheless, he is your firstborn, Maharaja Pandu. The first in the new generation of Kuru kings. His inheritance lies in the palace. You *cannot* deny him his right.'

Pandu sent him a twisted smile. 'Tell me, Mahamantri, what right does the son of a king who has abdicated have?'

'The last time the consecration rites were conducted was when you were crowned king,' Vidur said quietly. 'Not just as your eldest son, but as the first of his generation, this babe has the foremost claim on the throne…And this even Maharaja Dhritarashtra has acknowledged.'

'I am done with thrones, kingships, wars and politics.'

'I can see that,' Vidur said drily. 'This place is ideal for the way of life you have chosen, but a kshatriya must be brought up according to the tradition he is born into. This child's tradition is not of the forest, but of kingship. In time, he will need training to prepare him for the role.'

'There is no dearth of fine teachers here.'

Vidur nodded in agreement. 'And you, Maharaj, are still the best archer in the land.'

For a while after that Pandu was quiet but thoughtful.

Vidur did not stay long. Plying him with our simple hospitality, Madri and I showered him with questions. Our eagerness for news only revealed that, despite forsaking our earlier life, we had not been able to cut our links. 'Have you heard anything from Vraj bhumi?' I asked. 'What is the news of my brother Vasudeva and his wife?'

Vidur's face became sombre. 'They are still Kansa's prisoners in Mathura. He presides over a reign of terror. There were rumours that Princess Devaki gave birth several times, but the babies were all stillborn...Fear stalks Vraj bhumi like a pernicious curse, yet there is a growing hope that Devaki's eighth son will liberate the Vrishnis.'

'Do you think Kansa will allow him to live?'

'Narada muni may be a meddler, but his prophecies have never been wrong. Before it comes to pass, though, there will be some very turbulent times.'

Later, when we were alone, I cornered Pandu, 'What is the news from Hastinapur?'

His eyes flicked over me and shifted away. 'The maharani had a miscarriage.'

'Oh! But that's terrible.' He gave me a sharp look. I flushed. 'She has lost a child, my lord—what can be worse for a mother?'

'It wasn't a *child* she miscarried...It was nothing resembling a human, but a ball of flesh, hard as a rock.'

I gasped.

He nodded grimly 'The news of your son's birth upset her. She became violent, uncontrollable.'

When I was silent, he prompted, 'Don't you want to know what happened next?'

He told me then about the crisis in Hastinapur. The news of Yudhisthira's birth had, indeed, been welcomed, but in Dhritarashtra's household there had been a pall of gloom. The queen had cried all day and cursed her fate. She had banged her head against the bedpost, hit her belly repeatedly.

I was appalled. 'This doesn't sound like Gandhari Didi at all.'

Pandu shrugged. 'The desire for offspring is no different from any other desire.'

'But she was meant to reap a hundred sons.'

He shrugged again. 'They are working at it. Who knows—she still might.'

The rajmata, he explained, had called in her sole anchor in every crisis, the rishi Krishna Dwaipayana. I heard, with growing revulsion, how, on his orders, the ball of red flesh that the queen had delivered was washed under jets of cold water till it spilt into a hundred thumb-sized parts, and each part was incubated in an earthen jar filled with ghee and herbs. The jars were then stored in an undisclosed underground chamber. The sage had whispered secret mantras that, purportedly, gave rise to life inside the jars—his own grandchildren. Three months had passed. The royal physicians had put their fingertips to the jars and declared that they had detected heartbeats. Now the blind king and the blindfolded queen went often into the underground chamber where the embryos were housed, and the queen sang to her unborn children. He ended by saying that, lately, eerie sounds had been emerging from the chamber.

I shuddered. 'A hundred sons.'

'A hundred and *one*,' he corrected me. 'The queen's personal maid was delivered of a boy some months ago.'

Pandu's eyes moved to the baby sleeping in his simple bentwood crib. 'He will need a brother whose strength is far superior to any man born—it is time for you to invoke the next celestial, Kunti.'

After a moment, I asked, 'Who shall it be?'

'The lord of the winds. Vayu deva.'

We named the boy Bheemasen.

A few weeks after his birth, tidings arrived from the palace. Dhritarashtra's sons had been born. All hundred. I tried to imagine the scene: a hundred crying babies, a hundred wet nurses, a hundred names to choose. If I felt a twinge of envy at all, it was at the news that Gandhari had also got herself a baby girl, whom she had named Dushala. A daughter—I would have liked one.

❖

The births of his sons changed Pandu. As the babies grew into lusty infants he, too, regained much of his former vigour. It was not uncommon to hear him laugh out loud. One day, when Yudhishthira had learnt to walk, but Bheem was still crawling, I watched him fashion a toy bow.

'Aren't they a bit young for such games?' I asked.

'No harm in starting early. But I'm afraid neither of them is going to be particularly good at archery.'

I laughed. 'They are babies. How can you tell?'

'It's in their eyes. Neither of them has the archer's eye.'

Just then Yudhisthira, leading a small clay chariot by a string, came close to Bheem and squatted beside him. Bheem sat up with interest. The elder brother whose babyspeak was slowly becoming decipherable said, 'See, Bheemm... This is a ratha.'

Bheem looked at the toy for a long moment. Then he hauled himself up on his chubby legs, the soft flesh of his thighs rippling as he steadied himself, raised his foot and brought it down on the ratha, smashing it to bits. He turned around to stare into our shocked faces and bestowed a beatific smile.

Pandu burst out laughing. 'He may not be an archer, but I see the beginnings of a mace warrior.'

Madri looked at me in excitement. 'Didi, did you see? The baby just stood up—for the first time!'

But I was looking at my elder son. Yudhisthira's lips trembled, his face turned to me as if seeking an explanation for the smashed toy, or maybe it was reassurance. 'Come here,' I said softly. 'Let us go for a walk into the forest, only you and I.'

A few nights later Pandu said: 'Kunti, our next son must be the world's greatest archer. I have already chosen a name for him. Savyasachi. It means "skilled with both hands". He will be one who can string a bow with his left as well as his right hand—only the rarest of archers can do that. Or what about naming him Parantapa? *One who destroys his enemy with his concentration.* Focus is the prime quality in an archer…He must become an archer whose glory will last as long the sun shines. We could even name him Arjuna, what do you think? *The shining one.* In fact, Surya deva himself would make the ideal—'

'No,' I said, abruptly. 'Leave it to me—I want to choose the god this time.'

He became anxious. 'Who do you have in mind?'

I cast about for a name. 'Indra,' I said. 'The lord of the skies.'

'Excellent choice!'

On the day of the newborn's naming ceremony, the astrologer arrived with the horoscope. Pandu sat with him for a long time. Later, he said to me, 'This son of yours will be invincible and his fame will spread far and wide.'

'Does that make you happy, my lord?'

He frowned while choosing his words. 'It worries me, Kunti,' he said finally. 'A warrior's fame can only spread through battle. Your son's horoscope says it clearly: in his lifetime, there will be a great war that will end all the kshatriya clans.' With a sudden burst of energy and impatience, he added, 'He must be prepared for it.'

Soon after Arjuna's birth, a messenger arrived, not from Hastinapur, but from Vraj bhumi, the land of the Vrishnis. The message, a secret, told us that my brother Vasudeva and his wife had been blessed with a baby boy, born in the dead of night and shifted immediately to a hiding place. Kansa's spies and soldiers were on the rampage looking for him, but nothing was known about the infant. This news upset me. I was sad for my sister-in-law Devaki, and anxious for the baby. Pandu and Madri put it down to the broodiness new mothers sometimes feel, but for days afterwards I found myself thinking of that newborn far away and wondering about him. I found myself praying for him, as I had for *my* firstborn—that the breast that nursed him belonged to a tender woman, that she would shower him with love. That he would not lack for a mother.

❖

With two toddlers and one newborn in the house, my life had grown so full that there was no time to look up from the household chores. We had added more rooms, enlarged the kitchen and planted a vegetable patch to supplement our diet. As the requirement for milk increased, we got a second cow. All of this made for more work. Thus, when Pandu approached me once again with his demand for another son, I could not control my irritation.

'You know as well as I do that the shastras do not permit it,' I said. 'A woman who has been with more than four men is called a whore. Do you want the mother of your sons—' I stopped abruptly, as the significance of what I'd just said struck me.

'Oh…erm…yes,' he said, tugging his ear. 'I mean no… No, what I meant was that I hadn't seen it that way.' He looked at me inquiringly. 'How does it become four men?' Before I could think of a convincing reply, he nodded. 'Oh yes, I see! Myself and three others. But Kunti, an encounter with a celestial—is it the same as with an ordinary mortal?'

'The net result is the same, isn't it?'

He looked unhappy. 'If you say so,' he said.

15

I watched them—Pandu and Madri. I had learned to be unobtrusive about it. With the birth of his sons and the reawakening of his secret dreams, Pandu, like a dead man returning to life, had regained his earlier interest in her. He smiled more when she was around him and she, on her part, found more reasons to be around him. But she was mindful, I noticed. She had not forgotten the curse. If he came too close, a sudden wariness would enter her eyes and she would immediately withdraw, call out to a child or busy herself with a household chore. However, they were attuned to each other in a way that was, for me, disturbing. I could not help but draw a comparison: with her he was the man he would have liked to be. With me, of course, he was just himself.

It was late afternoon, the elder two boys had settled down for their nap. I was with Arjuna, rocking him to sleep. He was now ten months old and the first of his milk teeth had appeared. Whenever I could get away for a few minutes, I liked to spend time with him; he had a way of smiling with his eyes that I loved. Sometime I would catch a short nap too. Maybe that was why they spoke as they did, not secretly as conspirators, but as a husband and wife might, in the privacy of a bower not far from the window of the room where I was.

'Why are you so downcast?' he asked her.

'Am I complaining?'

'I know your every mood, dear one—something is troubling you.'

She sighed.

'Tell me,' he persisted. 'Frown lines detract from your loveliness.'

'Of what use is this loveliness?' she cried petulantly. 'God knows, I've tried to make the best of my situation.'

'What situation?' he asked, and then, as if tendering her a secret gift, 'I love you.'

'That doesn't change my situation,' she said. 'I'm nothing more than a maid. The patrani has delivered three sons, but what do I have?'

'You are their mother just as much as Kunti,' he said. 'Haven't you seen how their faces brighten when you are around?' He laughed and lowered his voice to a caress. 'Young though they are, all three have a healthy male's eye for beauty.'

'Don't think you can get away with just sweet words, my lord.'

'Sweet words are all I have…For now.'

'My family is superior to hers.' There was a note of aggression in her voice. 'I am younger and better looking. You love me, or at least claim to, more than her.'

It took me an instant to realize that she was talking about me. *Me.*

'Only a *little* more,' he interjected, teasingly. 'She's a good, kind woman. We are all together because she has made place for you in her home. She treats you as her younger sister, doesn't she?'

'And haven't I, too, made the best of my bad luck?' she demanded. 'I acknowledge that it was I who asked you for the deer skin—'

'That's history,' he interrupted brusquely. 'No one blames you, least of all Kunti.'

'Well then, if I am her equal, why can't I, too, be a mother?' Her voice took on a whiny note. 'Like her, like Maharani Gandhari...Why am *I* the only one who does not have a child? I want a child too!'

After a long moment he said, 'Why don't you ask her?'

'You want me to beg? Don't I have self respect?'

'Not beg, just request her...Why can't you do that?'

'I'm afraid to,' she said slowly. 'You know how domineering she can be, stubborn, as well. She likes to control everything. You asked her for another son, and she refused. *Her reputation!* She thinks only of herself.' She was silent for a moment, then said, 'The truth is, Aryaputra, she sees me as a rival. Always has, always will...No, don't shake your head. You may be the greatest archer in the world, but you don't understand women. She will *never* share the secret mantra with me.'

'Of course, she will,' he asserted, adding grandly, '*I* will make a request on your behalf.'

'Will you?' Her tone was eager, wheedling. 'Just *one* son.'

Like an itch that one cannot help but scratch, the conversation replayed itself in my mind. The story that one creates for oneself is different from the story others tell about us, but neither of them is true, neither false. The picture that had emerged from the exchange I had eavesdropped on was disturbing. I had told myself that, more than beauty, a queen needed to be clever, especially if her husband was anything like mine. But *domineering*? Was that my true nature, or just the way circumstances had made me? Hadn't we lost *everything*? Weren't we adrift? Who was there to take charge of our lives? Someone had to be practical. Yet the words rankled. *She thinks only of herself*. Had I been overassertive? Was Madri's compliance just a way of avoiding trouble? And below all these disturbing questions was the nagging thought, corroding my self-confidence: *After all that I've done for him, even now, he shares something with her in which I have no part.*

A few days later, he brought the matter up saying, 'Have you noticed how sad Madri often seems? Has she said anything to you about it?'

I shook my head. 'Not a word.'

'Oh…' The silence dragged for several moments. Then he said, 'It's almost as if a secret sorrow is rendering her hollow from within. She looks pale and listless.'

'Does she?' I tilted my head as if seriously considering his words. 'I think she looks even more fair than before. Haven't you noticed the ruddiness in her cheeks? It must be this healthy mountain air.'

He gave me an exasperated look. '*You* have three healthy sons, Kunti. That makes you more fortunate than she.'

'But they are *yours*,' I said, at once. 'You wanted sons—I invoked the gods only to please you.'

He smiled, reached out and held my hands. I pulled them away gently. 'We must not forget the curse,' I murmured.

His smile grew fixed. 'Kunti,' he ploughed on, 'you are the mainstay of this family, concerned not only about my welfare, but that of everyone in this little world of ours—even your sapatni.'

I laughed, giving up the pretence. 'She too wants a son... Is that what you're trying to say?'

He looked at me for a long moment. 'Envy is a fire. It needs only a spark to wipe out an entire forest. It can destroy everything we are trying to build, leave us in obscurity forever. Believe me, *I know*. The only way to prevent it is to be generous and give her what she craves. She will be forever grateful. One son is all she asks.'

'But will that be good enough for you?'

He did not reply.

❖

Pregnancy did not bring much pleasure to Madri. She craved foods that were impossible to obtain, and threw a tantrum when I failed to come up with them.

'Just *one* pomegranate,' she cried.

'Where do I get a pomegranate?'

'Are you sure Durvasa rishi didn't give you a secret mantra to get whatever food you desired?'

'No,' I laughed. 'Sadly, he did no such thing. That might have been more useful a boon.'

Her eyes flashed. 'You're mean,' she screeched. 'You hate me!'

'Hush,' I warned, glancing at the children. 'You're setting a bad example.'

She glared at me, hissing, 'Everyone cannot be as faultless as you.'

At times such as these she was infuriating, and I ignored

her. At other times she was a child seeking reassurance. 'What if I die while giving birth? Will you bring up my child?'

'Don't speak of such things. Women give birth to babies every day, every minute.'

'And often die in the process,' she muttered gloomily.

'Well, in that case I will happily bring up your son.'

She gave me an oblique look. 'And if I have more than one?'

'Doubtful,' I told her.

When the babies came I understood the meaning of that look. They were beautiful. One bright as dawn, the other swarthy as dusk. Nakul and Sahadeva. I did not say anything then, but several months later when Pandu approached me again I made sure my reply was loud enough to reach her ears.

'Don't plead for that deceitful, conniving woman!' I said. 'At your insistence, I gave the mantra which allowed her to invoke a god. I was generous. But what did *she* do? She called the divine Ashvin twins and got herself a pair of sons. Two for the price of one! That's how cunning she is.'

'But, Kunti—'

'I wasn't born yesterday, my lord,' I said, raising my voice a notch higher. 'I can see through her ploy. She plans to have more sons than I. That's her game.'

'What game?' he asked, genuinely baffled. 'All five are my sons, aren't they? They are all Pandavas, aren't they?'

'Yes,' I said. 'And you'll have to be happy with five. We are done!'

Madri didn't speak to me for a week, going about her routine with such an injured air that it made me want to smack her face. Pandu, too, looked downcast, but cheered up after a while.

'Five isn't a bad number,' he said. 'I would even say that it's a powerful number. Everything is made up of the *panch mahabhutas*, the five elements. In nature, too, five fingers make a hand, five toes a foot. We have five senses. There are five *tirtha sthans* that are considered most sacred, five gems that are the most precious. The calendar, too, has five parts to it. In history, five is a significant number, standing for the energy and dynamism of the *panch janah*, the five tribes from whom we have all descended. There are five implements a warrior can use to do battle. And now with the five sons that are the gifts of gods, I am the proudest father in the world. Yes, five is an auspicious number. I am satisfied.'

❖

We had a dozen years. They turned out to be, surprisingly, happy years. The best that I had known in my life till then, and the best I have known since. Once Pandu's hunger for sons had been satisfied, he settled down to the task of being a father. Watching him with his sons, away from the glare of his former life, I got the feeling that he came closest to being the man he had always wanted to be—a free man.

When the time came for the boys to be educated formally, we held the thread ceremony. Their education began under the tutelage of the rishis at the hermitage. At night, after they'd gone over their lessons and eaten the evening meal, they would surround their father and beg him for the stories of his earlier life. These stories fascinated the boys.

'Are there horses in Hastinapur?' Nakul asked.

Pandu shared a smile with Madri. 'That question could only come from a Madreya.'

Bheem implored: 'Please tell us again what they eat on festival days in Hastinapur palace?'

'Pitaji, how does a horse archer shoot an arrow while retreating from the enemy?' Arjuna wanted to know.

'Is war the only way one can acquire a kingdom?' Yudhisthira asked of no one in particular.

Sahadeva, the youngest, and the quietest as well, asked nothing at all, but smiled to himself.

'Now it's my turn to ask you five a question,' Pandu said. 'Having acquired a kingdom, how do you keep it together?' The boys were silent.

Pandu picked up five short sturdy sticks from the pile of faggots meant for the kitchen fire and gave each child one. 'Break it,' he ordered. Bheem did so easily, the other four with some difficulty. 'This is what happens when one is alone,' their father said. 'One can be easily broken.' Next he picked out five more sticks and handed them as a bundle to Bheem. 'Now break this in half,' he said. Bheem tried but could not. Pandu said, 'If you five remain together, no one can harm you or take away your kingdom…Remember this all your life.'

❖

Acharya Shuka, the boys' guru, had come to meet Pandu. 'When a pupil surpasses his guru, it is time for a change,' he said. 'Arjuna knows as much about archery as I do.'

'What about his brothers?' asked Pandu. 'Bheem still has some way to go. I was watching him with the mace. He could do with better control over his swing.'

Shuka shook his head. 'You haven't got my point, Rajan. Each of them excels at one skill. No one can throw a spear better than Yudhishthira; Bheem is a force to reckon with—with or without the mace; Arjuna is already the best archer I have ever seen. And the Madreyas are not bad as swordsmen. However, they all need to hone their skills. Competition is the teacher that I was talking about. A *gurukula* would be more appropriate. One of those institutions where other kshatriya princes go. Some healthy rivalry will develop the killer instinct.' He paused and looked around. 'This is not the right place for warriors.'

Spring had arrived early that year, unleashing a flurry of activity, like a painter driven mad by the discovery of new colours, spreading them across the canvas, discarding and starting afresh. Swans and ducks headed on a northward flight, the clear sweet warble of cranes filled the air. The taller summits were still glossed over by white swathes of snow, but on the lower slopes the ice had begun to melt and the cascades were in full gush, the silvery mist creating a fine net of moonstones, aquamarines and emeralds. Tender new shoots of grass were sprouting. The mango blossoms had appeared, their delicate yellow green contrasting with the deeper shade of the leaves. Below us in the valley, a herd of elephants stepped out of the forest to drink at the river. The scene had a timeless quality. *Yes, this is no longer the right place for us.* Even as the thought crystallized, a sudden anxiety filled me. A reluctance to let go of this tranquillity. What would it be like to go back into the world?

'It's Arjuna's birthday next week,' Pandu said to Shuka. 'We will have the celebration at the ashrama as usual.'

16

I think of that day as one that impaled me forever. Yet, I was not there when it came to pass. I did not see the eagerness in his eyes, nor did I hear the passionate endearments he said to her; those moments remain sealed forever in a lovers' pact.

❖

You, too, will feel fervent desire for the woman you love, and you too will die before appeasing it.

❖

Afterwards she said to me, over and over again, 'I *tried* to stop him, Didi.'

But I was beside myself with anger and anguish. 'Wretched woman,' I shouted at her. 'You took him away from me by your wiles, but that wasn't enough for you. Now you've taken his life too!'

'Not true,' she pleaded, shaking her head, tears running down her face. 'I did not invite him. *I did not*. I had just returned from my bath when he—I could not fight him off.

He was like a man possessed. He would not listen. There was an insane gleam in his eyes. Look! He tore away my garment. He grabbed my—'

'Be quiet!' I snapped. 'You expect me to believe that? You've destroyed *everything*...You were his death, nothing less! *After everything I did.*' I could not go on for the tears choking me.

When I was done weeping, I looked at him, at his face. The sun's rays found a gap in the canopy of deodars and illuminated a tiny patch of earth. His eyes. For a brief moment, that light in them that had first drawn me in, reached out again one last time to wrap itself around me. I put out my hand and gently touched him. His skin was still warm. I lowered his eyelids. But I could not erase the glow of desire on his face. Nor could I help thinking, *You never looked at me this way.*

'I, too, will follow my lord,' she said.

'Who are you to decide that?' I asked, coldly. '*I* am the patrani.'

'Yes, but you have never needed him the way I do.'

'Stop thinking only of yourself! You have two small boys.'

She began to shake her head. 'You are their Badi Ma, while I will always be Little Mother.' Her eyes were dark with a fresh pain. 'Where will they go now? What will become of them? I could never be as good a mother as you.'

I did not reply.

'It was my body that caused his death...Isn't it only fair that I should get rid of this accursed body?'

I did not reply.

'You will bring up my two as well, won't you?' she asked. 'Don't call them Madreya. They are yours now. Please call them Kaunteya…'

I did not reply.

'Forgive me, Didi.'

I did not.

PART THREE

The Kaunteyas

1

Eighteen years ago, I turned my back on Hastinapur's Elephant Gate; now, eighteen days after Pandu's death, I stand outside it. I was a queen then, I am a widow now, bringing home her husband's remains. A widowed queen with sons—and that, I suspect, will make all the difference. The decision to return has been mine, but it was made with serious misgivings.

A day after the dead bodies of Pandu and Madri had been placed on the pyre, the sages of Shatashringa forest appeared at my door. They were led by the oldest, a man reputed to be nine hundred years old. As always his expression was modest and grave, but on that day I detected some anxiety.

'Maharaja Pandu placed you in our trust,' he said. 'It is therefore our duty to restore you and your offspring to his family.'

'I must consult my eldest son.'

'We will wait for your answer.'

'Are you in two minds about going back to Hastinapur?' Yudhisthira asked.

I admitted that I was nervous about the circumstances under which we would be returning.

After mulling it over for several minutes, he said, 'The only other kinsmen we have are the Vrishnis. Would they provide us shelter?'

'They would, but that is all you can expect from them—a roof and the status of dependants. You would have no rights.'

He cocked his head to the side. 'How would that be different from our status in Hastinapur?'

'*Your* position alone makes all the difference,' I said 'You are not just the eldest son of the last consecrated king, but also the first of Maharaja Vichitravirya's grandsons.'

'Then Hastinapur is our home and the Kurus our family,' he said. 'We have to go back.'

'You five are the family,' I said, with more sharpness than I intended. 'Shatashringa is your home now.'

'Is brahmacharya what you intended for us?' he asked pointedly.

His candour unnerved me. 'Don't we have everything that we want right here?'

'Everything we need, perhaps, but not everything we want. We will never have everything we want. Here, there or anywhere.'

My trepidation grew. 'You are safe here…Who will protect you there?'

'We will learn to protect ourselves.'

I marvelled at how different he was from his siblings. Bheem had strength and brawn, but he was easily led; Arjuna was determined and intelligent, but he was too proud of himself; the two Madreyas, my babies, were charming, but also utterly self-absorbed. Yudhisthira was the odd one not only because he was unremarkable in appearance, but also because he was inscrutable. Discreet, level-headed and unassuming, but also strangely detached from everyone. Wise beyond his years, controlled in speech, but also crafty in the manner in which he manipulated his siblings.

'We do have well-wishers there, don't we?' he asked. 'Anyone we can count on?'

'The mahamantri is our friend, but his power is limited.'

'Can he be trusted?'

'Up to a point.'

'Well, then?'

'I suppose you are right,' I sighed. 'We will prepare to leave.'

❖

Dawn is breaking over Hastinapur. The sentries on the city's walls peer at us through bleary eyes, then gape in amazement. We make a strange sight: an army of ancient silver-haired rishis in nothing but deerskin, a lone woman in white, five boys ranging from sixteen to twelve, and a white-sheeted bier.

As word spreads about our arrival, the citizens begin to file out of the gates. The trickle becomes an outpouring. They come on foot and horseback, in carts and on litters. I cannot remember the last time I saw such a surge of humanity or even one as mixed. Men and women of the three upper classes share space with fisherfolk, leather-workers, weavers of ropes and baskets; courtesans and beggars, too, are in the throng. But everyone is strangely silent. They huddle some distance away, looking at us and whispering among themselves, waiting for the next scene to unfold. The sages have kept me and the Pandavas in the centre of the group, shielding us from curious eyes. Nakul has fallen asleep, his head rests on my lap. Sahadeva, though drowsy, is trying desperately to keep awake. Some distance away, the older Pandavas sit in a loose triad of their own, not talking, tired from the journey, but below the fatigue I sense the contradictory feelings, of despair and numbness, that come when the reality of death sinks in. *Now what?*

Arjuna has taken it the hardest. For some unfathomable reason, he blames himself for the accident—that was what I called it—because it happened on his birthday. For seventeen days now, he has walled himself in with his sorrow. He is barely eating, and whenever I try to make him swallow a morsel, he complains that his stomach hurts. His eyes are red from lack of sleep and he says it is because nightmares bother him, but we have heard him crying to himself. He is withdrawn and irritable when anyone tries to talk with him, and not even the dazed misery of the two orphaned Madreyas has evoked the compassion in him that it has in the others. Bheem grieves, too, but he is stoical about it. He searches for tasks that will allow him to spend his emotions. On our way down from the mountains, he carried the two Madreyas almost all the way on his shoulders. And every night, Yudhisthira has lain with them on either side of him under the open sky and told them stories, in his calm voice, about the constellations shining above.

'Are they too up there?' Nakul asked one night. 'Are they looking down on us?'

The breeze dropped as if waiting for the reply. 'Yes.'

'Can they see us?' persisted Nakul. 'How will they see us—Pitaji and Chhoti Ma—when it is so dark here?'

'They will see us by the light of our deeds,' replied Yudhisthira, proving once again that he is never short for an answer.

I have not told any of them what Madri had shared with me before she died. I explained her death to Nakul and Sahadeva by saying that she had accompanied their father to *swarga loka,* so that he would not be alone. They seem to have accepted it. When I look at their sweet, trusting faces, I do not see the sons of my rival, but two young children set adrift in this world. My heart trembles, stirred by disquieting memories that have been rekindled after all these years. Despite the tiredness of limbs, my slumber has been troubled by confusing dreams. I wake up feeling wretched, but the sight of my sons around me, the sound of their breathing, steadies me. You will not feel abandoned, I promise them silently. *You will never be alone*.

As Sahadeva finally loses his battle with sleep, I draw him close and pillow his head on my lap. Sensing his gaze on me I look down. The expression in his eyes is enigmatic. What does he think about, this solemn, secretive youngest child? He has a special place in my heart. It is the melancholy in his eyes—the eyes of an old soul. I stroke his hair gently and smile at him. He gives a small sigh and, after a few minutes, closes his eyes in sleep.

We do not have to wait long. There is a flurry of activity near the Elephant Gate. The crowd parts to make way, bowing in reverence as three men approach us. Pitamaha leads. The blind king is supported by the mahamantri. Behind them are the queens. Pitamaha bows before the sage who has led our procession and performs the arghya. 'Welcome,

Rishivar,' he says. 'This kingdom of the Kurus, its wealth and we ourselves are at your disposal.'

The sage, a man with bare feet, unkempt hair and a skeletal frame, nods regally, as if he is quite accustomed to these offerings of entire kingdoms, but thinks nothing of them. He eyes the smooth, dapper Kuru royals silently for several minutes. 'The sovereign of this vast kingdom was, as you know, Maharaja Pandu,' he says. 'He adopted the forest life and settled in our midst. There the gods themselves blessed him with sons.' Though he does not raise his voice it carries well over the silence. 'I present to Hastinapur the eldest of the Pandavas, Yudhisthira, child of Dharma, born of Maharani Kunti.'

Yudhisthira steps forward and touches his forehead to the ground, saluting both his elder kinsmen and his countrymen. After him, his brothers are presented with the mention of the names of their divine fathers. Only for Arjuna does the sage add an extra sentence, an extra name, perhaps because he knows the power of a name: 'This son of Indra, known as Dhananjaya, will be the finest archer the world has ever seen.'

I glance through the corner of my eyes at Arjuna. He is taut as a strung bow, his face impassive. The Madreyas are presented next; at the sight of them, so young and endearing, a huge hissing sigh rises from the crowd.

'These are the Pandavas,' the sage says. 'Through them, Pandu, a righteous man, revived the line of the Kurus of Hastinapur. Their birth, development and scholarship in the Vedas and Vedangas will, no doubt, give you pleasure.' There is a barely noticeable change in his tone, which drops a note lower, a beat slower. 'Virtuous Pandu has departed from this life, leaving behind these sons. His junior queen Madri could not bear the separation from her lord, and chose to accompany him into the next world.' He points to the bier. 'There lie the unburnt portions of their mortal bodies. Please conduct the appropriate funeral rites for the late king and his queen, hold the ceremonies that will enable him to join his dead ancestors...Then you must receive his chief queen Kunti and his sons with the honour that is their due.'

The eyes of the world turn to us: the five young boys, the woman in stark white with her head covered. It takes them a few minutes to realize that the sages have gone—dissolved into thin air. There is not even a gasp of surprise at this evaporation that they will later wonder about. *Did it really happen that way?* Maybe it will become one more odd detail in a very strange day, like being presented with the sons of the gods, and the white-sheeted bier under which lay the half burnt corpses.

Dhritarashtra addresses the mahamantri, making sure that he is loud enough for everyone else too. 'O Vidur, the king has left us lamenting.' Grief chokes his voice, tears shine in his eyes. 'But we must take heart from the presence of his sons, the five Pandava princes.' Judging from the reaction of the multitude, these are absolutely the right words. And the next are even better. 'We charge you with arranging the funeral ceremonies befitting the royal status of Pandu and his queen Madri. Spare no expense. Give away freely cattle, gems and cloth in their name. Make sure that Kunti's wishes are taken into account in the funeral of Madri.'

In short, he commands Vidur to organize a royal spectacle to beat all others. The crowd approves. It is something to look forward to.

The administrative wheels start churning. The palace is in a flurry of activity. A site has been chosen on the banks of the Ganga. Wood is piled for the pyre, ghee stocks are put together, fresh flowers are supplied to deck the hearse and to weave into garlands. Only the odours make this a different occasion, very different. Sandalwood and crushed marigold. The scent of death.

My sons and I have been put, almost as an afterthought, in the guest wing. From a three-roomed hut perched on a mountainside to the sheer sprawl of this place. The boys are slightly intimidated by their new surroundings. Though they have grown up hearing about Hastinapur, they had imagined nothing on this scale. They gawp like village yokels, staying close together for comfort, afraid of doing or saying the wrong thing. Unused to servants, they do not know how to command like princes, but merely to request humbly for a service. Their modesty and politeness has melted many hearts, but their cousins, the hundred sons of Dhritarashtra, are icy in their contempt.

Naïve as my sons are, they are protective of me. Young as they are, they have sensed that something inside me has finally buckled. They are careful to stay close at hand, gentle in the way they address me, taking care to demand nothing, but serving me in unobtrusive ways: urging me to eat a morsel, slipping a shawl around my shoulders when I begin to shiver, and when I lie still with my eyes shut for too long, they check surreptitiously to see if I am breathing.

I feel as though I am being taken apart and reassembled, but nothing works the way it should. My heart is dead. My brain takes note of details but does not understand what they mean. The days are filled with a twilight. I float on the hours, kept buoyant by *nothing*. There is no need to get out of bed, and having got out, the bed seems like a life discarded, broken and empty. I no longer differentiate between sleep and wakefulness, between who I was and what I am now. In this middle ground, my wounds are raw and the pain so crushing that it is, by itself, an opiate. I will myself to feel. Or not feel. The royal women come to condole with me. They weep at the sight of my fatherless children. Voices, atonal and distant, give me advice, thin and flimsy solutions on how to carve out a new life for myself. You must learn to live for your sons, I am told. *Live?* I share the world-between-worlds where the soul of my husband waits till it can join his pitris. In this half in, half out state I feel that I am still tied to him, still filled with the old tenderness and the ever-present hollow ache, but also separate, like marginalia. How different is this from that life we lead together? Scenes from the past beat like slowing pulse in my memory. Could I have lived them differently? Yet, as the final rites come closer and his body is taken by his family and the priest, I am panicky, as though all purpose is being snatched away from me. *Who shall I be? How will I live?*

His body is cleansed and dressed. His body is placed on the hearse. The cortege leaves the palace, it travels the long route to the riverbank. Musicians, bearers carrying yak-tail fans, priests in pristine white dhotis, soldiers, and finally the hearse under the royal white umbrella, make the solemn journey. But the grand display is sobered by the grief of the populace. There is no drama in the wailing, no simulation in the tears. They flow with such abundance that it seems enough not just to cleanse the dead ruler once again, but to revivify him. Their sorrow re-crowns him. It needs to create a narrative. Nearly twenty years ago, he redrew the borders of this country and brought glory to the Kurus. Whatever they are today is due to him. The decades that have passed since he left Hastinapur have made no difference to the high regard in which he was held.

At the riverbank, the sun is sinking. The kinsmen of the deceased wait for the last prayers to be chanted. Then a figure separates himself from the royal family. He is a man of average height and indeterminate age, yet possessing an impressive demeanour. Lean and dark-skinned with a narrow, austere face. He is a brahmin sage, Krishna Dwaipayana, the dead man's biological father. As he lights the pyre, lotuses are rained on it by the crowd; the smell of ghee fills the air. Black smoke rises in a dense cloud, forming a grey cord that carries the soul to its ancestors. Over the crackle of dry wood catching fire rises a bone-chilling wail, a woman's keening. Ambalika breaks the ranks of the royal women and rushes towards the rising flames. '*My son, O my son!*' She falls in a faint.

Twelve days pass on the riverbank. The Pandavas spend the hours with their kinfolk, not just the Kurus, but also the Madras and the Vrishnis who have come to attend the *shraadh*. The five boys receive the condolences with a composure that others find astonishing. Questions quietly buzz, like a hornet's nest disturbed: Where exactly have these boys been all these years? Don't they seem more like brahmins than kshatriyas? Who taught them the Vedas? What else have they studied? And the most scurrilous of them all—how does any man, even a king, get 'gods' to father his sons? Are they really demigods?

On the thirteenth day the shraadh ceremonies are held for the salvation of the dead souls. Water and *pinda,* cooked rice and sesame seeds, is offered to the pitris as a way of clearing all debts. On the mortal plane something more substantial is needed to feed the thousands of brahmins who are thronging to the place. Food grains, spices, fresh vegetables and fruits, milk, curd, ghee and butter are supplied to the makeshift kitchens where an army of cooks are at work. The kitchen fires burn, cauldrons are on the boil, tantalizing aromas rise. The meal is ready, the leaf plates laid out in long rows, the brahmins seated. We serve them, ask for their blessings, give away gems and cloth.

It goes on and on…

❖

A whole month had gone by since that day, the last day of my husband's life. The world had changed and I was back in Hastinapur palace, in the rajmata's rooms, summoned there for the last time. Ambika and Ambalika were already present when I entered. The news was shocking. Satyavati was going away to spend the rest of her years in a hermitage and she was taking Ambalika with her.

'Why are you leaving?' I asked, tearfully. 'Your great grandsons need you more than ever.'

Satyavati was a shadow of her former self. A crumpled old woman, her indomitable will finally broken. 'There is no other way left for me,' she said, her voice raspy with grief. 'I cannot watch the destruction of my own family.'

'What destruction?' I asked with apprehension. 'Was it wrong of me to come back with my sons?'

'No,' she said. 'You did the right thing. This is their home. But, as you can see, everything has changed. Happiness fled when Pandu left the palace eighteen years ago, but no one was ready to believe it. Not even I. Maybe the seeds of decay were planted much before that and were lying in wait, though we did not see it like that. Stasis has this effect, it preserves the illusion of happiness.'

'But change does not necessarily have to be for the worse...All I want is a safe place for my sons to grow.'

'*All*?' The glint was back in her eyes. Sharp, ironic. 'It can never be all, Kunti. Don't fool yourself.'

'What—what do you mean?'

'Those hundred grandsons of Ambika were unchallenged till now,' she said, glancing at Ambika, who shrank. 'Duryodhana, the eldest, has grown up believing that the crown is his private property, held in safekeeping for him by his father till he is old enough to wear it—he was nurtured on that belief.'

'We need your wisdom now to hold us together,' I said. 'Please reconsider your decision.'

From her expression, I gathered that I had touched a chord. 'I would stay,' she admitted with a rueful look, 'but nobody has use for my wisdom. Dhritarashtra is blind not just by sight, but in his perception as well. When Duryodhana was born there were terrible omens and Vidur begged Dhritarashtra to do away with the babe. For the good of everyone, he said. But Dhritarashtra did not listen. Love for his firstborn has made him not just blind but deaf. As for Gandhari…' She stopped and gave a dismissive shake of her head. 'And now, Krishna Dwaipayana has advised me to retreat to the forest unless—' Her voice trembled. 'Unless I want to witness the annihilation of my own race.' She shut her eyes, but the tears escaped down her cheeks. 'Those were his exact words. *They will destroy each other*.'

My heart was beating like a drum. *What have I got into? What have I led my sons to?*

'Ambalika will accompany me,' Satyavati said. Without glancing at Ambika, she added, 'Her elder sister is free to stay here or come with us.' Her cold tone made it clear that blame, if any, must accrue to the elder daughter-in-law who shut her eyes at the precise moment she conceived and was, therefore, responsible for all that followed. She stood up; I was being dismissed. I bent to touch her feet and she blessed me. 'I have spoken to both Gangaputra and Vidur about it,' she said. 'These rooms are yours now. This is your home. I pray that you will find peace, solace and strength in this space.'

A day later, while the palace was still asleep, the three women left in the pre-dawn darkness, passing through the city gates unnoticed, never to be seen or heard again.

2

Gandhari had changed. The poise that I had so envied in the early days had sharpened into a quality of alertness. She rarely left Dhritarashtra's side. Her senses, combined with a woman's intuition, were now more acute than his. The servants were wary of her. She was known to deliver severe tongue-lashings at the slightest mistake. However, when she came to visit me, she was all charm, all grace, and every inch the reigning queen.

'Are you comfortable, Kunti?' she asked in a silvery, considerate voice. I assured her that I had everything I needed. She sat quietly, slowly turning her head this way and that to get an orientation of the room. After a while she sighed deeply and reached out for my hand—almost dropping it in surprise. 'How rough your skin feels!'

I responded by withdrawing my hand.

She bit her lip in mortification. 'I'm sorry. I didn't mean to—'

'It's all right,' I said with a laugh. 'I am not ashamed of the life I've led.'

'Now you're only making it worse for me, Kunti,' she chided. 'Years in the forest may have roughened your hands, but I will not believe the same of your heart. You are the kindest woman I know.' Lowering her voice, she added, 'How easily you've accepted the sons of your rival as your own.' Dhritarashtra's peccadilloes with the dasis were well known; Gandhari, it was rumoured, ensured that only the oldest crones served him.

'But they were always my own,' I said. 'Madri was a mother to my sons as well.'

Gandhari said, 'Your elder brother-in-law is struggling to come to terms with his loss. He and Pandu were very close. He says it to me often enough in these precise words, "I am where I am today because of Pandu".'

And I am where I am.

'He is particularly keen that the Pandavas should be happy in the palace.' She hesitated before adding delicately, 'All this must be new to them.'

'They will adapt.'

She chewed her lip. 'They are so well brought up. Pitamaha is most impressed with Yudhisthira, who appears mature beyond his years.' A bitter note entered her voice. 'It is unfair to make comparisons with one's own child, but Duryodhana, I fear, is much too used to having his own way. Maybe the company of your eldest will teach him something, though I must say,' and here she was all acid, 'your other son Bheemasen is quite destructive.'

I sighed. 'What has Bheem done now?'

'Oh, I don't mean to complain,' she demurred at once. 'It is just that he is so much bigger and doesn't know his own strength…Does *everything* have to be a competition?'

'With Bheem it usually is,' I said, with a little laugh. 'But it's only harmless fun. It is best if you and I stay out of these children's squabbles, Didi.'

'You are right,' she said, her tone milder, more reasonable. 'We all need time to get used to—' she floundered for second.

'This new situation,' I said. 'It's difficult for you and Maharaja Dhritarashtra as well, that we have come back.'

Her denial was immediate. 'No. Not at all! Maharaja Dhritarashtra is keen to do his duty by his younger brother's sons.'

That shows me my place.

'Oh, I nearly forgot to tell you what I'd come here for,' she said. 'Duryodhana has invited the Pandavas to Pramanakoti.'

'Where is that?'

'By the river. Duryodhana is quite excited about the excursion. He has even got Pitamaha to agree to it. It would be a good way for the cousins to get closer.'

'My older boys are quite responsible,' I said, 'but Nakul and Sahadeva are a bit young to be without adult supervision. Are the servants accompanying them trustworthy?'

She smiled and patted my hand. 'You worry too much, Kunti. The boys don't want the servants to stay once their work is done. My brother Shakuni will keep an eye on things.'

❖

'Duryodhana dislikes us all,' Sahadeva said flatly. 'But it's Bheem Bhaiyya he cannot bear.'

I was intrigued. 'How do you know that?'

'I just do.'

I turned to Yudhisthira. 'Is that true? Can't you keep a check on Bheem? Stop him from needling Duryodhana.'

He grinned. 'Bheem is a force of nature, Ma. He means no harm. Duryodhana is quite touchy.'

'He is jealous,' declared Sahadeva.

'Hush,' I chided him. 'He is your cousin.'

Yudhisthira was thoughtful. 'I'll tell Bheem to go easy on Duryodhana,' he said.

A day later my anxiety seemed unwarranted. Bheem and Duryodhana had joined forces in planning the excursion to the riverside. The day of the outing was clear and bright. As the chariots, packed with chattering boys, rolled away from the palace, I felt a sense of lightness. *It's going to be fine,* I told myself. *This is a fresh start for all of us.*

Hours later my words came back to cut me to shreds.

❖

'We've got hundreds of men out there,' said Vidur. 'They are scouring the riverbank for miles.'

The fear in my heart grew stronger. *I'll never see him again.* 'They've killed him,' I said abruptly. 'Sahadeva was right. Duryodhana hates Bheem and his uncle—'

Vidur gave me a quick look of warning. 'I share your apprehension,' he said in a low voice. 'Duryodhana alone would not have been able to hatch this scheme. Shakuni is the brain behind it. But you must not reveal a word of your suspicion—remember, you are still quite new here.'

I stared at him in disbelief. 'I am going straight to Pitamaha.'

He shook his head firmly. 'That would place your other sons in danger too.'

'But—but *why*?'

He did not answer my question. Instead, he said, 'The royal astrologer has studied Bheem's birth chart and predicted a long life.'

Yet my mind could not stop running through the possibilities of what could have happened. One thing I was certain of—this was no accident.

'At lunch, Duryodhana sat beside Bheem. He encouraged him to eat dishes that were especially served to him. Then he challenged Bheem to a competition. "They call you Vrikodara," he said. "Let's see how much you can eat, Wolf belly." Kheer by the bowlfuls was the challenge. Shakuni Mama served them and kept the score. We were all laughing at them and when Bheem won we all cheered and Duryodhana, his face wreathed in smiles, embraced him. Later we went out to play, but Bheem was very drowsy. He just lay down on the cool sand under a tree and said he needed a nap. When it was time to return we couldn't find him, though we searched everywhere.'

The hours slipped by. Vidur's wife, Parashavi, spent much of the time with me. Her quiet presence was calming. A second night passed, then a third. They were still looking for him. He was not on the riverbank. Was he in the forest? *He is in the river*. To dispel the ghost in my mind, I said it aloud to Vidur.

'At Pramanakoti, the river is very deep,' he said.

He cannot send divers into the water, he is saying.

Seven harrowing nights passed. Gandhari came to see me. I listened to the platitudes and thanked her for her concern. On the eighth night the moon was barely a nail shaving in the sky. One by one the lamps dimmed, till just the one in the window remained. Suddenly, the lamp went out. A heavy shadow slipped into the room. My heart stopped and then began to thump wildly. After a moment I whispered, 'I'm here.'

A low chuckle. In the next instant, I was grabbed, lifted clean off my feet.

'Put me down!'

'Not till you guess where I've been.'

'At the bottom of the river,' I said, annoyance and relief making me sound furious.

'Guess who I met there,' he chortled.

'Put me down,' I ordered him, a little louder now. His brothers were stirring and sitting up. Arjuna, who had a cat's eyesight, gave a whoop and jumped onto his errant brother's back. They fell to the floor in a scuffle. I made my way to one of the lamps in the wall, added more oil and raised the wick. The flame brightened the huddle of faces. Five, I counted. All safe.

The story Bheem told us was amazing. He had spent eight days at the bottom of the river with deadly water snakes. They bit me all over, he said, showing us the tiny fang marks on his arms, neck, torso, thighs. How had he survived their lethal poison? 'Survive?' he hooted. 'I will survive any snakebite for life. I owe it to that wretch Duryodhana and must not forget to thank him.' He turned to his brothers. 'Do you remember how he was egging me to eat that "special kheer"? Every mouthful was poison, a slow acting venom that made me feel heavy and sluggish. It would surely have killed me if he hadn't shoved me into the river. When the water snakes began to bite me, I started feeling better, the drowsiness disappeared.'

'The snake venom would have worked as an antidote to the poison in your body,' Yudhisthira pointed out.

Bheem nodded. 'That's what Vasuki said.'

We were aghast. *Who*? 'The king of the Nagas,' whispered Yudhisthira, clearly impressed. 'Did you meet him? Where?'

Bheem's grin widened as he turned to me, 'In Bhogavati, the city of the Nagas. And your great grandfather Aryaka, too, was present.'

Before he left, the Nagas gave Bheem an invaluable gift by allowing him to imbibe, as much as he could hold, of their secret elixir. When he finally lifted his head from the bowl, they said he would now possess the strength of a thousand elephants. 'What to speak of Duryodhana,' said Bheem, flexing his arms. 'I can now take on all hundred of them single-handed. Just see what mush I'll make of them.'

'You will do no such thing,' said Yudhisthira with a severe look. 'You will not speak a word about what happened to you.'

Bheem scowled. For a moment it looked as if he was going to challenge his brother. But his mood changed, he brought his hands together and bowed in mock obeisance. 'As you wish.'

The Pandavas were very careful now. The only time they met their cousins was when they went for lessons to Acharya Kripa, and then they would go to great lengths to avoid a confrontation. I was aware that they were chafing at the curb Yudhisthira had placed on them. Competing with their cousins had sharpened their teeth, they had tasted blood, and now that the attempt to murder Bheem had come to light, they were thirsting for revenge. It was around this time that the hundred sons of Dhritarashtra began to call themselves by a new patronym—the Kauravas.

'But we are all Kauravas, aren't we?' Arjuna asked. 'King Kuru was our common ancestor. Then why have they appropriated the name for themselves?'

'It doesn't matter,' Yudhisthira said, with a dismissive shake of his head. 'The only true Kaurava left is Pitamaha.'

Around this time, too, Vidur began to give Yudhisthira lessons in a new language. What this language was and who spoke it we did not know. Yudhisthira refused to tell us. Meanwhile, the word had gone around that Pitamaha was concerned about the further education of all the princes. They needed to be inducted in the intricacies of warfare. He had been making inquiries about the different gurukulas across the land. I prayed that he would not send my sons too far away; I could not bear that. One day it appeared as if all the prayers had been answered. The guru entered our lives.

Son of Rishi Bharadwaja of the Angirasa clan, disciple of the redoubtable Parshurama who was also Pitamaha's teacher, Guru Drona was received with open arms in the Kuru court. I was curious to see this man who had been chosen as the all-important preceptor to my sons. On the day he was to be presented in the sabha, I made it my business to watch the proceedings from the queens' gallery.

The man who stood before the throne did not have the austere look of a brahmin, nor the calm, reflective detachment of a teacher. He was handsome, self-assured and proud. His speech was clipped. His eyes, deep set and dark, missed nothing. Pitamaha requested him formally to accept the Kuru princes as his disciples. 'I place all the wealth of the

Kurus at your feet,' he said. He promised the brahmin their undying gratitude and loyalty. Acharya Drona accepted these words silently, with an air of condescension. Then Pitamaha announced that he would build a gurukula for Drona and his princely disciples. At this Drona looked appreciative. He seemed even more pleased when Pitamaha announced the customary gifts of land, cows, slaves and grain. 'Is there anything else we can offer you, Acharya?' asked Pitamaha.

Drona nodded. 'I have a purpose in my heart,' he said unhurriedly. 'A lesson I want to teach someone. My disciples must promise me that when their training is done, they will achieve this purpose for me.'

'It shall be so,' pledged Pitamaha, on behalf of the Kurus.

3

For a brahmin, Acharya Drona took to the pomp and regalia of court life with surprising ease. Though he ran a large gurukula for the princes on the outskirts of Hastinapur—on prime land by the river—he found the time to appear regularly in the Kuru sabha. His seat was next to Pitamaha. The acharya's wardrobe reflected this new exalted status. Thin cotton was replaced by fine linen and rich silks. Diamonds glistened in his ears and the rudraksha beads around his neck had the glitter of gold in them. The emaciated look disappeared, his skin glowed from oil massages and his hair was smooth and well-groomed.

As months slipped past, there was little news from the gurukula, other than that the princes were doing well. When I inquired if I could visit my sons, I was told courteously that Acharya Drona had put the princes on a tough regime; visits from mothers, particularly, were not encouraged.

One day, the mahamantri came to me with a request. Following the rajmata's departure, he said, the welfare schemes for citizens that she had started had languished. 'You are the rajmata now. It would be good if you oversee the work. Maharani Gandhari does not leave the palace, but you might like to get out for a few hours...Also, there is no harm in being known as the mother of the future king.'

It was gratifying that despite my long absence from Hastinapur, I was still remembered and welcomed in the larger world outside the palace. Pandu's untimely death and my own position as a widow and single mother earned me public sympathy; everywhere I went, women would approach me freely and inquire about my wellbeing, invite me into their homes.

While life in Hastinapur went on as usual, in Aryavarta there was an upheaval. Kansa was dead—killed by sixteen-year-old Krishna who had freed his parents, Vasudeva and Devaki, and reinstalled Ugrasena as the leader of the Vrishnis. Jarasandha, the emperor of Magadha, had sworn to avenge his son-in-law's death by destroying Mathura and the Yadavas.

❖

Drona announced in court that the martial training of the Kuru princes had come to an end. A tournament would be held to showcase their skills. It was all anyone talked about for months, the preparations for the games and the facilities that were being created for them, the weapons and horses that had been procured, the invitations that had been sent to other kings in Aryavarta, the extensive seating for the citizens according to their class, and the luxurious pavilion for the royal ladies. Gandhari and her daughter Dushala, too, were busy planning their wardrobe and jewellery for the event. They constantly solicited my views.

'Chachi, this dove grey will suit you nicely,' said Dushala, unravelling a bolt of silk before me. 'You could offset its depth with that beautiful nine-strand pearl necklace that you've kept for your eldest daughter-in-law.'

'Not just kept,' I laughed. 'I've kept it *aside*...All eyes will be on the princes. Who is going to look at an old woman like me?'

'We aren't old,' Gandhari immediately countered. 'And the royal enclosure will get its share of attention too.' After a moment, she said, 'Arjuna is sure to win the archery contest, so they say...you will have to receive his salutation, at least.'

'And those of Nakul and Sahadeva,' Dushala added with a giggle. 'They will surely win the good-looks contest.'

Gandhari's lips tightened. 'Don't be frivolous,' she snapped. 'And don't speak out of turn.'

Dushala curled up like a scorched leaf. It was a constant source of bewilderment for me that Gandhari, who was an overly tolerant mother to the hundred sons, was so hard on this one daughter, constantly admonishing and rarely praising her. Despite that, Dushala had grown up to be a sweet-tempered and cheerful young woman, virtues that made her a favourite with everyone in the palace. She had recently been betrothed to Jayadratha, the ruler of Sindhu, a kingdom to our west. When Dushala had gone from our company, I said to Gandhari, 'I will miss her when she leaves for her husband's home.'

A spasm passed over Gandhari's face.

'I know what you think,' she said. 'That I'm unkind and unloving, that I constantly reprimand her...She's a girl, Kunti, just as you and I once were. Did our former life prepare us for this existence?' I was silent. 'You know what the world does to daughters,' Gandhari continued. 'My parents loved me, but when the time came, I was married off to a sightless man. You, on the other hand, chose your husband in a swayamvar, but he renounced his kingdom, became a hermit and you had to follow him into the forest. Who can say what Dushala's husband will turn out to be? Self-restraint is her only protection in this savage world. It will train her to follow her dharma, irrespective of the circumstances.'

'But why do you starve her of *your* love?' I cried. 'Why do you tamp that glow in her?'

She became very still, as if gazing into the depths of her own being. There was an air of desolation about her. After a long while she said, 'Distance between her and me is necessary. She is my flesh and blood, but she must not become *me*. She was created from leftover scraps by Krishna Dwaipayana because—after a hundred sons—*I* wanted one girl. A child in my own image. My little vanity! If I show my love, as you say, the boundaries may dissolve and she may become like me. Worse she may attract the same fate to herself…That would be unbearable!'

The room suddenly felt airless. Fate and duty. Was one's entire life meant only to be crushed between these two?

❖

The stadium was packed, not a seat to be had. Though friendly contests were a tradition among kshatriyas, nothing on this scale had ever happened before in living memory. The crowds had started at dawn, contingents from the different quarters arriving early in order to get the best seats in the designated stalls. They brought with them an air of festivity and a desire to be awed.

It was Drona's moment of glory. He had dressed for the occasion in pristine white. With him was his son Aswatthama, a strange, aloof boy with a jewel in the middle of his forehead and a loud trademark laugh like the whinnying of a horse. Just as Drona had taken to court life easily, Aswatthama had discarded the former discipline of a brahmin household and embraced princely ways with alacrity. He had been befriended by Duryodhana and his closest sibling Duhsashana.

The contest opened with the blare of trumpets. The gates to the arena swung open and the Kuru princes entered, in order of age, led by Yudhisthira. There was a noisy round of applause from the spectators and someone shouted, 'Here is the next king of the Kurus.' In the king's enclosure, Pitamaha and Vidur looked pleased at the disciplined turnout of the princes. The Kauravas lined up to salute the king and their mother, the queen. Gandhari stood and held up her right palm in blessing. Then Pitamaha stood up, brought his conch to his mouth and, with its ululation, declared the tournament open.

A display of equestrian skills followed. Gandhari plucked at my sleeve and demanded to know what was going on. 'What is happening? Tell me, what is happening.' All through the chariot races, the archery and fencing competitions, I gave her a running commentary. Then, as the participants for the next event entered the arena, a hush fell over the stadium. There was a strange tension in the air.

'What is next?' asked Gandhari.

'A mace fight between Bheem and Duryodhana,' said Dushala. 'They are evenly matched.'

From the outset it was clear to all that this was not a simple sparring between rivals, but a deadly battle between enemies. Duryodhana and Bheem looked like a pair of masked dancers as they slowly circled facing one another, bodies glistening with oil and sweat, their expressions an identical snarl. One or the other would suddenly strike out, a swift glancing blow that would evoke a collective gasp from the audience. Several tense minutes passed. It was clear that Duryodhana was the more agile opponent, but Bheem was the stronger of the two. In the king's enclosure, I could see Vidur describing the scene to Dhritarashtra. Pitamaha looked impassive as usual, Kripacharya was grim-faced, but Shakuni, the prince of Gandhara, could barely hide his delight when Duryodhana got behind Bheem's guard and struck him a mighty blow. Bheem staggered and fell to his knees. 'What's going on?' asked Gandhari, holding my wrist and shaking it. The crowd had begun to murmur angrily. One half of the stadium, supporting Bheem, cried 'Foul, foul!' However, Duryodhana had an equal number of supporters to egg him on. Gandhari repeated her question. 'What is happening?'

'Your son is trying to murder mine,' I said. 'Again.'

Gandhari gasped. Dushala, too, turned to me with a shocked look. I stared straight ahead. Duryodhana was pounding at Bheem with the mace. Drona shouted something at his son Aswatthama, who ran to the duellists and separated them. 'The guru commands it: stop right now. You must obey the guru!' he yelled. The trumpets rang, signalling that the mace fight had been ended abruptly. In the king's enclosure, Pitamaha was slowly shaking his head. Vidur and Kripacharya looked grave, and even Dhritarashtra's enthusiasm seemed dampened. Out on the field, both Duryodhana and Bheem looked defiant as they went back to their respective sides. The drums began to beat again. Drona re-entered the arena. Silence fell. 'Dearer to me than my own son is Arjuna, master of all arts.'

As Arjuna stepped forward, a deafening cheer went up, the loudest we'd heard so far. Seeing him like that, a slim, solitary figure in the middle of the field, bow in hand, armour plate glinting in the late afternoon light, tears blinded me. I was reminded of Pandu and the glory he had dreamed of for this Pandava. The next hour went in a blur as Arjuna demonstrated his skill with the bow and arrow, arming them with secret mantras, aiming at a variety of targets. His arrows started fires, amassed thunderclouds, brought down rains, whipped up dust storms. We watched till it seemed that there was no further magical feat left for us to witness. Arjuna was the finest archer in the world, this we had witnessed.

By now the sun was fairly low in the western sky, obscured partially by a bank of blue-grey clouds. Deep pink shadows stretched their fingers across the arena. A few of the spectators had begun to rise from their seats and make their way to the exits, when at the main gates there was a scuffle between the guards and a man whose entry they were trying to stop—unsuccessfully. From a distance it was hard for me to see the newcomer's face. At that moment the sun emerged from the clouds, a fiercely blazing orb lighting up the field. I saw that he was an archer, tall and strapping. His flowing hair, catching the rays, seemed aflame, like a lion's mane. Something about his stance and the look on his face made me uneasy. Drona was still in the field. Around him stood the Pandavas. At the other end of the field was Aswatthama, by Duryodhana's side, with the remaining Kauravas surrounding him. As the intruder approached, Drona seemed to recognize him, his face darkened. The newcomer sketched an indifferent salute in his direction. His gesture in the direction of the king's enclosure was more respectful. He turned towards Arjuna.

'Kaunteya!' he said, his voice carrying to every corner of the hushed stadium. 'You've performed your wonders and dazzled this multitude. Now watch me do everything you did *and* do it better!' He shot an arrow into the sky. A garland of lotuses flew out of the blue heavens and threw itself around Dhritarashtra's neck. There was a stunned silence. The newcomer bowed deeply to Drona. There was a heavy touch of irony in his gesture, as if it was the master and not the pupil who was his adversary. He was a kshatriya—that proud bearing, the disdainful air could only belong to a born warrior—but who was he? Everyone looked at Drona, who nodded slowly, giving his permission, with obvious reluctance.

The challenger then proceeded to make good his promise, repeating everything that Arjuna had done—and with more precision. When the display was over, the Kauravas raised a cheer and the spectators responded, but there was complete silence from the guru and the Pandavas. Arjuna stood to one side, staring pensively at the ground. I knew that look: his heart was in a boil, his eyes burning with tears of humiliation. Bheem tried clumsily to put an arm around him, but Arjuna shook it off and moved further away.

Meanwhile, Duryodhana had rushed across the field to greet the stranger. He embraced the man in full public view and said, 'Welcome, mighty warrior! It is my good fortune that you are on *my* side. I am yours to command and the kingdom of Kurus is yours to enjoy!'

The warrior acknowledged the offer with an unsmiling nod. 'What I would really enjoy is a one-to-one combat with Kaunteya over there.'

'Wonderful!' Duryodhana's crowing laugh echoed around the stadium. 'Share the good things of life with me, and yes, do bring down your opponents!'

This was clearly too much for my third son. Face flushed with resentment, Arjuna said loudly, 'If it is combat you want, let me assure you that an unwelcome guest and an uninvited speaker are sent packing in the same manner. As you are both, prepare to leave.'

The warrior, as though acknowledging the deeper implication of Arjuna's words, took his time to reply. 'This arena belongs to all, not just you alone,' he said evenly. 'Let us not waste time on words. Let your arrows speak—for a change. Let them do the talking, Kaunteya, till the moment I choose to silence you, once and for all, by striking off your head.' Glancing at Drona derisively, he added, 'Under the watchful eyes of your guru, of course.'

No one spoke a word. No one moved. We were aghast at the man's bold manner and speech. Acharya Kripa and Pitamaha were conferring quietly. They stood up and made their way to the centre of the arena where all the participants waited for the next scene to unfold. The sun blazed on the setting, its deep glow falling directly on the mystery man.

He came forward to greet Pitamaha, and in that movement of his, I recognized the breastplate of gold and the earrings that I had seen only once, a long time ago.

My blood drained away, my knees trembled. I knew I was falling and then, mercifully, there was complete darkness. The dizzy spell must have lasted only a few minutes. I came to slowly, with a strong smell of sandalwood filling my nostrils. Though I was still shaky, the blur of faces looking down at me separated into distinct people: mahamantri, his wife Parashavi, Dushala, several maids.

Vidur? What is he doing here?

His gaze on my face was steady. There was something at the back of it. 'Slowly, Bhabhi,' he said. 'You fainted…Here, drink some water.' I sipped the water that a dasi offered.

'Are you all right, Kunti?' Gandhari asked. 'Was it the heat?'

Still looking at me, Vidur said with quiet emphasis, 'You don't have to say a word. Not a word.'

He knows! I lowered my eyes. 'Yes,' I murmured. 'It must have been the heat…I'm all right now.'

The maids fanned me. Vidur asked Parashavi to stay by my side and left. I felt as though a strong tide had swept me off and I was powerless to stop myself from going under. There was a strange sense of paralysis over me, an exhaustion. Nothing made sense. *After all these years? Now? Why now? Oh god, what should I do?*

'Listen,' Dushala said. 'Kripacharya is speaking.'

I could not bear to lift my head. I shut my eyes, but the words could not be shut out.

'It is the custom for all opponents in the arena to make

their identity public,' Kripacharya said. 'This is Arjuna, the third son of Maharaja Pandu and Maharani Kunti. He belongs to the Chandravanshi house of Kuru. His guru is Acharya Drona.' He paused and began to speak at a slower pace, 'Now tell us who you are...the names of your father, mother and guru...and the royal clan to which you belong. After that, if Arjuna deems you a fit opponent, he will fight you.'

A buzz ran around the stadium, but the challenger was very quiet. 'Tell us who you are,' Kripacharya said patiently. 'You must introduce yourself.'

'I am Radheya.'

Radha's son.

Kripacharya shook his head once as if to indicate that this information was of no significance. 'As you well know, the son of a king will not fight with anyone of a lesser lineage. Who is your father?'

'I am also known as Karna.'

Drona muttered something to Kripa who gave him a startled look. However, before he could speak, Duryodhana stepped forward and addressed him. 'According to the scriptures that you've taught us, Guruvar, three kinds of men can claim to be kings: those of royal birth, heroes and generals of armies. *Bravery* is the hallmark of a hero, *not* birth. And bravery does not belong to kshatriyas alone. If Arjuna thinks that it is below him to fight someone who is not a king, I will give away the kingdom of Anga-desh, which was given to me by my father, to my friend here. He will be crowned king immediately. Let us see how Arjuna refuses to fight him!'

There was resounding applause from the spectators. I could hear Vidur protesting to Dhritarashtra, 'Please stop him, Maharaj. This is anarchy. Duryodhana has no right to give away Anga-desh to anyone!'

Dhritarashtra was unperturbed. 'Who has the right, Mahamantri?'

Vidur was taken aback. 'Only you, O Rajan.'

'In that case, I endorse Duryodhana's gesture—let this man Karna be crowned king.'

There, before our very eyes, the priests were called in, the mantras chanted, holy water and rice grain dribbled as per rites. A white umbrella was produced, and the symbolic yak-tail whisks. Finally, a gold crown was brought. Duryodhana placed it on Karna's head.

'You are the king of Anga-desh,' said Duryodhana. 'Now go fight Arjuna.'

The crowd roared with delight. '*Anga raja ki jai.*'

The newly-crowned king looked as if he couldn't believe his eyes and ears. He kneeled before Duryodhana. 'I will never forget this,' he said. 'How can I ever repay you?'

Duryodhana raised him up and, with his hands on Karna's shoulders, said, 'Repay me with your friendship.'

'So be it,' said Karna.

It was Duryodhana's finest act, without a doubt, and all Hastinapur recognized it. Hearing her son's name being hailed again and again by the crowd, Gandhari's face was wreathed in smiles. 'See how they praise my eldest born!' she said.

Someone said, 'Look, a man is entering the arena…Who is he?'

The trespasser was old and grey-haired, dressed in a simple dhoti. He hobbled with the aid of a crude stick towards Karna, asking loudly, 'Is it true, Radheya? Have they made you a king? My son a king?'

For an instant, the newly-anointed king froze. His shoulders slumped as if in defeat. Slowly placing his bow on the ground, he came forward to meet the old man, and when they were quite close, fell to his knees. The man embraced him and ran his hand over his son's head in a gesture of affection. Suddenly he grew aware of all the personages standing there, and uncertainty and nervousness filled him. He brought his hands together and bowed low before Pitamaha, who acknowledged this respectful salutation with a curt nod.

'What's going on?' Gandhari asked. 'Who has come into the arena now?'

For a moment no one replied, then one of the elderly ladies of the royal entourage said, 'Adiratha. He used to be Maharaja Shantanu's charioteer. Radheya is no kshatriya. He is a sutaputra.'

In the arena, Bheem laughed. 'A sutaputra, are you?' His words were addressed to the outsider, but his gaze included Duryodhana. 'A bow looks odd in your hands. A horsewhip would be more appropriate. As for being crowned king of Anga-desh, well, even a lowly cur sometimes has the fortune of getting at the butter meant for a sacrifice, but that does not change his status an iota.'

Radheya received the insult by raising his head and staring at the sky as if seeking vindication. None came.

Duryodhana gave a roar of outrage. '*How dare you!*' he

shouted at Bheem. 'Does anyone seek to know where the source of a mighty river lies? It is no different with the lineage of heroes. A hero is known only by his strength. Even the pedigree of gods and gurus is not known. Take your own guru Drona. Wasn't he born in a water pot? And what of Kripacharya? The story is that he sprang from a clump of grass. Do we ask these venerable men questions about their ancestry? And if we do, then shouldn't we start by raising a few questions about you and your siblings as well?'

There was a deathlike hush.

'Just look at Radheya,' Duryodhana said. 'Can a doe give birth to a tiger? Everything about him proclaims his superiority. He does not deserve to rule just Anga-desh, he is born to rule the world. Look at those kundalas in his ears, that golden coat of mail. Can you not recognize a man of noble birth?'

Barely had Duryodhana finished speaking, when the entire crowd began to cheer lustily. 'Let Radheya and Kaunteya fight each other. That will settle the matter,' someone said. It became a demand. *Let them fight. Let them settle it right now.* But Kripacharya pointed towards the western sky where the flaming eye, as if having seen enough for one day, had begun its descent and was now speedily withdrawing into another dimension. A grey curtain fell over the sky. 'It's over,' Kripacharya said with obvious relief. 'The contest ends at sundown.'

Dronacharya and Pitamaha started to walk back to the king's enclosure. The show had, indeed, ended.

❖

At the royal dinner that followed, there was a sense of victory among the Kauravas. Present beside Duryodhana as his guest of honour was Karna. If Arjuna was aware of the oblique glances cast in his direction, he ignored them.

Just prior to the dinner, the Pandavas had gathered in Yudhisthira's chamber for a discussion. When it was over, Yudhisthira came to me. 'Arjuna refuses to attend the king's dinner,' he said, visibly upset. 'Speak to him, please.'

'What is his reason?' I had asked dully.

'You were there,' Yudhisthira said. 'You saw it, too. How Duryodhana gained advantage over us.'

'What advantage?' I asked frowning. 'It was only a tournament.'

'Is that what you think?' Yudhisthira said in disbelief. 'Then you must be the only person who does so. It was an out-and-out war. With Radheya on his side, Duryodhana has the advantage of the best archer in the land.'

I stared at him with anger. 'We don't know anything yet about this…this Karna, but you know Arjuna. How can you undermine your own brother?'

'You saw what Karna did. He was superior. Acharya Drona knows this, too, and that is why he did not admit Karna into the gurukula when he came begging for a place. Acharya told him to leave as he is not of royal blood, but everyone knows that he will never be guru to anyone who may outshine Arjuna.' He stopped and looked at my face curiously. 'They said that you fainted.'

'It was the heat.'

'We should thank our stars that the sun sank when it did,' he said. 'Even Arjuna knows deep down, though he will never admit it, that in Karna he has met his match. But it is not just that alone that fuels his outrage. He believes that the sutaputra insulted Guru Drona in the arena with the manner in which he swaggered in and spoke today. You know how Arjuna reveres the acharya—I shudder to think of what would happen if Karna and Arjuna were ever to meet in direct combat.'

They would kill each other. 'I cannot understand what has got into you brothers. Can't you learn to live in peace with your cousins?' I said sternly. 'We returned to Hastinapur because it was your father's kingdom and your ancestral home. You have every right to be here, but you have to coexist with that lot. There *is* no other way.'

He shook his head with regret. 'There might have been a chance of that, just a slim chance, if the sutaputra hadn't turned up today from nowhere.'

'Don't keep calling him that!'

Yudhisthira looked at me in surprise. 'I'm sorry if I've upset you, but what else should I call him?'

'I don't wish to see Arjuna or anyone else right now,' I said. 'Tell him from me that there was no winner and no loser today. He must get through this evening's dinner without any more scenes.'

Karna's presence at the dinner irked others too. Pitamaha acknowledged his greeting with supreme disdain, and the two preceptors, Kripa and Drona, looked right through him. All the older noblemen took their cue from this treatment and gave him a wide berth, except for Shakuni, who fawned over him in a sickening manner. Vidur was polite but distant. As for Dhritarashtra, he was all warmth and graciousness, and

Duryodhana saw to it that his guest was properly looked after. Servants fell over themselves in pouring out the wine and offering the choicest meats. The recipient of all this attention was, I sensed, uncomfortable. He remained aloof, barely smiling at the jokes of the jesters who performed that night. His responses to friendly overtures from the Kauravas were perfunctory. He drank moderately, but ate very little. The only time he seemed animated and relaxed was when Duryodhana engaged him in conversation. His face was transformed when he smiled.

He is alive. How will the Pandavas react when they learn who he really is? They will not see a thing beyond what is obvious to all: a sutaputra. They will not be able to live down the shame of it. It has taken us years to make a place in Hastinapur, and nothing is settled yet...I must not put my sons' future in peril. One false step and I will pull everyone with me deeper into this quicksand...He is Anga-raja now, a ruler in his own right, but Yudhisthira and his brothers are still dependant on their uncle. The past cannot be retrieved. No reparation. No repair.

It was time for the speeches. Pitamaha spoke first, thanking Drona for the flawless training imparted to the Kuru princes. He was in the mood for nostalgia and wove in anecdotes from his own younger days. He said that watching Arjuna in the arena had reminded him of Pandu. At this, Dhritarashtra, quite drunk by now, burst into noisy sobs. Winding down hurriedly, Pitamaha said that he had no worries now that he had seen the Kuru princes in action. Hastinapur was in safe hands. Finally he thanked the acharya again and said that the Kurus would never forget the debt they owed him.

The preceptor stood up. He waited till the hall was completely silent. 'The time has come for dues to be paid,' he announced.

'Name it, Acharya,' said Bhishma, with a grand wave of his right hand.

'Dhrupad, king of Panchala,' said Drona. 'I want him in chains before me.' He looked straight at Arjuna and raised an eyebrow. 'Will you get him for me?'

Arjuna stood up and bowed before speaking. 'It would be an honour, Gurudev, but I don't want my hundred cousins to feel deprived. Permit them to make the first attempt to capture the king of Panchala.'

The acharya looked amused and nodded.

Duryodhana and his cohorts cheered lustily. 'Tomorrow,' they shouted. 'We'll get him for you tomorrow.'

❖

For a phlegmatic brahmin, Drona had a high sense of drama, the kind that inspired the court bards to compose their finest narrative poems. The story called *Drona's Revenge* was sung so often that I, at least, was bored to death. Nevertheless, I sat through the performances trying to look enthralled, as well as gratified, whenever the part that Arjuna played in the capture of Dhrupad was sung.

To be honest, it was a grim tale. It began with the camaraderie fostered in a gurukula between a prince, the scion of a powerful kshatriya ruling family, and a studious intense brahmin boy. When the studies were over, they parted. The prince promised the brahmin that, when he inherited his father's kingdom, he would share half of it with his friend. In time, the prince became king, while the brahmin earned a livelihood as a teacher. So poor was he that he did not own even a cow. His only child, a boy, had never tasted cow's milk. One day, hearing about its sweet taste, the child demanded a drink of milk. His harried mother turned on her husband in frustration and asked, 'Of what use is all this learning of yours when you cannot provide something as basic as cow's milk to your son?'

The brahmin, a touchy man, left the house immediately. He headed for his old friend's kingdom, and once in his court reminded the king of the old promise. 'I don't want half your kingdom,' he said. 'But I'll accept a place in your court.' Was the sight of the shabbily-dressed brahmin who spoke in such familiar terms an embarrassment for the king? Were there sniggers among the courtiers at the outrageous demand? What else would compel the king to say: 'Don't be absurd, Brahmin, in bringing up that childhood friendship. We aren't children any more, nor are we equals. As I can't send you away without anything, I'll give you a cow or two.' The brahmin turned on his heel and retraced his steps. However, he did not go home. He went to Hastinapur where, he'd heard, they were looking for a man who would teach the Kuru princes how to fight.

Drona's revenge came years later when his erstwhile friend, Raja Dhrupad, stood before him, in chains, a prisoner of war. The common view, or rather the commoners' view, was that Dhrupad richly deserved what he got. But the question that Dhrupad had first asked Drona in the crowded assembly, *How can there be friendship between those whose status does not match?* was echoed with genuine puzzlement in kshatriya gatherings. What was *not* right about it, they asked each other.

What no one recognized was that knowledge is a great equalizer. A brahmin with the secret knowledge of the most potent weapons in the world was, by no means, powerless. Drona had walked out of Dhrupad's court and sold this knowledge to the Kurus, who, unlike Dhrupad, respected it and him, as well. The *gurudakshina* that Drona asked from the House of Kurus achieved two gains: Dhrupad was delivered to him in chains and, coincidentally, Arjuna retrieved his reputation as the finest archer in the world. Duryodhana and his brothers had not succeeded in the first attempt; in fact, they had been roundly thrashed.

In his moment of triumph, Drona believed he was being magnanimous when he said to the humiliated king, 'You do realize, don't you, that your kingdom is now mine and your life, too, is at my mercy? However, I am a brahmin and it is my nature to forgive. You may have forgotten the friendship that sprang between us when we were both disciples in my father's ashrama, but I remember it well. I want us to be friends again. How can there be any friendship between those who are not peers, you asked me once. I am a teacher and I gave you the answer in the form of a lesson. Now that is done, I am returning half your kingdom to you.' They said he looked wistful as he added the final sentence, 'We are equals now, and I hope we can be friends again.' It was missed by no one, however, that the noble brahmin returned the southern half of Dhrupad's kingdom, keeping for himself the more prosperous region in the north where he established the capital Ahichhatra. Now Drona was truly a king and his stature rose even higher in the Kuru court.

These events brought another issue to the forefront: who would be the next king to sit on the throne of Hastinapur? Even though the borders remained safe and the administration functioned well, the hiatus caused by Pandu's departure had not been filled. The citizens were pressing for the appointment of the yuvaraja. While Duryodhana had his supporters, the popular choice was Yudhisthira. That he was the eldest son of Pandu, who had extended the borders of the Kuru kingdom and singularly brought it to its present powerful position, was not forgotten. Yudhisthira's modesty, his stable nature and calm demeanour, too, won him many backers. It was common knowledge that Pitamaha, whose opinion many respected, favoured Yudhisthira. Finally, Dhritarashtra was left with no option but to name him the yuvaraja and we had a small ceremony to make it official.

Shortly after this event, an important visitor arrived—Balarama, the eldest son of my brother Vasudeva. He brought us news: outraged by Kansa's death at the hands of Krishna, Jarasandha had attacked Mathura with his full might. Krishna had saved the Yadavas by leading them to Dwaraka on the western coast where he had established a beautiful city. Though Balarama was the elder, whenever he spoke of Krishna, it was hard for him to hide his adulation for his half-brother. Looking at him, a burly, unsophisticated young man with an aloof air, I asked him if Krishna was anything like him. He laughed out loud. 'We couldn't be more different.' After a moment he added, 'There is no one like him. You'll see it for yourself.'

The threat posed by Jarasandha would only grow with time, Balarama said. Determined to prove his hegemony over the entire land, the emperor of Magadha aimed to capture a hundred kings and behead them as an offering to the god Mahadeva. Listening to all this, I got the feeling that the daily life which so absorbed us in Hastinapur was inconsequential. Yet that everyday world of our mean little rivalries, petty ambitions, our struggles and triumphs was all that we knew. However, there were changes in this world too. Pitamaha and Drona started to transform the Kuru army by increasing its strength, and introducing better weaponry—battle axes, spears, swords, maces—and new battlefield tactics. In the broad plain outside the city gates, the soldiers practised manoeuvres from dawn till dusk.

Balarama, a renowned mace warrior, was persuaded to give lessons to both Duryodhana and Bheem. That he favoured Duryodhana as a pupil over Bheem was clear from the beginning. Yudhisthira admitted that Duryodhana was a better learner, had shown great progress under Balarama's tutelage and was now a superior mace fighter. Bheem laughed and upped his quota of milk and eggs. Around this time Drona chose to give his most powerful weapon to Arjuna. The *Brahmashira astra* was an arrow with the capacity to annihilate the world. It was a gift from the gods meant to be used once, and returned when its work was done. In return Drona asked for a peculiar fee. 'When the day comes for you to face me on the battlefield, you will not hesitate to kill me.'

Arjuna said to me, 'I agreed because he called it gurudakshina but it was a strange request. It's not likely that I will ever have to face my guru on a battlefield. Acharya had a soft, regretful expression on his face, as if he was saying goodbye...But we aren't going away, are we?' He laughed at the idea.

A week later we knew that we were, indeed, going away.

4

Yudhisthira broke the news.

'My uncle gave me no choice,' he said. 'He is spending a fortune in building a palace for us in Varanavat. He wants us to go there for the festival of Pashupati. Apparently, it is a big event.'

'I've never heard of it,' I said.

'They talk of nothing else in the court,' Yudhisthira said. 'At least four different noblemen spoke of it to me today.'

'What did they say?' asked Bheem.

'Now that I am the yuvaraja, I should get to know the country and its people. The festival at Varanavat attracts common folks from every corner.' He stopped and a fox-like sharpness entered his eyes. 'I do wonder why I, my mother and my brothers are being pushed into this. If the festival is, in fact, such a momentous occasion as the courtiers are making it out to be, why is Duryodhana not being urged to attend it too?'

'Good question,' said Sahadeva.

'It could be a ploy to send us away,' Bheem said.

'Send us *far* away,' said Nakul. 'Even the swiftest horse rider would take four to five days to reach Hastinapur from Varanavat.'

'They want to finish us,' Arjuna said, his voice sharp with anger. 'They want to lure us to a faraway spot because it will be easier to get rid of the bodies…Fewer questions.'

'Don't talk wildly,' I said, trying hard to quell my own rising panic. 'Who are *they*?'

'Duryodhana and that idiot Duhsashana,' said Arjuna. 'Possibly their uncle Shakuni, maybe even Radheya.' He sneered. 'They think that now that they have the sutaputra with them, they are invincible.'

'You know that Pitamaha, Vidur and the two acharyas would never support any such scheme,' I said. 'They did not approve of Karna's coronation.'

'Could they stop it?' Bheem countered. 'Nor will they stop Duryodhana's plan.'

Yudhisthira nodded. 'Our uncle Dhritarashtra calls it a holiday, but the truth is that we are being sent away. It may be that Duryodhana hopes to consolidate his position here in our absence.'

Just as Dhritarashtra consolidated his in Pandu's absence.

Yudhisthira's normal composure remained, but it disguised inner turmoil. He was never easy about taking a decision unless he had weighed all its consequences. Yet he could be stubborn. I got the feeling that he was worried about how it would look if he refused this offer from his uncle and benefactor.

'If you have no choice but to accept it, then do it with good grace,' I said.

❖

It did not smell right, the house, but the man showing us around seemed to find nothing wrong. His name was

Purochan. A portly man in his fifties, bald and fleshy-faced with beetling eyebrows. He called himself a trader, but had the cold eyes, silver tongue and smooth falseness of a courtier. The rumour was that he was Duryodhana's henchman.

'What do you trade in?' Bheem asked.

The man smiled—a lot. His teeth, stained red from chewing betel nut, had two front-ranking members missing. Whenever he opened his mouth to speak, a generous spray of spittle accompanied his words. 'Timber,' he said, happily. 'Plenty of it around.' The house was surrounded by a dense wood of palash trees. In bloom, they looked from a distance like a forest on fire.

'How is the hunting here?' Arjuna asked.

Purochan's smile widened. 'Plenty of that too,' he said. 'Panther, wild boar, deer. You won't run short of sport or meat.' He looked at me with a sidelong glance and an unctuous note entered his voice. 'I've managed to get a very good cook. A local man, but trained in the palace kitchen at Hastinapur.'

Bheem curled his lip. 'The palace kitchen had dozens of cooks,' he said. 'Will one man be good enough for us? I don't like to be kept waiting at meal times. Hire a couple of assistants to help him.' He glanced in my direction. 'Our mother will need several maids as well.'

'My wife can help out,' Purochan said, reluctantly.

'I don't want to trouble your wife,' I said. 'She looked after us very well for the week we were attending the festival, but we cannot impose on her hospitality.'

'No imposition,' Purochan spat the words out. 'An honour to serve the rajmata.'

'That's settled then,' Bheem said. 'A maid for our mother and at least three assistants for the cook. They can do double duty as servants in the house.'

Purochan stiffened. 'Difficult,' he said, stroking his double chin. 'This house is far from the town. That is an advantage and a disadvantage.'

'We will manage without servants,' Yudhisthira said, his tone pleasant but firm.

Purochan looked relieved. He hung around for several minutes more, smiling a great deal, but watching us all the time. 'Have you seen all the rooms?' he asked. 'Are you satisfied? We have used only the best materials in the construction. The frescoes on the walls, have you seen them?'

'Yes, thank you,' Yudhisthira said. 'Everything is in order. If we need anything, we will call you.'

'I'll be within hailing distance,' promised the trader. 'Just give a shout.'

When he had gone, the brothers began to speak at once, but Yudhisthira held up his hand in warning. 'We shall be very comfortable here,' he said in an extraordinarily loud voice. 'This Purochan is a good man. We should trust his word.' We looked at him baffled. He pointed towards the door. It stared back at us silently. The smell that had put me off in the beginning began to thicken. My head was swimming. Nakul reached my side just as my legs gave way. 'Open the windows and doors!' he said urgently. 'Ma needs fresh air.'

Sahadeva went to the door and slowly opened it. There was no one outside.

'The room does smell funny,' Bheem said, tapping a pillar,

then scraping at its surface with his nail. He sniffed at it. 'Ghee?' he said, puzzled. He rubbed his fingers and stared at them. He held out his hand for us to see. His fingertips were reddish.

'Lac,' said Yudhisthira calmly. 'He deals in timber and lac. Those palash trees out there are for producing the resin. Vidur Chacha gave me a hint just as we were leaving. Apparently, one of the clerks accidentally brought to him the bills to be cleared for ghee, oil, wood, jute fibre, lac and other...combustibles.'

'Poison and drowning didn't succeed the last time with me,' said Bheem, wrathfully. 'So now they mean to kill all of us by fire...We should leave, Bade Bhaiyya.'

Yudhisthira shook his head. 'Where will we go? Duryodhana has spies everywhere.'

Bheem sent him an exasperated look. 'Then let us go back and stay in that slimy toad Purochan's mansion. He won't set his own house on fire.'

'He'll think of another way. He is coldblooded enough for that and I'm sure he has been paid very well.'

'Someone will surely help us,' Arjuna said. 'Duryodhana can't buy everyone.'

'He has the keys to the Kuru treasury.'

'Well, then!' Bheem threw up his hands. 'Since you have all the answers, Bade Bhaiyya, pray tell us what we should do.'

'Nothing,' said Yudhisthira. 'Purochan will not act immediately. We have been here only a week and that time was spent in attending the temple festival and in meeting the people. The goodwill towards us is at its highest. He will wait several weeks, even months.'

Arjuna pursed his lips. 'We must find escape routes through the forest. When the time is right, we will need them.'

'How will we know that time?' I asked.

'Vidur Chacha told me that he would arrange for someone to help us,' Yudhisthira said. 'Meanwhile, it would be good for us to remain in the public eye.'

'We should have people coming and going all the time,' said Bheem. 'We could hold pujas and feed the poor.' He gave a wicked grin. 'All paid for by our revered uncle, the king.'

Purochan pretended to be pleased by our activities. However, after several weeks, it was clear that our sojourn was anything but restful for him. He felt the pressure of keeping a watch on us and it made him short-tempered. Yudhisthira discovered that the man had a weakness for dice games and invited him to play every now and then. More often than not, he'd end up losing, which improved Purochan's mood a great deal. 'The prince has no head for the game,' Purochan would say, with a patronizing smile.

Before long Vidur's man arrived. We hid him in an inner chamber. He was a wiry compact man of indeterminate age, his features indiscernible under a short beard. He spoke only to Yudhisthira. The language he used was the one that Vidur had taught Yudhisthira years ago. Whatever he revealed satisfied my son. 'He's a miner,' Yudhisthira said. 'He's going to dig us a tunnel from your chamber, Ma, that will lead to a safe spot in the forest. Purochan snoops around our rooms, but he will not dare to enter yours without permission.'

I looked at the little man who was to be our saviour. Where had Vidur found him? He glanced at me once—a beady-eyed intelligence shone through—before shifting his gaze away.

I did not see the miner again, though the food and water kept for him was regularly replenished. It was reassuring to know that he was at work, but at night when the servants left and only Purochan remained, drinking heavily in his chamber near the front door till he fell asleep, I would lie awake beset with doubts.

The decision to return to Hastinapur had turned out horribly wrong, but where else could I have gone but to my husband's kin? Wasn't Hastinapur the natural home of the Pandavas? Yet, hadn't I been propelled there by my own secret desire? My husband had been the king, Yudhisthira as the eldest in the next generation had every right to become the yuvaraja and then the king—hadn't I assumed this? Blinded by my own wish, perhaps, I had not stopped to think that conditions in Hastinapur, too, had changed while we were away, nor could I have foreseen the high degree of hostility we would have to face. The rajmata's parting words had, indeed, come true: *Duryodhana, the eldest, has grown up believing that the crown is his private property, held in safekeeping for him by his father till he is old enough to wear it—he was nurtured on that belief*. I had a strong suspicion that this plan to get rid of us had Dhritarashtra's tacit approval. Those who wanted us dead, and had gone to such lengths to ensure it, would not rest till they had accomplished their purpose. Even if we were to get out of this situation alive, where would we go? Who was there to help us? How would it end?

Tired of thinking, I would sit by the window and stare at the sky, at the millions of twinkling points of light, and wonder about the mysteries of fate. In those dark hours, episodes from the life I had led played out before me like flickering shadows on a wall. The journey that I had begun as a day-old babe, cast out of her mother's arms and her father's heart, had made of me a lifelong exile, looking not for a home so much as for refuge. Every journey that I had made had only taken me deeper into this strange banishment. But now there were my sons to think of. *I must keep going. I cannot give up*. Gradually, the darkness would fade, and my tears dry up. The rosy glow of dawn meant that another long night had ended. As the breeze picked up and liquid birdcalls filtered through the silence, as my sons stirred, I, too, would find myself ready to face whatever lay ahead. Prepared to do whatever was needed.

❖

I am a murderer.

I am a mother.

The nameless bold-eyed Nishadha woman who came to my door that evening was a mother too. I was sure that I had never met her before, but something about her was familiar. She asked for food. A party of pilgrims had eaten at the house that day, we had plenty of leftovers. I placed a leaf plate and asked her to sit down. She looked back towards the palash trees and made a sign. To my surprise, dark shadows emerged, half-naked, barefoot—her sons. Five. The oldest, with aquiline features and furtive shifting eyes, was in his thirties; the youngest, about fifteen, had an incipient moustache. They wore loin cloths and carried bows. The servants had left for the day so I did the serving. Hearing the noise, Purochan came to the back of the kitchen to investigate.

Over the last few weeks the man had grown edgy; his drinking, too, had increased. At night I would hear him walking around the house checking that all the doors and windows were latched. Observing his behaviour I got the feeling that he was close to completing the task for which he had been paid all these past months. He had ordered a fresh supply of kindling even though we still had plenty. It had been stored right next to the *chulha* in the kitchen. When I had protested that it was a hazard and asked him to have it removed, he had given me an insolent look. I pretended not to see it, but later I spoke to my sons, and they shared my fears. Yudhisthira said he was waiting for a sign from the miner that the tunnel was ready. A few days later he said that it was. He looked at me and the look said, *Now it's up to you.*

On seeing the Nishadha woman, Purochan said nothing. She glanced at him briefly before she continued eating, but something intimate, knowing passed between them in that look. Her youngest son stiffened and seemed to bristle at Purochan's presence, but the others remained indifferent. After Purochan had gone, I asked the woman where she lived. She pointed vaguely in the direction of a hillock. On top of it was a small settlement of crude beehive huts. I asked her if her husband waited at home, and if she wanted some food for him as well. Her reply was a short coarse laugh, as if the very idea of a husband was amusing. Her sons continued to chew their food impassively, but the youngest seemed discomfited; he lowered his head.

'Stay the night then,' I said to the woman. 'I have some work for which I will give you raw rice and oil in exchange, but it can wait till tomorrow morning.'

A gleam entered her eyes. Her sons had eaten their fill. The eldest belched and got up to throw away his leaf plate. He looked at me and said something to his mother. I caught the word 'liquor'.

'Tell Purochan to give it to you,' I said to her. 'But tomorrow you must do my work.'

Hours later, when darkness had settled on the forest, we could still hear them. They were all drunk, even the fifteen-year-old. As the night passed, they grew more boisterous, shouting and singing snatches of songs. Purochan had joined in the drinking and the revelry. His jokes got bawdier, the woman shrieked with laughter.

I looked out of the window. A moonless sky. The night was a void that had engulfed the forest. Would it allow us to survive? It was well past the midnight hour when there was a knock on my door. My sons quickly slipped in, all except Bheem. They rolled up the mat that lay over the tunnel entrance and pulled the slab up. In the dim glow of a lamp, I saw the deep hole and quailed. 'Bheem is setting fire to the house,' Yudhisthira whispered. 'He will be the last to enter the tunnel. Arjuna will go in first, then you, Nakul and Sahadeva. I will follow as soon as Bheem arrives and—'

'I am not leaving till he is here,' I said.

Sahadeva gave me a quick hug. 'We'll all leave together,' he said.

Dawn did not show its face in Varanavat that day. Thick black smoke billowing in the skies cast a shroud over it. After all these years, in my nightmares I see that fire, the flames sneaking out of the doors and windows, racing across the floors, licking along the walls. I hear their evil crackle, as if celebrating their freedom. The heat rises in a wave, it singes my hair. A gust of wind blows burning straw towards the palash forest where lac trapped within the trees catches fire, making fiery torches of the tree trunks. And now, as the red blaze rises, a different kind of dawn appears, fierce and hot, the dawn of the last day of our lives. From now on, we will be dead to the world. A river awaits us. We rush towards it. When I trip over a twisted root, Bheem lifts me up and carries me in his arms. Arjuna leads, stopping only to get his bearings. His eyes meet mine and I am reassured by the look of resolve in them. Sahadeva tires and Bheem lifts him onto his shoulder. At last, we hear the river, its soft susurration. A boat with a prow shaped like an eagle's head bobs on the waters. A lone boatman waits. Yudhisthira uses his secret language. The boatman replies. He takes us across to the opposite bank. And we are back in another jungle, plunging deeper and deeper into it through its tangled vines. In my nightmares, the fire follows us, its hot breath licking at our heels. *It is only a matter of time...*

5

Kuntibhoja's daughter and her sons had perished in a fire. The Pandavas and their mother were no more. A state funeral had been held on Dhritarashtra's orders—obviously, no expense was spared. A countrywide mourning had been announced. Prayers had been said for our souls. Yet the feeling of being relentlessly pursued did not leave us.

It was always there in the forest, where the silence was unnerving and the echoes of our own breathing seemed to stalk us. But it was strongest in the human settlements where all eyes were on us as we walked in, a poor brahmin woman accompanied by a son or two—we were careful never to be seen as six. It may have been the mood of the times, the sudden appearance of a posse of horsemen galloping on the country roads, stopping and questioning, or maybe it was the prolonged feeling of persecution that pushed out every other instinct in us but the one to stay alive. We avoided the settlements as far as possible, remaining within the jungle. Not that we were free from danger there. It lurked in the bushes and shrubs, squeaking and rustling, it watched us with sharp hidden eyes, sometimes it crawled or slithered by at arm's length, but it was still a lesser danger. Cruel and amoral as Nature is, it is not malevolent.

In Hastinapur, thousands of brahmins were fed during the shraadh held for us. But we were reduced to foraging for food and water. We spent nights without sleep. Our clothes soon became tatters and our spirit was made ragged by our homeless, hopeless state as we wandered god-knows-where-all. In that no-time which we inhabited, Bheem was our strength. Were it not for him, we would surely have perished. The vitality that he had inherited from his father Vayu, the brute strength that he had been given by the Nagas, and his own uncomplicated nature combined to make him our mainstay. Even Yudhisthira, who had always secretly scorned him, and Arjuna, who hadn't bothered to hide his sense of superiority, gained a new respect for Bheem's indefatigable effort in keeping us going. As for the Madreyas—whom he carried on his shoulders when they were young—they had always loved him the best.

Bheem was the first of my sons to get himself a wife. Hidimbi was nearly as tall as he was, dark-skinned, slim-waisted and sinewy. She belonged to a forest-dwelling tribe, the Rakshasas, who had their own gods, and were a law unto themselves. Her brother, Hidimba, was a savage with a taste for human flesh. He sent her to kill us, but Hidimbi fell in love—with Bheem. The bestial brother, enraged at this betrayal, challenged Bheem to a fight. It was a fair fight and he lost. Hidimbi's love for Bheem multiplied due to her admiration for his strength. Yudhisthira told her to leave us alone, as a marriage between a kshatriya and a rakshasi was not approved of by either side, but Hidimbi persisted. She asked to speak with me in privacy. Yudhisthira advised me against it. 'This isn't the right time for diversions. What purpose will this alliance serve? Bheem will have to leave her anyway.'

'Have you noticed that ever since she's been with us, we've had it easier?' I pointed out. She had been helping us in small but significant ways. Gifts of food were regularly left for us. Once or twice, when we'd lost our way, she had guided us back. 'Let me, at least, hear her out.'

'I love him with all my heart,' she said. 'You know what that means, Mata, don't you? You, too, have suffered these pangs.' Her light brown eyes were surprisingly gentle as she looked into my face. 'He is all I have ever dreamed of. I am ready to leave my family and my clan for him.'

'He could be happy with you for a while,' I said. 'But he cannot live the life of a forest-dweller forever. He is a kshatriya.'

'Not forever,' she said with a quiet smile. 'A week or two—if that is all I can have with him, it's still better than nothing at all.' She hesitated, her face flushed. 'You know what a woman feels when she looks at a man and wants only to have his baby.'

I saw that she was open and vulnerable, just as I had once been. Yet, is it possible to love someone and not expect something in return?

'I will keep him only as long as it takes to give him a son,' she said, her eyes clear and honest. 'If you are proud of him you will be prouder still of your grandson.'

I allowed myself a smile. 'Now you are making me an offer I can't refuse.'

We agreed that Bheem would be hers for a year, till the child was born.

It was a magical time for them. The tenderness that I had always suspected lay beneath my son's unruly and loud exterior now surfaced. As her pregnancy advanced, Hidimbi would come and sit by my side. I'd place my hand on her distended belly and feel the nudge from my grandchild. 'He wants you to tell him what his father was like when *he* was a boy,' she would say.

The baby came, bigger than any newborn I have ever seen. Not a single hair marred the smooth round of his head. I loved him on sight. The parents named him Ghatotkach. *One whose head is as bald as a water pot.* When the time came for us to leave, I was truly sorry.

❖

The rakshasa Hidimba had preyed on unfortunate travellers who passed through his patch, but he had rarely strayed out of the forest. However, that did not mean that the open countryside with its fields and villages was safe. The kingdom through which we were passing was notorious for being poorly governed. Its ruler had moved away after tribes of rakshasas and asuras, who were, by nature, not inclined to obey laws, began to run amok. The Pandavas, seeing the fear, misery and inactivity in the settlements talked about the anarchy, they chafed to do something, but there was little they could do.

We were travelling as a family of brahmin ascetics, dressed in bark, studying the Vedas, living off alms given in exchange for a blessing. We got so good at it that Yudhisthira would often pontificate under the local banyan in whichever village we were that day. He rather enjoyed these public engagements. An important benefit from these discourses was a regular supply of offerings: fruit, grain, vegetables. It was enough for us to keep body and soul together, though Bheem, who ate more than the rest of us combined, always complained of being hungry. Even in those diminished circumstances, food was a source of pleasure to him. 'Look at what we've got today, Ma,' he'd say, putting down a bunch of plantains or a pot of buttermilk.

'Whatever it is, you five must share it,' I would reply.

One evening, just as I was preparing to cook khichadi, we had an unexpected visitor in Krishna Dwaipayana. It took me a moment to recognize him. The last time I'd seen him was at the funeral of my husband. Then his head and beard had been shaved off. Now the hair was done up in a two-tiered top knot and the long, silver-white beard that reached his chest was clearly his pride and joy. When we realized who it was and that it was *us* he had come to see, we ran about in a fluster for the welcoming rituals. Yudhisthira offered the arghya before we led the muni into the cave that was our shelter for the night. If he noticed how humble our surroundings were or how meagre our hospitality, he was gracious enough to not comment. However, Yudhisthira, probably out of sheer nervousness, apologized profusely.

The sage gave an understanding smile. 'I wasn't expecting anything else,' he said. 'I've known about everything that you've gone through in the last eighteen months, ever since the sons of Dhritarashtra ensured that you were banished.'

If you've known, why have you not said a word against it?

Without looking at me, he said, 'In my eyes, the five Pandavas and the hundred sons of Dhritarashtra are one and the same. But it's only normal for humans to be sympathetic to those who are in trouble, especially if they are young and at risk. I came to see you because I don't want you to lose heart. You've done well, so far.'

How much further and for how long?

'I have a suggestion,' he went on in the same measured tone. 'Go to the town known as Ekachakra. You will like it. Live there discreetly for a while. I will come to see you again.'

The Pandavas were a bit overwhelmed by this visit, but they performed all their duties as hosts. Just before leaving, the sage had a private word with me. 'I'm pleased with the way the Pandavas have turned out,' he said. 'They will rule their ancestral kingdom one day.'

❖

'This is all we have to offer,' said the brahmin's wife.

Two bare, fairly large rooms on one side of the small open courtyard. Beyond them lay the back garden where plantains grew in tight green bunches and a green vine, covering the byre's thatched roof, produced gourds aplenty.

'It will do,' I said. She seemed so anxious to please that I smiled.

'It was my grandfather's house,' she said, her face brightening with pride. 'Built for a large family. Now there's no one left except us.' After a moment she added, 'We have our own cows, too. You won't have to worry about milk. And you must help yourself to the vegetables in the kitchen garden.'

'Do you manage all this by yourself?'

'With help from my daughter.' She looked at the doorway

behind me and a girl of thirteen or fourteen quietly entered and touched my feet. 'Her name is Mamata,' said the brahmin's wife.

The girl had inherited her mother's slender frame, narrow face and large, contemplative eyes. However, the mother's mouth had a permanent downward curve to it. The front door creaked open, a pattering noise was heard, followed by the dull *thunk* of a ball hitting the earthen floor. It rolled in over the threshold and was followed by a lad of six or seven. He stopped short on seeing a stranger. The mother's eyes lit up. 'My son Shankar,' she said.

'There are five brahmins waiting under the neem tree at the corner of the lane,' Shankar told his mother. 'One of them looks like a mountain.'

The brahmin's wife shushed him 'Ask them to come in,' she said. To me she added, 'Don't cook till you are settled in. I'll make enough for all of us.'

'It will be too much work,' I protested. 'The mountain needs a lot of food or he'll turn into a mole hill.'

The boy and his sister giggled. The mother, too, smiled. 'I hope you'll be happy here,' she said shyly.

Ekachakra, built around a large square tank, was a settlement of brahmins. It was fairly prosperous, but a little too quiet. The houses on our street were big and well maintained, but many of them were shut. Sound carried far in the silence. I'd wake up in the mornings to the soft wet swish of the brahmin's wife milking the cows. She'd talk to them, using endearments that she never used with her children. She would clean out the shed, wash her hands and feet at the well and come into the house. After a while the aroma of milk reaching a boil would fill the air. By this time her husband would return from his ablutions at the temple tank, the girl Mamata would be up and sweeping the courtyard, the young boy would begin reciting the previous day's lesson to his father. Every now and then, the brahmin would stop him and gently correct the pronunciation of a word. He was a polite but reticent man who didn't seem to mind being bossed over by his wife. These people and the simple rhythms of their household charmed me, as I, too, went about my daily routine: washing myself with water from the small cistern in the back, lighting the lamp in the altar, starting on the cooking chores under the green shade of the jackfruit tree. After the morning meal, my sons would leave, returning only at dusk with the grain they'd got as the day's *bhiksha*. The placid routine of our life in Ekachakra worked like a cure on me.

One day, about three months into our stay, Bheem, complaining of fever and body ache, stayed back on Nakul's advice. It was late afternoon and he was dozing when the quiet was broken by a loud wail from the other side of the courtyard. It was cut short abruptly, but I heard a soft whimper and the sound of sobbing. I made a move to get up.

'Leave them alone, Ma,' said Bheem, without opening his eyes. 'It wouldn't be wise to meddle.'

I sat back reluctantly, but the weeping did not stop. 'They've been very good to us,' I said. 'We cannot act indifferent.'

'Bade Bhaiyya has advised us to mind our own business,' Bheem said.

'At least let me find out what's wrong!'

He sighed. 'Nothing is as it seems, even in this peaceful village.'

'What do you mean?' I asked, alarmed.

'Nothing,' he said and turned on his side.

I crossed the courtyard. The brahmin was speaking to his wife: 'I asked you to leave this village, but you said you couldn't abandon your ancestral home. What sense did it make to stay on when your parents were dead and you had no immediate family? Some of your own relatives have left, yet you remained tied. You loved every corner of the house, the trees in the garden, the taste of the water, you said. You wouldn't listen to me. And now it's too late...Our turn *had* to come—' He stopped, as though overwrought. 'What choice do I have?' he asked, brokenly. 'I can't send you, my wife, to your death. Nor can I send my young son to his death. As for this daughter of mine, she was given to me as a pledge from the gods, how can I sacrifice her? It would be easiest to give myself up...I see no way out.'

It was the longest speech I had heard him make. After a few moments, his wife spoke. 'I admit to my fault. But I'm not going to allow you to go.' He murmured something. Her voice rose in anger, a harried note entered it. '*Why* don't you listen to me? If you were to die, what would become of me? I would not be able to bring up these children in the right manner. How would I, as a poor widow, marry this girl off into a good family? How would I keep your son safe from harm? How would I keep *myself* safe? Tell me! Just as stray dogs, if given a chance, pollute the ghee meant for the sacrifice, men who have lust in them defile the body of a woman who is without protection. You say you will not let me go but, as usual, you are being impractical. It makes sense that I should be the one to die.' A new note, of bitterness, entered her voice. 'I have done all my duties by my parents and by you. Given you children. Fulfilled my desires, be it for the water or for the fruit from the garden—it's easiest for everyone if I go.' She faltered. 'You—you can always marry again...it is not a sin for you, but for me it is.'

For a few minutes no one spoke. Then I heard the girl Mamata say hesitatingly, 'Pitaji, Ma—please don't weep. Neither of you need to think about death. My brother is too young, he needs you now. And you will need him when you yourself are old. But I am your daughter and you will give me away one day in marriage. A parting from you is written in my fate. So, I beg you, let me go now. Let me be the sacrifice. I would be happy with that destiny, as it is the answer to all your problems.'

More than all the words I'd heard from the parents, the young girl's speech struck a chord in me. Pushing open the door, I entered the room. They looked up. 'I knocked,' I said brusquely. 'Please—tell me the reason why you are all so upset.'

❖

It was unlike Yudhisthira to be furious, but that evening his face was like thunder. 'How could you do it?' he asked, his voice low, shaking with anger. 'You've sacrificed your own son for someone else's child?'

'They were *all* going to die together,' I said calmly. 'I offered to send Bheem instead.'

'What sense does that make? We *need* Bheem.'

'Bheem's strength will keep him safe.'

He snorted. 'How can you say that when you didn't even know what the danger was?'

'Evidently, you did,' I said sternly. 'You knew all along that this town was being terrorized by a rakshasa. Why didn't you tell me?'

He shifted his gaze. 'We didn't want to worry you.'

'Why don't you just say that you didn't want to get involved in somebody else's problem? Is this how we repay their hospitality?'

Arjuna made a gesture of wanting to speak. I looked at him questioningly. 'Yes,' he said. 'We've known that an asura named Baka has settled in a cave outside the village. In the beginning, he'd abduct victims at random and no one knew who it would be next. The people of Ekachakra came up with the solution of making one human sacrifice, by turn, from every household so that Bakasura would spare the rest,' he said. 'The arrangement has suited them because they have some control over who gets chosen as the sacrifice. In return Baka does not allow any other of his ilk to prey on them. It's a covenant *they* made—the townspeople. What role do we, as outsiders, have in it?'

'I cannot believe my ears!' I said. 'Is this *your* view?'

He glanced at Yudhisthira. 'We conferred among ourselves,' he said.

'Debated it like good brahmins, no doubt. You've lived as brahmins for so long that you've started applying scholarly knowledge to everything. Have you forgotten that *you were born kshatriyas*?' Arjuna flushed deeply but remained silent. 'Don't justify it by calling it a covenant. When it comes to tackling tyranny, all the rules in the shastras fly out of the window, do you hear me?' I turned on Yudhisthira. 'As for you, Yudhisthira, cramming high wisdom in your head has left no space for common sense. Didn't your father din it into you that a kshatriya's first duty is to protect the weak? Why else does he always bear arms? Who can be more helpless than an entire family that decides to end its very existence rather than let any one of their number go? I heard that innocent seven-year-old-boy talk about how he, alone, would go and face the rakshasa and kill him. A childish boast, yes, but for all it's worth that was the only spirited response I heard from *that* family.' I took a deep breath. 'And now I've come to know that my own five sons, all grown up and able-bodied, would much rather pretend to be deaf, mute and blind than fight! Do you still call yourself kshatriyas?'

'You should have waited till we returned, Ma,' Arjuna said.

'Whatever I did, it was after careful reflection,' I said. 'We may be fugitives, but if we forget our dharma, we are nothing. This house has been a haven. We've had a few months of peace, a chance to recover our strength. Our hosts have treated us with respect and kindness. This seemed the only way of repaying our debt.'

'We could have talked it over,' Arjuna said. 'We brothers would never disobey your command. If you wanted us to fight Baka, we would have done it, but to send Bheem alone there was not wise.'

'You and Yudhisthira always seem to think that Bheem, because he laughs and jokes all the time, doesn't have a brain between his ears,' I said. 'When he was fighting

Hidimba, you, Arjuna, couldn't stop yourself from shouting instructions from the sidelines. He didn't need your help then. He doesn't need it now.'

Yudhisthira changed tack. 'You are right,' he said. 'Bheem will rid this village of Baka. But what happens after that? Everyone will know we are not brahmins. They've heard about the Pandavas' tragedy even in this place. We must flee again, hide in the jungles, sleep in caves, worry about our next meal.'

'No,' I said. 'I promised to help the family on condition that they do not reveal a word. The brahmin may have his suspicions, but he will think up a story to satisfy his neighbours.'

They looked unconvinced.

The next morning, the body of Baka was found lying in a field outside the village.

6

Draupadi. Panchali. These were her names; they tell you about her genealogy and the kingdom she came from, but they say nothing about her. Other names do that: Yajnaseni, because she emerged from the sacrificial *vedi*; Krishnaa, because her skin had that rare coppery glow never again seen on a woman. The rumours of her mysterious birth caught on like a forest fire in summer, but it was a tale that the bards had stayed away from. It was too dark.

For months after his humiliation at Drona's hands, the story went, Dhrupad, the king of Panchala, had searched for a means to get even. As Drona was known to be indestructible, Dhrupad had sought the help of those sorcerers who practised the dark arts. He had found two brothers, priests of sinister repute, who agreed to materialize for him a son who would kill the brahmin. An esoteric secret ritual had been performed; it produced a handsome warrior prince, but along with him came his beautiful dark-skinned sister, who, a celestial voice said, would bring about the fall of the kshatriyas and the end of the Kurus.

'The fall of the kshatriyas seems like a boast, but I'm

all for her if she's going to bring down the Kauravas,' said Bheem. 'She must be some woman, this Panchali. Wonder what she looks like.'

Men, everywhere, were wondering about her. Now that she had stepped out of the flames, a full-fledged woman with her feet lined with the auspicious red dye, the next buzz was of her loveliness. The fragrance of blue lotus, eyes with the radiance of dew on a flower, long, flowing tresses, pearl-like teeth, coral lips, reed-like waist, thighs like that of a doe. In sleepy little Ekachakra, too, men dreamed on. I sensed the longing and the restlessness that had come over my sons. I saw how their ears pricked up at the mention of her name, and pretended not to see their callow efforts to conceal the slow burn of curiosity mingled with desire behind the brotherly banter.

Krishna Dwaipayana hadn't forgotten his promise to visit us; he arrived one morning. 'The time is right for you to move,' he said. 'Go north. Go to Panchala. Dhrupad is holding a swayamvar for his daughter. All kshatriyas are invited.' Now that direction had been given to their ardour, the Pandavas, as if sensing the end of a stage in their lives, were reluctant to leave. The seer, recognizing this as trepidation, told them a story—about a nameless virtuous maiden who prayed to Mahadeva for an accomplished husband. Thinking that repeating her request would make it stronger, she did so. Five times. And the great god, in his unfathomable wisdom, said to her that, in her next birth, she would be the wife of five men.

The moral *I* got from this unlikely story only reiterated what I already knew: *Be careful what you wish for—you just might get it*. But, my sons, I formed the impression, had got an altogether different message.

❖

Kampilya, Dhrupad's capital city, was bursting at the seams. Not a room to be had. We were turned away from eight or nine places before Bheem, in exchange for his labour, got us an empty hut in a corner of the potters' *basti* outside the city gates. He was contracted to fetch cartloads of clay every day from the riverbank. Everyone was busy in the potters' quarter. Wheels spun all day as utensils—bowls, pots, plates, cups—and thousands of oil lamps were shaped and fired in the common kiln. An enterprising toymaker had created a whole range of dolls in the likeness of the princess Draupadi and her fireborn twin Drishtadyumna. On the eve of the swayamvar, Arjuna returned with the clay doll of an archer. He placed it before me.

'It's you!' I said, startled.

'There's gossip that the Pandava princes did not die in the fire at Varanavat,' he said.

'But—those bodies?'

He shook his head. 'Not bodies. Bones. The bones only say that the dead were human. There was nothing to say *who* they were.'

I was silent.

'In this series of dolls there are four others. Can you guess which one sells the most in the market?' I could not. 'Bheem,' he said, with a grin. 'The boys just love him. Even Jarasandha comes second.'

'And the girls?'

'Nakul and Sahadeva.'

'They have good taste, but I hope the princess will employ good sense when it comes to selecting her husband.'

'The princess will have no choice,' he said with a shrug. 'She is only the bait to pull in the best archer in the land.'

There is only one. 'Any serious contenders?' I asked without looking at him.

'They are all in the running. Jarasandha, Shishupal, Shakuni, Duryodhana and that Radheya.'

Yudhisthira, entering the hut, gave Arjuna a look of exasperation. 'Karna has a legitimate right to compete,' he said. 'The invitation was sent to all kings.'

Arjuna gave him a disbelieving look. 'Kings govern their own kingdoms, Bade Bhaiyya, they don't sit in the court of another king as hangers-on. The sutaputra has adopted the dress code and mannerisms of a kshatriya, but that doesn't change the shade of blood flowing in him. He'll remain a charioteer all his life.'

'Are you worried that the charioteer may get the princess?' Yudhisthira's tone was mocking.

'Aren't you?'

Yudhisthira looked away. A vein throbbed in his temple. 'There isn't a man alive who doesn't want this prize,' he said slowly. 'My sympathies lie with the man who wins it.'

He was thinking of the celestial prophecy—with longing, but also with dread. 'You are in hiding as brahmins now,' I said. 'Only kshatriyas are eligible to participate in the swayamvar of a princess.'

Arjuna's expression turned obstinate. An eternity passed

before Yudhisthira said, in a quiet, reassuring tone. 'We will be in the brahmins' enclosure, Ma, as spectators.'

❖

When Dhrupad laughed Drona out of his court, he was a king. When he lost half his kingdom to Drona, he was still a king. However, hatred for his arch enemy had limited his imagination; it had made of him a merchant. When Yajnaseni, the fireborn maiden, stood before him in all her brilliance, all he could see was merchandise. All he could think of was how to use it to his advantage. It was Dhrupad who made his daughter a commodity. He called it a swayamvar, but it was an auction that he held for her.

Like the proverbial dutiful daughter, she accepted her father's will and stood by the side of her brother Dhrishtadyumna, looking not unlike a clay doll, waiting patiently with the garland in her hands, as each of the suitors tested his skill on a spinning target. What was she thinking of as she watched them try their luck and fail? Did she feel unease about the outcome? Did she pray for one particular man to win? When it came to Karna's turn, how did she gather the gumption to say in that packed stadium, *I will not have a suta for my lord*? In a gathering of kshatriyas, for a woman to coldly insult a man in this way stunned everyone. Duryodhana looked daggers at her and there were disapproving murmurs from others. The mood began to sour. There were grumbles that Dhrupad, with his arrogant daughter and his unwinnable contest, had deliberately intended to humiliate his peers. Finally, there remained not a single kshatriya who had not tried to string Shiva's bow. Tried and failed.

To make matters worse, a young man sitting in the brahmins' enclosure stood up and asked if he could participate. The kings frowned. The contest was strictly for kshatriyas, but several brahmins—encouraged by the poor show from the kshatriyas—nodded their approval. They quoted the examples of Parashurama and Agastya, both brahmins who were expert in the martial arts. Dhrupad shrugged and said that, as far as he was concerned, *any* archer could take a shot. The young brahmin approached the bow, strung it and shot five arrows into the target. Before anyone could react, the princess went to him and placed the garland on his neck. There was complete silence in the stadium. Then there was pandemonium. The kings collectively began to abuse Dhrupad and Dhrishtadyumna. 'At that point, Nakul, Sahadeva and I left,' said Yudhisthira, who described the events to me. 'We came straight home to tell you the news.'

'Did Arjuna take your permission before he entered the arena?' I asked tersely. Yudhisthira did not reply. In his stillness, something altered, like a tremor. 'Where is he now?'

'The last I saw of him, Karna had challenged him to a fight.'

My heart sank. 'And Bheem?'

'He had uprooted a tree and was fending off Jarasandha.'

She hasn't even crossed the threshold and look at the trouble she has caused!

It was dusk. The light entering the hut through the window disguised the starkness of our dwelling. My mind was in a whirl. To calm it, I lit the chulha, waiting till the dry sticks caught the flames properly and began to crackle. I put a pot of dal to boil, adding, as an afterthought, a little more water to it. I wondered what Bheem would have to say today. He complained when the dal was too watery, but his brothers never said a word. They ate without fuss whatever was placed before them, grateful for even something as plain as parched grain. They had accepted everything from my hands. Was it about to change?

Arjuna has won her. Dhrupad will expect him to marry her. But how can he marry when his two elder siblings remain unmarried? He may do what Bhishma did when he brought home the princesses of Kashi and offered them to his brother, but Vichitravirya was just the one sibling. Here there are four others. What of them? Every one of my sons is captivated by the idea of this woman and secretly yearns for her. Now the fantasy will present itself in flesh: a smile, a flashing look, an arched eyebrow, the curve of her chin, the tender mouth. What will proximity to such a woman do to my family?

A wife's first duty is to her husband, but a mother cannot single out among her children. Sibling rivalry was the slow poison that killed Pandu: it has rendered us homeless, we fear for our lives. Gold, woman and land, they say, are the three causes of squabbles in any family. The woman is about to arrive. I cannot turn her away. How shall I receive her?

Bheem's voice interrupted my reverie. The words were what he said every day, no different. 'Ma! Look at what we've brought home today.'

Without turning around, I said, 'Whatever it is, share it equally among your brothers.'

❖

'How can my daughter have five husbands?' Dhrupad asked icily. 'What does that make her?'

'The chief queen of the Pandavas,' replied Yudhisthira urbanely.

'For that she needs to marry only you,' Dhrupad said. 'Why don't you marry her? Or nominate one, *anyone*, of your brothers.' He stuck out his chin. 'Don't think of anything so preposterous as sharing her. I will not allow it!'

Yudhisthira remained calm. 'In that case, none of us will marry the princess. You can keep her.'

Dhrupad's face turned purple. 'You—you are a kshatriya! You know how big an insult that is. I have no choice but to avenge it by putting all five of you to death.'

My sons sat very still.

Yudhisthira rubbed the side of his nose. 'The point I'd like to draw to your attention, O Rajan, is that *you* put her up as a prize,' he said. 'The prize was won fairly by Arjuna. Now, when Bheem made the announcement to our mother he was playing a joke. But he said what he always says, "Ma, look at what we've brought home today," and she replied—'

Dhrupad interrupted him with a disgusted wave of his hand. 'I know, I know...I've heard the words repeated innumerable times. *Share it equally among your brothers*. Your mother is a remarkable lady, but even she has admitted that it was unintended. Don't you see? It is not to be taken literally. You need to make an exception now and then, or it can be disastrous!' He stopped to sip a little water.

Sitting in the queens' gallery, I felt sorry for him. No doubt he regretted the day Drona entered his court. Had he made an exception then, he'd still have had his entire kingdom and we wouldn't be having this difficult discussion. The same thought probably occurred to my sons, for I noticed that the twins exchanged amused glances; Bheem sniggered, but Arjuna, to his credit, kept a poker face. I stared at him. He looked pale. He never spoke much, but since the evening before when he had brought the princess home, he had seemed morose. *He doesn't want to share her.*

'Your majesty, I am a man of truth,' said Yudhisthira.

'Yes, yes, we are all men of truth,' Dhrupad interrupted testily. 'But we are talking of dharma here. Of morality, decency, honour, virtue, duty, doing the right thing and all that.'

'*All* that,' echoed Yudhisthira pensively. 'Yes, it is rather too much, isn't it? Not to make too fine a point of it, Rajan, but we could carry on this discussion till the cows come home and not agree on what exactly *is* dharma. Yet we are all trying to live honestly and do the right thing. Towards that intent, our mother's words are the only truth we brothers recognize. To us, she is the first and foremost of teachers. Our mother is the epitome of purity in body, mind and heart.' He paused. 'I must tell you that in the northern branch of our family, the Kurus, this is, in fact, the tradition...In an unconventional situation, such as ours, it is safest if one sticks to what is tried and tested.'

'Unconventional! It's unheard of!' protested Dhrupad. 'Give me one precedent, outside the northern Kurus that you speak. Just one example among civilized people.'

Yudhisthira nodded. 'Not one, I'll give you two. From the Puranas, no less. Attitudes were a lot more flexible then.' He unwinded a long-forgotten yarn about the birth of Prajapati

Daksha from Marisha who was the common wife of the ten Prachetas.

Listening to it, Dhrupad looked a bit dazed. When the story ended he was silent for a moment, then he said uncertainly, 'But wasn't Prajapati born from the mind of Lord Brahma?'

'You know the Puranas,' said Yudhisthira blandly. 'They offer different versions of the same tale.'

'So what does one believe?'

Yudhisthira smiled faintly and shrugged. 'Whatever suits.'

'And what is the other example?' Dhrupad asked. 'Very briefly, of course.'

'There is the tale of a woman name Jatila,' Yudhisthira began.

Fortunately, there was an interruption. The guard outside the chamber announced that the muni Krishna Dwaipayana wished to see the king. Dhrupad and his son Dhrishtadyumna rushed out to perform the welcome ritual.

'Saved by the white beard!' said Bheem, with a look of relief.

The sage was ushered in. When he had been comfortably seated, he nodded at us, as though just noticing our presence. 'I was passing by,' he said. 'I felt I must congratulate you, Dhrupad. It's only right that I should welcome your daughter, my first granddaughter-in-law, into the family.'

Presented with this new addition to the confusing welter of kinships he was about to acquire, Dhrupad was at a loss. 'Erm…er…Munivar, it is an honour…but.' The seer raised an eyebrow and waited politely for him to continue. 'These young men want to make her their common wife!' Dhrupad burst out. 'How can I, the father of the bride, allow that?'

The seer stroked his beard. 'I see your problem, Dhrupad,' he said soothingly. 'Any normal father would be as concerned, but you aren't a normal father, are you? She was not born from your loins nor did she emerge from your wife's womb. While her brother was your *manasaputra*, born out of your desire for revenge, you got her as an additional benefit that you couldn't wait to capitalize on. You wanted Arjuna at any cost,' he paused before adding with some amusement, 'and now you've got more than you bargained for. Five for the price of one!'

Dhrupad flushed deeply. 'But in the eyes of the world she is my daughter,' he said. 'Her reputation will affect mine.'

'Reputation!' The rishi made a rude, dismissive sound. 'Don't be an old woman.' His gaze moved over the gathering and rested on me, thoughtfully. I felt an uneasiness. 'Look at Kunti. That Pandu was not the birth father of the Pandavas is an open secret, yet it has made no difference to the respect she gets. Her sons honour her, not because they are idiots, but because they know she is wise and loves all five equally. Unconditionally. Family unity creates a good reputation.'

I tried to look unaffected, as modesty bids a woman who is being praised to her face. Vyasa turned to Dhrupad and said with sad reproof, 'You have never looked beyond the tip of your nose, Rajan. Never imagined beyond fantasizing about the terrible things you will do to Drona...Take a long view, is my advice to you.'

Dhrupad forced a smile. 'I cannot. I am an ordinary man, Munivar, not a seer.'

The rishi stroked his peerless beard. 'This was ordained,' he said. He narrated the story he had shared with us in

Ekachakra, ending with, 'Shankar bhagwan granted her the husband she asked for—times five.'

Dhrupad wasn't convinced. 'It may have been ordained, but how is it going to work?'

Then Vyasa came up with the solution that was eventually adopted. Each of the Pandavas would have exclusive access to Panchali's chamber for a year at a time. I saw that the suggestion pleased my sons. Though no one had discussed the issue, it had exercised everyone's mind rather strenuously. Dhrupad was still unhappy, but he gave in with as much grace as he could summon.

'We will prepare for the wedding,' he said.

❖

She held herself with a catlike grace, proud and distant. Her face and features were formed with exquisite symmetry, her body had the thrust and pertness of youth, her skin the sheen of polished wood. But it was her hair, springing like a sacred river from the widow's peak, cascading down the length of her back to her knees, a glossy black-brown shade, rich, wavy and voluminous, that aroused in me, for a moment, a feeling of pure envy. Her eyes stared at me with cold defiance. This was the first time Draupadi and I were alone together. I had asked to speak with her.

'You've put me in an impossible situation,' she said. 'I chose Arjuna. *Only him*. When you understood that your second son had spoken in jest, why didn't you take back your words?'

'Because my sons had taken them to heart,' I said frankly. 'Each one had made *you* his heart's desire.'

'You don't think that it is improper for a woman to be the common wife of five men? It doesn't bother you that the world will call me loose?'

'No one will dare...'

She tilted her chin. 'That doesn't answer my question.'

I sighed. 'Something difficult and intricate is being asked of you.'

'Difficult and intricate!' she rolled her eyes. 'I am going to be parcelled out between five men. How many people must I be?'

Sidestepping her question, I said, 'They say you came to light from the depths of the vedi fully grown, but surely you were born somewhere else.'

A flash of irritation crossed her face. 'So you too think that I'm a freak show,' she said. 'Just like everyone else here! They asked me: What do you remember of your past life? Who are your parents? Which country do you come from? How old are you? What is your name?'

'And what did you reply?'

'I have no memory of the past.'

How lucky! No nightmares or sleepless nights. No agonizing or pretending.

She went on with some annoyance. 'They named me Draupadi! Awful name! Panchali is a shade better. Only one person has picked the right name to call me by. A name that is *me*.'

'Who is this person?'

'Krishna of the Vrishnis. Dhrupad's friend.' She looked at me sideways. 'They told me that you are his aunt, but I would have guessed it anyway.'

'How?' I asked, intrigued.

'Your feet are exactly like his,' she said. 'I noticed it immediately that first evening when I came to your house.' After a moment, she added, 'I have discussed it with Krishna and he said that what you have suggested would be an unusual arrangement, but the Pandavas are men of morals and they would never dishonour me.' She shrugged. 'I haven't been around long enough to know what to think of matrimony—with one man or many. Raja Dhrupad has several wives and so does Krishna.'

'It isn't quite the same thing for men.'

She raised an eyebrow. 'Well, like so much else, all this is new to me. I *came to light,* as you just said, just about a year ago. Dhrishtadyumna was sent off immediately for military training, but they didn't quite know what to do with me.' She stopped and looked at me as if uncertain whether to disclose more or not. 'Raja Dhrupad's patrani is *very* proper. She doesn't say it, but I know she finds me odd—the way I sometimes laugh out loud and even the way I speak my mind. She would like me to be more demure, keep my gaze lowered before men, titter in a ladylike way. She wants me go to the temple with her, learn to play a musical instrument or sing. She said this is how royal women amuse themselves.'

'Most royal women,' I said, 'but not all.'

Puckering her brow, she asked, 'Does it have to do with competing for one man's attention all your life? Is that why the patrani seems so fed up all the time?'

'It has to do with marriage itself,' I said. 'Marriage does tend to dispel women's illusions about men.'

'And vice versa?'

'Probably,' I said. 'But men have the freedom to create other alternatives for themselves.'

She looked at me curiously, waiting for me to elaborate. Never mind, I thought, she'll learn. Men are men, but the world, in my experience, requires us women to be something different from what we really are. *Be the first to rise and the last to go to bed. Never eat until everyone else has been fed. Don't stare anyone in the eye. Never ever speak your mind.* I debated whether I should pass on the list of dos and don'ts that had been stuffed into my head during my growing-up years. What good had it done me?

'Dhrupad thinks Arjuna is exceptional,' she said giving me a mischievous look. 'If it were possible, he'd marry Arjuna himself. He's that enamoured with him.'

'Well, Arjuna *is* a brilliant archer.'

'But he's not the only one. There is Karna, too,' she said. 'Everyone feared that he would win me. But Krishna hinted that I could protest; only that would stop Karna. If I did not I would end up a widow, he said.'

My mouth was suddenly dry. 'Why do you say that?'

'Krishna called it the destiny that the sutaputra must fulfil.' She looked at me, troubled. 'If we *know* that something terrible lies in wait, shouldn't we do our best to avoid it?'

'We should, but oftentimes fate allows us no choice,' I said with some bitterness. 'Our vision is limited, and our actions that seemed right at the time turn out—differently. Despite all our efforts, there is a certain inexorableness that is set in motion without our knowledge...Destiny never reveals how it works till its work is done.'

'So what does one do? How does one act? Or does one not act at all?'

'Not acting at all is never a good idea.' I thought of all we'd gone through in the last year. Weren't we alive through our own effort? Hadn't we seized opportunities and created choices for ourselves? We had chosen a path, but hadn't the path too chosen us? It had led us here. Where would it take us next? 'I don't know...' I tapered off. 'One must try to do the right thing, but also for the right reason—only, it's never that simple.'

It was a lame answer, but she accepted it.

'Krishna says that you must train your mind to let go of whatever it is that you fear to lose,' she said.

Krishna.

I thought back to the brief meeting we'd had with him in the hut soon after Bheem and Arjuna arrived with Panchali. The moment was fraught because of the words I had uttered. Yudhisthira was troubled, Bheem angry and Arjuna clearly miserable. Disregard my words, I said to them. But they wouldn't listen to that either. Everyone was talking at the same time, when there was a knocking on the door. We froze. Bheem opened the door. Balarama stood on the threshold. With him was a slim, dark man dressed in pale yellow. I had known him at once even though I'd never seen him in my life before. Why did my heart lift like a bird rising into the blue skies? He touched my feet and called me *Bua*. One word, but it was everything to me. Blessing him, I had kissed his forehead and rested my own briefly on his manly shoulder. A serenity entered my heart, a fulfilment that spilled over in foolish tears. Was it due to the affection and respect I read in his look or was it the deep, lifelong yearning in me to belong somewhere, to someone? To call someone my own?

'What do they call you at home?' I had asked him.

He had smiled. 'When I was in Gokul with Yashodha Ma, they called me The Butter Thief.'

'And now?'

'Govinda,' he had said with a light shrug. 'Gopala. The Cowherd. It is what I am.' He had talked briefly with his cousins, telling us that the news of our deaths in the fire had cast a terrible pall over the entire land. He expressed his happiness at how events had turned out. He had to leave, he said, but he'd be in touch. *You'll never be alone again.*

Dragging myself back to the present, yet disturbed by the turn our conversation had taken, I asked Panchali the question I had come to ask, 'Do I take it that you are agreeable to this arrangement?'

She studied my face. 'Did your sons put you up to this?'

'Yes, they did,' I said. 'They want you, but they want you to know that they will always respect your wish—whatever it is.'

Her expression was unreadable. 'No,' she said with firmness. 'It is *your* will that they are bowing to. I don't like it, but I will accept it.'

7

The waiting game began. News had been sent to all the royal houses that the wedding of Dhrupad's daughter had been solemnized. There was a cautious response from everyone, but the Vrishnis had sent cartloads of wedding gifts. Months passed. Finally a messenger arrived from the House of Kurus. A very special messenger: Vidur. He came bearing an overly-generous wedding gift of gold jewellery for Panchali and an invitation to visit. 'The king has asked me to convey his deep sense of happiness at hearing that the Pandavas and their mother are safe,' he said.

Dhrupad smiled sardonically.

Vidur continued: 'He is delighted to learn that the princess of Panchala is now a daughter-in-law of the Kurus. The alliance is even more fortunate in that it has brought these two great ancient families, the Kurus and the Panchalas, together. Hastinapur looks forward to welcoming the new bride, the Pandavas and their mother.'

'That's up to the Pandavas to decide—and their mother, of course,' said Dhrupad, with a polite but cursory nod in the direction of the queens' gallery where I was sitting with Panchali. 'I'm happy to have them here for as long as they'd like to stay. But if they wish to visit their ancestral home, I will not keep them.' He looked at Yudhisthira as if to say, Your turn.

Yudhisthira, always circumspect, said, 'We rely on you, Maharaj—we'll do whatever you advise us.'

Dhrupad turned to Krishna. 'What do you think, Vasudeva?'

'I think that they should go,' said Krishna.

Dhrupad nodded in agreement. 'If the sons of Dhritarashtra know what's healthy for them, there will be no trickery this time.'

Krishna laughed. 'Who knows, some good may actually come out of the visit.' As an afterthought, he added, 'It's high time I paid *my* respects to the House of Hastinapur. I will accompany my cousins.'

❖

Entering the Elephant Gate in a procession for the third time, I could not help but be reminded of the earlier two occasions. The difference was that on each of them I had believed I had come home, but this time there was no such illusion. Though Hastinapur welcomed us warmly, those living in the palace made it clear that we were guests on a short stay.

Gandhari gave a small reception for the bride. I had learned that Duryodhana, too, had got married recently—to Bhanumati, a princess of Kalinga, whom he had, in the old tradition of Pitamaha, abducted from her own swayamvar. From Bhanumati's plump, smiling face, it appeared that she had no serious quarrel with this form of marriage and had, in fact, endorsed it by falling in love with her husband.

At the reception, Panchali was courteous to everyone but also slightly reserved. Dressed in a ruby red sari with a border of pearls and a gold bodice, she was, undoubtedly, the centre of attraction. Bhanumati was clearly an admirer, but Gandhari, I thought, was chilly towards my daughter-in-law. Her behaviour puzzled me but I said nothing. The reason for the coldness became clear a short while later when we were summoned to a special sabha called by Dhritarashtra. There, in front of Bhishma, he announced his decision: The kingdom was to be divided. The Pandavas were given Khandavaprastha.

'It delights my heart to think of the sons of Pandu restoring the old capital of the Kurus—of kings like Nahusha, Yayati and Puru—to its former glory,' he said, looking anything but delighted. From Pitamaha's satisfied expression, I judged that he had forced the blind king's hand. Duryodhana's face looked like thunder.

'Former glory!' said Bheem when we were in our chambers. 'He has given us a jungle and a barren parcel of land. A scrap thrown to a beggar. And now he can't wait to see the back of us!'

'He has never been as unpopular as he is now,' said Arjuna. 'The people blame him for the incident in Varanavat. He was forced into making this division because he cannot risk offending us now that everyone knows we have the support of Panchala,' he looked at Krishna and smiled, 'and the Vrishnis.'

Krishna turned to Yudhisthira. 'You aren't worried, are you, Bade Bhaiyya? I noticed that you accepted the king's decision with good grace.'

Yudhisthira gave a short laugh. 'Did I have a choice?'

'You did,' Krishna said quietly. 'Dhritarashtra is no fool. He knows that the kingdom is not *his* to divide. There is only one rightful claimant to the throne: you.'

His words subdued us. They brought home the fact that for the first time in its long history, the kingdom of the Kurus had been broken in two parts. The question on everyone's mind was: would it stay this way? Echoing the thought, Bheem said, 'Did you notice Duryodhana's expression... Even that little patch was too much for him to part with.'

'When it comes to giving it to us, even a needlepoint of land is too much for our brother Duryodhana,' said Sahadeva.

'Hush now,' I said. 'What's done is done. Let us look ahead.'

Dhritarashtra ordered a coronation ceremony to be held. It was a private affair. As soon as it was over, we left Hastinapur.

❖

The founding of the new kingdom—the groundbreaking ceremony, the raising of the walls, the city built, tanks dug, trees planted and gardens laid—was an exciting time. Krishna persuaded Vishwakarma, architect of Dwaraka, his own city on the western coast, to design this one for us. In time, settlers came to our kingdom: communities of weavers, dyers, potters, carpenters, timber dealers, jewellers and tradesmen established their separate quarters. Outside the city's walls villages sprang up as farm workers cleared land for cultivation, dug the soil, and sowed the seeds. The rains came on time, the first crop was cut by the king. We celebrated with a feast. The wasteland that had been Khandavaprastha gained the bustle and colour of human activity. It took the contours of a city. The Pandavas renamed their kingdom in honour of Indra as Indraprastha. With its flower gardens and singing birds, its marble buildings and golden-roofed shrines, it duplicated the grandeur of the eternal city in the heavens.

We forgot, I now think, that here on earth, time consumes everything.

When I think of those years spent in Indraprastha, I see them now as a gossamer-fine web of dreams that held us for a while in its lattice. We believed that we were happy. The worst was over, I told myself. Yudhisthira had his kingdom; his brothers thrived. When grandchildren made their appearance the clan would grow. The Pandavas had made their place in the sun. Pandu's spirit would surely be satisfied. Now that my family's fortunes were revived, there was a strange lethargy in me. It evinced itself in body aches, rash and a low fever that would come and go. The royal vaidya prescribed potions and rest.

One day my old friend, the sairandhri, arrived. A bit thicker at the waist, crow's feet around the eyes, but otherwise the same. Laconic, cynical and true.

'I don't need you now,' I said, a little sadly.

She gave me a long look. 'When was the last time anyone dressed your hair?'

'My life has changed.'

'For the better,' she agreed. 'Mother of five sons!' She looked around my chamber critically. 'Why such a spartan existence for the rajmata?'

'For a widow this is fine.'

She gave a derisive snort. 'Had the king not died you'd probably still be in the mountains with your sons play-acting at being brahmins.'

'You are trying to rile me,' I said tiredly. 'But I don't have the energy to get angry with you.'

Her face grew gentle. Without asking permission, she picked up a comb, undid the simple knot at my nape and slowly began to run her fingers through my hair. It was a long time since anyone had touched me with so much affection. I sighed and closed my eyes, something inside me loosened. Tears travelled down my cheeks; it was a relief to let them go. She finished styling my hair and held up a mirror. I was startled to see the difference it made. The reflection that gazed back was graceful, serene but pensive.

'You are one of those few lucky women who look better with time,' she said.

I was surprised and pleased at the compliment. 'You're wasted on me,' I said. 'On the other hand, my daughter-in-law has the most beautiful hair.'

'So I've heard,' she said nonchalantly.

That evening, when Yudhisthira and Panchali sat down to have their meal with me, her eyes went to my face and hair immediately. 'It suits you,' Panchali said. I told her about my old sairandhri.

'You have the job starting tomorrow,' I said to the sairandhri. 'Same old job, but a different queen.'

She sniffed. 'I'll take the job because I need it,' she said. 'But for me there will only be one queen.'

❖

Panchali and I shared a relationship characterized by decorum and courtesy. I would have liked it if there had been more warmth between us, but it wasn't in her nature to seek close friendships with women. Besides, she had not quite forgiven me. Yet common concerns frequently brought us together. She had no experience of running a royal household and sought my advice. I was careful always to offer it only as a suggestion.

She was a quick learner. In time she became very good at getting things done. She was an astute judge of character and always seemed to get the right person for the job. She made an excellent consort to Yudhisthira, complementing his philosophical, unpretentious persona with the vigour and glamour of her own. Authority suited her, she enjoyed it. She had a head for planning and accounts, was decisive, knew instinctively how to get work out of the palace staff, when to censure and when to praise. In Yudhisthira's company, she grew adept at argument. Often, I'd hear them wrangling amicably over some quote from the shastras or a legal issue that had come up in court.

Panchali had accepted all five Pandavas, but somewhere in her heart she had enshrined the romantic image of the handsome young archer who had won her hand. I was aware that she bore a secret love for Arjuna—a feeling deeper than the affection she had for the others. In time, as she heard of his philandering ways, the liaisons with women like Uloopi and Chitrangada, she grew resigned and wiser. As these affairs were carried on far away, she chose, sensibly, to ignore them.

Her jealousy surfaced only when Arjuna brought home

my niece Subhadra as his bride. He had been travelling around Aryavarta. While on a visit to Dwaraka, he had, in his impetuous fashion, fallen in love with Subhadra at first sight. However, he was a guest of the Vrishnis and well aware that the girl's brother Balarama would most likely take a dim view of his growing love interest. There had been talk that Balarama had wanted his favourite pupil Duryodhana as his brother-in-law. Did this add an edge to Arjuna's interest? At the back of his mind there may have been the memory of the fracas at the swayamvar in Kampilya, and a desire to show off again, because he eloped with Subhadra. As Krishna was their accomplice in the plan, it worked out smoothly. Balarama, though upset with Arjuna's action, was eventually soothed. He saw, too, the willingness of the bride and agreed to the match.

When we heard the news of the nuptials, everyone wondered how Panchali would take it. She had made it clear at the very beginning to her five husbands that what they did outside was their own business. In her domain she would not tolerate a rival. I was concerned for her. Years ago I had gone through exactly the same situation. I knew firsthand how devastating sexual jealousy could be. It didn't help that Yudhisthira declared, rather tactlessly, that he saw the alliance with the Vrishnis as beneficial, in the same way that the relationship with Panchala had worked to our advantage. Nor did it help that the rumours of Subhadra's charm and beauty had already reached us. As a last straw, when Subhadra arrived, it was clear that she was in the early stages of pregnancy. It was also clear that history was repeating itself: Arjuna and Subhadra shared something very special, the way Pandu and Madri had, in another lifetime.

I saw the flash of pain in Panchali's eyes and felt for her. I searched for ways to comfort her, but could come up with nothing that would get past the prickly exterior she had developed of late. When she did not attend the havan held to mark the bride's arrival, I did not say a word, nor did I allow Yudhisthira or Bheem to censure her for this serious breach of etiquette. Though the rituals were conducted without her, the songs sung, the feast held, I, for one, kept thinking of Panchali alone in her chamber, shunning food and drink, speaking to no one.

'She'll get over it,' Yudhisthira said, with some irritation. Arjuna remained cheerful, blatantly unapologetic, but Bheem, I noticed, was unusually subdued. It was her year with him and he alone made repeated efforts to approach Panchali, begging her to eat something. For his trouble he got it square on the forehead, with a silver *paandaan*. He emerged out of her chamber groaning and rubbing the spot, but also muttering in reluctant admiration, 'What a woman!'

Finally, the second wife herself brought peace to the situation. A combination of fury spent, a growing awareness that there was little she could do, the co-wife's humility and her close resemblance to Panchali's dearest friend Krishna, all worked together to bring about a change of heart. When she emerged from her chamber, Panchali was her old self—imperious, decisive, dignified. I wonder, did no one but me sense the new belligerence in her? Did they not see the glitter that would enter her eyes when she was defied, the way her lips tightened into a thin line when anyone argued with her?

Were they deaf to the sharp criticism in her words? Or was it that, being men, they thought that a woman's bitterness was inconsequential, tedious and best disregarded? Being men they didn't realize that there is a certain zest to anger, a kind of clarity which eludes one otherwise.

Subhadra gave birth to a boy whom Krishna named Abhimanyu. After the baby arrived, he began to spend a lot of time in Indraprastha. It was clear that the child was the draw. Always laughing and joking with everyone, Krishna was especially tender with Abhimanyu. Whenever it was time for him to leave, he would hug the little boy, kiss his cheek and tell me, 'Take good care of him, Bua. You know how to raise warriors. Make him the best fighter in the world.' Was there a tremor of pain in his words? With Krishna, one never knew. It is human nature to look for patterns. They provide an explanation, or maybe it is reprieve that we yearn for.

In time Panchali, too, in quick succession, gave birth to sons, five bonny babies, one from each husband. Motherhood failed to blunt the sharp edge to her nature. On the contrary, being busier than ever, she had little time to spend with her sons. They would be presented to her every morning by their nurses after they'd been bathed, dressed and fed. She'd run a quick critical eye over them, like a senapati inspecting the troops—tuck back a wayward curl, straighten a slouch, correct a pronunciation—and tell them to carry on.

'Go and play,' I once heard her say. 'Whatever *that* is.' Catching my raised eyebrow she said with a shrug, 'How would I know? You forget that I, like my brother, had no childhood.'

❖

At first I thought it was a bad dream, a return to that night of horror when we escaped from the blazing house surrounded by the burning plantation of palash trees. I sat up in bed and realized that it was no dream. Acrid smoke thickened the night air. Looking out of the window I saw a flickering red gold thread stretch along the horizon. It took me a moment to understand that the Khandava forest was on fire. *Good! I've always hated that place, its ugly shadow.*

The story that emerged was this: Krishna, Arjuna and their wives had gone on a picnic along the river Yamuna. It had been an afternoon of pleasure with boat rides, drinking the brew made from fermenting mahua flowers, frying and eating fresh fish. A gaunt brahmin with a fierce gaze appeared seemingly from nowhere. He claimed that he was starving. It was no ordinary hunger, he said, but something gigantic, demanding immediate satiation. Only the fat of creatures, the flesh melting off bones would do for him.

'A brahmin who wanted to eat flesh?' Yudhisthira asked incredulously when we heard the story.

'A Fire God who wanted to swallow a forest,' replied Arjuna. 'Govinda saw through his disguise, of course. Agni devata wanted a meal from us. How could we refuse?'

'But he could have got his own meal, couldn't he?' Yudhisthira asked. 'Fires usually swallow forests without any trouble.'

Apparently, Khandava was a protected forest, under the aegis of no less a god than Indra. Whenever Agni had tried to consume it, Indra had thwarted him by emptying the clouds and quenching the flames with torrential showers. 'I saw an opportunity, Bade Bhaiyya,' said Arjuna, with a disarming smile. 'Agni deva mentioned, in passing, that he had some rather special weapons. I needed a new bow. He had one—the Gandiva. More advanced, lighter and quicker than anything I had seen. For a bow like that, I needed an unending supply of arrows. To carry all this weaponry, naturally, I needed a new chariot.'

'With horses?' Nakul interjected eagerly.

Arjuna smiled. 'Six white steeds,' he said. 'They shall be the pride of your stable.'

'A celestial bow, unlimited arrows and a chariot.' Yudhisthira turned to Krishna and asked silkily, 'And yourself, Vasudeva? Did you get nothing out of this unholy deal?'

'Only a discus,' replied Krishna with a straight face. 'And a rather insignificant mace.'

Yudhisthira was aghast. 'For a handful of weapons you two butchered thousands of living creatures?'

'A few escaped,' Arjuna admitted.

'And we rescued the odd one,' added Krishna with a quick grin. He went to the door and gestured to someone waiting in the passage to come in. The man was light-skinned with delicate, almost feminine features and limpid brown eyes set in a narrow, bony face. He had a short curly beard. He didn't look like he came from these parts. 'His name is Maya,' said Krishna. 'He wants to build you a palace.'

'But I don't need one,' Yudhisthira said, irritably.

'What about an assembly hall?' asked Arjuna, adding, 'I know, I know—you already have one. But it's not big enough, and quite honestly, Bade Bhaiyya, it's a bit drab. Now Maya here designed one for the king of the asuras. And it sounds like just what we need.'

Maya broke his silence. 'I could do better than that, my lord. For you I would create a marvel. The envy of all three lokas.' He looked at Arjuna with such fervent longing that the twins winked at each other and Krishna hid a smile.

Panchali leaned forward. 'What exactly would you do for us? Give me details.'

He flicked a glance in her direction with no real interest. 'No. *You* give me the details. I will give you your heart's desire.'

'Walls of gold studded with gems?' she asked.

He nodded. 'A ceiling of turquoise and lapis lazuli. Aquamarine for pools,' he said, rippling his long fingers through the air to help us visualize better. 'That deep translucent blue women seem to like so much. Steps of marble inlaid with mother of pearl. Lotuses of gold.'

'What about real pools?' I asked, half-joking. 'With real lotuses.'

'Why not?' he said, adding with slight condescension, 'I suppose you'll want streams, too, in which you can float millions of lamps at dusk. Self-lighting lamps. You shall have your own *Akashganga* to rival the one in the sky.'

'Full-length mirrors?' asked Nakul, eagerly.

Maya's smile bordered on a leer. 'Mirrors that talk. They will say to you every day that you are the handsomest of all.' He looked at Bheem. 'And for you, my prince?' he asked, in a voice like a caress. 'A gymnasium is what you'd like? What do you say to a wrestling ring where you can test your strength against the strongest of the gandharvas—beckoned at your will, of course?'

'Actually, what I'd really like is a kitchen,' said Bheem,

not sure if we were being serious, but getting into the spirit of things. 'Smokeless chulhas, pots that don't burn the food, knives that never need to be sharpened, dishes that don't get dirty.'

'Done!' Maya said. 'Dream on, dream on...*anything* is possible.'

'Stables for ten thousand horses,' said Sahadeva. 'Stalls that clean themselves out; an unending supply of hay, jaggery and gram; warm air in winter and cool air in summer.'

'That's a good idea,' nodded Panchali. 'We could use it in the palace too. Mosquito-free air...Do you think you could do that?'

Maya chuckled softly. 'I love you all. You ask for so little.' He turned to Yudhisthira and announced with an air of flourish, 'And especially for you, O Rajan, I will build a great *dyutasabha*, a gaming hall.'

Yudhisthira was taken aback. 'Just a nice throne room will do,' he said stuffily.

'That goes without saying,' said Maya. 'But wait till you see the dyutasabha. It will dazzle your eyes.'

'I don't play dice all that much,' Yudhisthira protested.

'All great kings dream of a dyutasabha,' Maya said. 'Dicing is only for the greatest of the great.'

❖

Khandava *vana* took fourteen days to burn. A strange battle raged between earth and sky, fire and water, Agni and Indra. Black smoke from the blaze climbed into the sky, immediately rainclouds amassed. Arjuna threw up an umbrella of arrows to stop the rain. Below, the forest burned, flames shooting out, while in the heavens, lightning crackled an angry response. The fire devoured everything: elephant herds, stags in the flush of their youth, pregnant does, nestlings too young to fly to safety. The wind howled, carrying on its heated wings the agonized cries of all those dying creatures. Thunder raged above. We watched the scene from the palace's windows, Yudhisthira, Sahadeva and I.

'Did we do the right thing by burning down the forest?' Yudhisthira asked, with a worried frown. He was Dharma's son, after all. Weighing and re-weighing actions and consequences was second nature to him.

'How else will your kingdom advance?' I countered. 'Indraprastha is growing. We need the land.'

Yudhisthira's face grew taut with disapproval. 'We need to prune our needs.'

'The burning of Khandava forest can also be seen as the settlement of an old wrong,' said Sahadeva.

Yudhisthira stared at him. 'What old wrong?'

'The unfairness of Yayati to his heir Yadu.'

Sahadeva was referring to the tradition of the Chandravanshi kings, by which an heir was appointed only if he was deemed worthy. It had first been broken by Yayati. 'That was a long time ago!' I said, surprised that Sahadeva should bring *that* story up. It was one of the many that Kuntibhoja had told me.

Of all the Chandravanshi lineage, none was more colourful than Yayati, the son of Nahusha. He had two wives and managed to keep this a secret for several years, even though the second woman was the maid of his chief queen, Devayani. Furthermore, he had sons through both.

When Devayani discovered the truth, she went straight to her father, Shukracharya, and complained. Shukra, preceptor of the asuras, was a powerful man. Devayani wanted him to punish Yayati severely. Shukra cursed his deceitful, pleasure-loving son-in-law with instant old age, but later relented when Yayati begged him to withdraw the curse.

'I can't do that,' Shukra said regretfully, as he rather liked Yayati and thought his daughter was being unnecessarily vindictive. 'What I can do is allow you to exchange old age for youth. If one of your sons is willing to take on the burden of fulfilling the curse he will become old in your place, and you can remain young and enjoy the pleasures of life for as long as you like.'

Yayati had five sons. He went to the eldest, Yadu, the heir to the throne, with his request. To his disappointment Yadu refused the barter. One by one, the next three sons refused as well. Finally, without much hope, he went to the youngest, Puru. What words were used to persuade Puru is not recorded, but the boy agreed. The next instant he was an old man, bent, emaciated, white-haired, half-blind with cataract. And Yayati found himself in possession of an even younger and stronger body than before. He used it to enjoy all the sensual pleasures till he grew tired of them, when he re-exchanged his youth for old age again. To Puru, who had regained his youth exactly as he had given it up, in reward for his filial devotion, Yayati gave his kingdom. The other four sons left the land and founded their own dynasties. The eldest, Yadu, the deposed yuvaraja, was the ancestor of the Yadavas. Puru, the favoured son, had established the capital, Khandavaprastha, but his descendants could not rule from it for very long. The place fell under a curse and had to be abandoned. Hastin, a descendant of Puru, created a new capital at Hastinapur.

Yudhisthira became thoughtful. 'You could be right,' he said to Sahadeva. 'But I have a feeling that the story will not end here.'

'It is over,' I said, though deep down, I, too, was uneasy. From the first time I'd seen it on my way to Hastinapur as a bride, Khandava vana had always had that effect on me. There was, I realized, an unsettling correspondence between Yudhisthira's experience and that of my ancestor Yadu: both had been deserving but disinherited in favour of a younger brother, and left with no choice but to establish their own separate domain. *Has time erased nothing? Is it all buried alive as a snarled knot—lust, injustice, cruelty, bitterness, rancour? Has it all been growing and spreading for generations, waiting for the right moment to strike? Is* this *how old wrongs are set right?*

The grey skies gave a loud rumble. A strong gust of breeze swept into the room. I shivered. 'Close the window,' I said to the servant.

Sahadeva shook his head. 'You can't keep the storm out, Ma,' he said. 'No one can.'

That night, I dreamt once again of the fire at Varanavat. I saw the face of the Nishadha woman who had come to my door that fateful day. It was not a human face, but a bloodless mask concentrating, in its frozen features, an unmistakable hatred. Her eyes bore into me with such an intense malignity that I woke up with my heart thudding, in a cold sweat. Did I imagine the glimmer of satisfaction in their depths?

At dawn, when the forest was entirely burnt and all was quiet, rain fell in fat drops on the scorched earth, raising plumes of vapour that created a thin, clingy mist. Where there had once been a living forest, there was now an empty grey miasma that took several days to dispel.

8

From this distance, those ten years spent within the walls of Indraprastha seem like an idyll. What a blessing it was to wake up every morning and know that the day given to me was free of strife. But the walls that kept us safe soon became restrictive for my sons. They had developed the endurance needed for a protracted fight; they had none for a prolonged peace. The signs of restlessness became obvious, particularly after Narada muni's visit.

Sages visited us from time to time. They stayed for a few days, blessed us and went away. But, of course, with Narada muni it was never that simple. I recall my nervousness when he arrived, carrying his veena. However, Yudhisthira greeted him with genuine enthusiasm. The sage was quite the globetrotter and a source of the latest news from everywhere.

'Your father Pandu isn't happy in swarga loka,' Narada said.

Yudhisthira became anxious. 'Does he lack for anything?'

'A man may shed his body like a worn-out garment,' the sage said. 'But the same cannot be said of his wishes.'

'What does my father wish for, Munivar?'

Smiling faintly, the sage said, 'He wants the Pandavas to hold a *Rajasuya yajna*.'

Yudhisthira frowned. 'But that would mean conquering the world first. It would mean declaring war on kingdoms with which we have no quarrel.'

The sage's smile deepened. 'I am only the messenger,' he said. 'You must do as you think fit.'

❖

Bheem swung the new mace that he was trying out with Arjuna as his opponent. The two brothers circled each other like caged animals.

'The Kauravas kept us on our toes,' Bheem observed. 'Thrashing the living daylights out of you isn't quite the same thing as beating Duryodhana.'

Arjuna chuckled.

Overhearing them from the balcony outside my window, I was tempted to call the pair in and deliver a tongue-lashing, but I stopped myself. They were grown men. I'd done everything I could for them. Besides I, too, was restless. On Yudhisthira's suggestion, I had gone on several pilgrimages, and found that I rather enjoyed being on the open road again. It felt as if I was escaping; what, I couldn't say.

'Expectations,' said Yudhisthira—as though making a diagnosis—when I confessed the feeling to him after returning from Kashi. 'I feel their weight too. There are moments when I'd like to lay aside everything and leave... quietly. *Just leave.*' I was perturbed. He sounded exactly like Pandu had all those years ago. 'Ever since Narada muni visited us and planted the idea of a Rajasuya yajna, Bheem and Arjuna have not talked of anything else,' he grumbled.

'Have you consulted Acharya Dhaumya?' I asked, referring to our family priest.

'He thinks that I am eminently suitable to conduct the yajna and declare what he calls my "sovereign status".' Yudhisthira grimaced. 'Krishna seems to think so as well. He believes that it may well prevent a war in the future. I don't see how. Our relatives in Hastinapur would burn in the yajna of their own envy if we were to hold such an important sacrifice. Do we want to revive the old enmity?'

I did not reply.

'As you can see, I am being pushed towards a confrontation,' he said. 'I do *not* covet the position of an emperor, nor do I want the homage of other kings. It is too risky.'

'What is too risky?'

'Challenging Jarasandha of Magadha is the precondition to holding the Rajasuya sacrifice. Bheem is to take him on, with Krishna and Arjuna to support him.'

'Take *him* on?'

He saw my alarm and gave a grim nod. 'Yes. It is impossible to defeat Jarasandha through a military conquest.'

'What other way is there?'

'Krishna has something up his sleeve,' he said.

'What?' I asked nervously. 'They aren't plotting a murder, are they?'

'I have tried to reason with them,' he said. 'It will not go down well. Jarasandha has his allies. Our cousin Shishupal is his staunch supporter; Karna and Duryodhana are his friends. But Krishna believes that freeing those eighty-six—or is it eighty-seven?—kings that the Monster of Magadha has imprisoned will earn me the undying gratitude of all Aryavarta, and the royal houses will endorse my supremacy.'

Pique entered his voice. 'Krishna has an axe to grind. He wants to finish Jarasandha and knows that he cannot do it alone. But how can it be right for *me* to attack someone who has not harmed me or my kingdom in anyway? Jarasandha has left us well alone.'

'What does Panchali say?'

'*She*!' He sounded even more annoyed. 'She agrees with them. The last hurdle, she calls it, on the way to everlasting glory…There's no end to the fireborn lady's ambition. She's already planning the celebrations.'

'You are clearly in the minority,' I said mildly.

'At least you see my point of view,' he said, brightening. 'Tell them that it is not advisable. Command them to drop the scheme. They will listen only to you.'

'But what reason can I give them?'

A sharp, knowing look entered his eyes. 'You are with *them*,' he said coldly, and walked out.

❖

Jarasandha's gory death at the hands of Bheem inspired many artistic compositions, including a dreadful play that was performed at the celebrations that concluded the Rajasuya sacrifice. I thought it was in terrible taste, but my sons laughed at me.

For the yajna, six sacrificial altars were built. Vyasa, the grandfather, arrived together with hundreds of priests who came to chant the Vedic hymns that went on non-stop for days. The smell of ghee burning saturated the air. Food grain poured in by the sackful to feed the ten thousand brahmins who were honoured with gifts of cloth and herds of cows.

Earlier, horsemen bearing invitations had been sent to every kingdom in Aryavarta, and acceptances piled up daily, creating an administrative nightmare.

Nakul went with an invitation to Hastinapur. It was graciously accepted. Pitamaha and the mahamantri represented the king; they were accompanied by the yuvaraja Duryodhana, his closest sibling Duhsashana, Shakuni, Aswatthama and Karna. The acharyas, Drona and Kripa, were there as well. As family, the Hastinapur party was assigned important duties, of which they eagerly took charge. They were full of wonder at the grandeur of Indraprastha, particularly the assembly hall that Maya had created.

It was a long building painted an austere white on the outside, but filled with unimaginable surprises. Many of its architectural marvels were designed to mislead: false doors and windows, fake fountains and crystalline pools complete with turtles and silvery fish, artificial groves of tall trees where birds called out from perches hidden in the foliage and the scent of wildflowers floated in the air.

'I hope the Kauravas eat their hearts out,' said Bheem when we first inspected the completed sabha.

Nakul laughed. 'And if envy doesn't finish them, there's always you,' he said. 'I've put you down in a friendly wrestling match against Duryodhana. Now that you're on a winning spree you could tear him from limb to limb, just as you did Jarasandha.'

'One day you will,' said Sahadeva.

I turned away from them, disquiet simmering in my heart. Hastinapur had left us well alone all these years, though Duryodhana's spies probably reported everything back to him. The Rajasuya sacrifice was intended to end all wars and bring the kings together under one sovereign. Everyone agreed that no one other than Yudhisthira had the requisite qualities of a *samrat*, but the constant bloodthirsty talk from my sons bothered me, as did the lavish preparations. It was wasteful. When had we become so pretentious? When I voiced this concern to Yudhisthira, he, usually the model of rectitude, brushed it off.

'Everyone is expecting a show, Ma,' he said airily. 'We must not disappoint them.'

Beyond him, through the open windows, I could see a train of elephants from Magadha trudging towards the new treasury building. This had been going on for days, the emptying of Jarasandha's hoard into our treasury and the arrival of tributes from all the freed kings. The sudden affluence had dazzled even Yudhisthira. 'Dhrupad was speechless at the size of the booty,' he said.

'It's folly to put Duryodhana in charge of receiving the tributes,' I said.

Yudhisthira shook his head. 'We suffered at Duryodhana's hands earlier because we were powerless. The game has changed.' Slipping an arm around my shoulder, he added, 'Stop worrying and learn to enjoy our success. Think of how happy our father must be.'

I *was* thinking of Pandu, remembering the day he had returned victorious from his battles and filled the coffers of Hastinapur—just to prove to the world that he was not lacking in valour or virility. He had made his point, but what had it finally got him?

The priests proclaimed it successful, but I felt that

nothing good came from the Rajasuya yajna. Strangely, it was only on the final day, after the coronation in the grand hall of a thousand gold pillars, that the façade of unity and bonhomie began to crumble. For the seven days preceding the coronation, the guests had enjoyed the festivities—friendly contests, dicing games, theatre, music and dance performances as well as the long sessions of drinking and eating.

Besides showing a brief presence at one or two of these events, I had remained in my apartment. It was here that I welcomed my Vrishni kin. I met my brother Vasudeva for the first time. Kuntibhoja and Purujit, too, visited me. My foster father wept openly and even Purujit seemed overwhelmed by emotion. They dredged up forgotten memories of a simpler world where concerns had been limited to the mango crop, the number of milch cows and the extension of the palace. I got the feeling that little had changed in Kuntibhoja's palace, except that the rajmata had departed for her heavenly abode.

For the coronation of Samrat Dharmaraja Yudhisthira, I was required to be present. The first sign of things going wrong came when the newly consecrated samrat had to choose a guest of honour from the most eminent men in the assembly. Pitamaha, the Elder of the Kuru clan, was asked to name the person who should be offered the arghya. He named Krishna of the Vrishnis. There was an immediate buzz in the gathering. The assembled kings had clearly not been expecting this. Sahadeva dutifully stepped forward with the pot of water to wash Krishna's feet. Before he could commence this ritual, my other nephew Shishupal, the king of Chhedi, shouted from the opposite side of the hall, that Krishna, a mere chieftain and not a crowned king, did not deserve the honour; it was an insult to 'real' kings like Dhrupad, as well as to respected gurus like Drona. He then launched into a long tirade which sounded like the ranting of a disaffected man, but seemed to, surprisingly, contain a core of truth: Who *is* Krishna to be given this respect? Is he a priest, a teacher or a king? Several kings in the gathering began to mutter that Shishupal was right, while others argued against it. Towards the end of his rant, Shishupal said, 'Honouring Krishna like a king is as improper as conducting the marriage of an impotent man.'

An uncomfortable silence fell on the gathering.

Sitting beside me in the queens' enclosure, Subhadra wrung her hands. 'Why is he spoiling everything? Why?'

I will not go into the details of what followed. Pitamaha politely but firmly reminded Shishupal that he was a guest. At this Shishupal turned on the Kuru elder and began to abuse him. My sons were immediately up in arms, but Pitamaha himself and Yudhisthira, too, controlled them. In all this, Krishna was as calm as a rock against a stormy sea. While Shishupal heaped insult upon insult, Krishna studied the fingers of his palm, as if counting off something.

'You have reached one hundred,' he said musingly to Shishupal. 'A hundred misdemeanours that I promised your poor mother I would pardon you. You could apologize now, but to expect that much good sense from you would be a mistake.'

Shishupal curled his lip. 'You think I care about your opinion?'

What happened next was so sudden that, later, no one

could exactly describe it. Something flashed across the space between the two men. A silver blur lasting an instant. Whatever it was, it severed Shishupal's head. Blood spouted from the wound, it sprayed the pillars and the floor, the fallen head rolled away. We saw with horror that the eyes were wide open, the ears twitched, the mouth gaped, the tongue still worked and a long gurgle of red emerged from the lips. The decapitated body lay still, a glow rose from the chest, a spot of brilliant light. It moved through the air towards Krishna and became one with him. This we witnessed.

❖

That very day Krishna was gone. One by one, the other guests, too, left. The leave-taking was taciturn, as if they could not wait to get away. Only the Kauravas loitered. Yudhisthira naïvely believed that they stayed on as a show of family solidarity and was grateful. Given a free run of the palace, Duryodhana was everywhere, mesmerized by the sabha that Maya had built. He openly said that he wanted one just like it. The chief architect was summoned from Hastinapur to make a note of the features that Duryodhana wanted exactly replicated. As the days passed and the note-taking became voluminous, the architect had the appearance of a beleaguered man. 'Absurd!' I heard him mutter once or twice. 'Nothing but folly!' But fear of Duryodhana made him do as bid.

Karna, too, was clearly unhappy to linger, though he stayed out of loyalty. His inherent awkwardness among kshatriyas had always made him brusque. Years of living in Duryodhana's company had made him arrogant. Several of the kshatriya kings who were also our guests had treated him like an imposter and snubbed him. Instead of calmly ignoring them, he had grown surly, so that even those who were neutral to him were forced to comment on his poor social skills and give him a wide berth. Among my own sons, Yudhisthira was unfailingly courteous to him, Bheem was contemptuous, while Arjuna avoided him. Nakul and Sahadeva laughed at his gawkiness, but admired his skill as an archer. He had won every competition, they said, yet he expressed no gratification in the applause. The servants informed me that, at the banquets, Karna drank too much, but barely touched the food. Though he did not play dice, he was fascinated by the game, or perhaps it was the air of the dice hall that held him, like many others, in thrall.

Maya, the master of illusion, had built the dicing hall to a deceptively simple design with a high-vaulted roof supported on stately columns of black marble. The room was circular, shorn of embellishments, designed to amplify sound. Each throw of the dice was audible. My sons later said that the sound of the dice led to a strange kind of intoxication. *Magical*, was the word that Shakuni had used to describe it. Yudhisthira had been visibly pleased. Shakuni's skill at the game was legendary and the other kings had been desperate to play with him.

I did not like the dyutasabha. 'Your life can go to pieces here,' I had said to Yudhisthira when he had first shown me the dicing hall, soon after it was ready.

He had shrugged it off. 'It's just an amusing way to pass time. What is lost today may be won back tomorrow. There is nothing harmful or immoral in it.'

Night after night, he played dice with his cousins; during the day he was too listless and ill-tempered to attend to any of the administrative matters. When Panchali asked, exasperatedly, if the Kauravas had made Indraprastha their permanent address, he said, 'Don't spoil it, Panchali. This is the first time they have shown friendliness towards us.'

Panchali sent him an angry look. I would have taken her side had she asked my opinion, but she did not. Neither did Yudhisthira. It was a relief, then, to know that the Kauravas had suddenly departed. Yudhisthira was at a loss to understand the reason why. Indeed, there was no reason given. But, in the women's quarters, word spread that something unpleasant had triggered their exit. The sairandhri told me about it. She had witnessed the incident.

The maharani was sitting in the balcony when one of her retinue said: 'Oh, look, we have a visitor.' It was the Kaurava prince, with him was Karna. They had entered that part of the Maya sabha that was known as the Queen's Courtyard. Maya's creativity was all the more beautiful here because it was subtle: fine gold filigree work, cool pavilions of pale jade, a pool of indigo blue lilies. The maharani was clearly displeased at the intrusion, but when a maid offered to warn the men off, she had turned her head away without answering. She stood up and was about to go in when there was a loud splash. The ladies-in-waiting burst into gales of laughter. Duryodhana, assuming the lily pool to be one of Maya's crystalline showpieces, had walked into it. The pool was real. He sat there, looking wet and foolish, among the lily pads. The maharani had said in a carrying voice: 'Looks like the blind king's son is blind too!'

The sairandhri frowned when she repeated the words to me. 'Someone should have taught the maharani better manners,' she commented.

'What was the prince's reaction?'

'Duryodhana did not look up. But Radheya, who was helping him out of the pool, stared at the latticed balcony. His face was the picture of fury.'

The Kaurava party had left within the hour.

9

It's only a game, the blind king said. He likened it to life. Fate pitches us into different circumstances, we are nothing but pawns. Yet the play carries on. The mahamantri protested: dice games played within the family can only lead to its ruin. But my son Duryodhana insists on inaugurating the new dyutasabha by inviting the Pandavas, the doting father said.

'Doting father or dotard king?' I asked, when I first heard of the invitation, from the man who had brought it to Indraprastha.

'Possibly both,' replied Vidur unhappily.

'And Yudhisthira has accepted the challenge?'

'With reluctance,' Vidur said. 'It's all in the nuances. It was worded like an invitation, but it was a command from his father's elder brother. He felt he could not refuse.'

'I have heard Panchali berate him for his love of dicing despite the fact that he is no good at it. He lacks the gambler's instinct *and* the gambler's faith in winning.'

Vidur looked alarmed. 'Then he must not play at all.'

'Who will play against him?'

'Shakuni, probably,' said Vidur. 'He came up with the

idea in the first place. Duryodhana, Duhsashana and Karna took it to the king. The Evil Four, I call them.'

I gave him a bitter look. 'It is starting all over again, isn't it, the old enmity? Where will it end?'

There was an uncomfortable silence. Then Vidur said, 'There will be witnesses this time. The king himself, Pitamaha, Acharya Drona...Duryodhana will have to stay within limits.' His words lacked conviction. After a moment he asked, 'Will Yudhisthira not listen to you?'

'He did not even think it fit to ask my opinion,' I said angrily. 'He listens to Panchali, though. But *she*, what does she really know of the Kauravas?'

At dawn the next day, the Pandavas left for Hastinapur. *It's only a game*, I told myself. *A ritual.*

❖

Yudhisthira staked a collar of pearls churned out of the ocean's depths. It was won. He staked a hundred jars each full of thousand gold pieces. Those, too, were won. He staked his regal chariot that had been the envy of all the kings. He lost it. A thousand elephants caparisoned in gold, slaves and slave girls, the partridge-dappled Gandharva horses, cattle, milch cows, sheep, goats, his kingdom, its fields and forests, a thousand chariots with golden shafts, the jewels his brothers and he himself wore, his brothers—the two Madreyas first, then Arjuna, Bheem—and finally himself. He lost everything. He lost us all. And when there was nothing left to lose, he went a step ahead and gambled his wife.

'*What* has been won?' cried the blind king, unable to believe his ears.

Panchali, wife of the king of kings, was brought into the dicing hall. A single cloth covered her, stained in red for she was in her period. She was dragged by her hair. Her cries of protest cleaved the deathly silence. Blind Dhritarashtra had turned deaf or maybe he, like everyone else, was rendered dumb by the awfulness of the scene that played itself out in the Kuru sabha. To say, as some say, that it was ordained is not just wrong—it is evil. Human beings engendered that situation, but who were they? Was it the cabal of four that planned it, the blind king who sanctioned it, the man who wagered his wife, or was it I? Was it my words, once uttered for an entirely different reason in a potter's hut, that ultimately heaped ignominy on the fireborn princess?

The truth *I* cannot walk away from is this: one Kaunteya staked her, while the other called her a whore and ordered her to be stripped. The sutaputra was the worst of the evil four, they said, bringing to the proceedings an unimaginable savagery. 'Remove her clothes,' he is reported to have said. 'Shame her in public for what else is a woman who cohabits with several men but a common whore?' Was it the revenge of a rejected suitor who had not forgotten an insult? Was it lifelong rancour against those responsible for all the injustices: the unknown noblewoman who had concealed her shame by abandoning her bastard son to his fate, the social order that would not recognize his merit but had favoured his only rival in the world, Arjuna? In one fortuitous moment, did all the hoarded acrimony of years finally find its outlet in those words? Or is it as Pitamaha said: 'Dharma is subtle. Indeed, when applied to a woman it is perverse. A man who has lost himself has no possessions left to wager, but if he is married, he still has a right over his wife.' Yudhisthira *had*, after all, staked her, Pitamaha pointed out. *He* had lost her.

Being a woman, however, Panchali had no use for the intricacies of manmade laws. Perhaps that is why the god within came to her help: though Duhsashana expended all his energy in the disrobing, he could not dishonour her. Finally, the blind king, rendered naked by his inability to stop what was going on, was shamed into action; he tried to make reparations by giving her a boon. She had the Pandavas freed and their weapons restored. She rescued my sons in their worst hour.

They left for Indraprastha shortly after.

They did not reach home.

A lone horseman brought us the news. Yudhisthira was ordered by the king to play again. Again, he could not refuse. 'I do what I must,' he said resignedly. 'It is my dharma to obey my uncle.'

This time the stake was simple but deadly. Win and you get the entire kingdom. Lose and you give up Indraprastha and go into exile for thirteen years.

My son, not surprisingly, lost.

Ten years in Indraprastha, the satisfaction of seeing my sons flourish as kings, my grandsons grow as princes, was it all, like the Maya sabha, a chimera? Gone in the blink of an eye, the way a dream is swallowed by the void the minute the sleeper awakens. How else had the Pandavas returned to where they had started? Destitute and homeless. Dressed once more in deer skin, united only by their resolve to live through this together.

I tried, Pandu. I have failed.

One more journey to Hastinapur. But this time the covered chariots passed through the Elephant Gates without being noticed. The horses' hoof beats clattered through the empty streets, the shops were shuttered. No lamps were lit that night. Slowly, out of the darkness, an outline emerged. The palace. When we alighted, Subhadra and the grandchildren were led away to their chambers, but I was informed that Gandhari wished to see me.

She did not keep me waiting. Nor did she waste time in commiseration. 'You cannot accompany them this time, Kunti,' she said. 'Your health, I have heard, is not very good. The king and I would like you to make your home with us.'

'That is kind of you,' I said stiffly. She waited for more, but I had nothing to add. For a few minutes she stood there, a thin, silent scarecrow whose classic beauty had been replaced by an unappealing severity of expression, a downward slant of the mouth that suggested a lifetime of disappointment. There was grey in her hair, but her posture was straight.

'It is unfortunate,' she said haltingly. 'But thirteen years will pass.' She made a gesture of helplessness. 'As women it is our destiny to suffer.'

Platitudes again. What else can she offer?

When I had been silent for too long, she said in an artificial brittle voice, 'All right then, I'll leave you now.' She turned to go, took a few steps and stopped. 'Kunti!' she cried. 'Tell your daughter-in-law that she cannot persist in this silliness.'

I pretended not to understand. 'What silliness, Didi?'

'Surely you've heard! That ridiculous vow of leaving her hair loose.'

I shook my head. 'I've only just arrived.'

'Oh! Well then, you will probably hear about it,' she said. 'But let me tell you, your eldest born staked her by name. What was the need to do that?'

'Why don't you ask your brother?' I said sharply. 'It was his idea. Do they stake their royal women in Gandhara that he thought of suggesting it here?'

She clenched her fists and bowed her head. '*Tell her*,' she whispered. 'Tell her to give up the idea of revenge. It will destroy us all, Kunti...I have never differentiated between your children and mine.'

'The king has.'

'The king!' She choked over the words. 'He is no king, he is a pawn. Fate is cruel to all, but cruellest to him. He clings to Duryodhana as if to a lifeline in a dark, endless tunnel. The sound of Duryodhana's tread, his laughter, his voice—this is all he lives for.'

'And that is why a daughter-in-law of the Kurus was humiliated in the sabha,' I said. 'And his dead brother's sons go into exile tomorrow morning.'

'A daughter-in-law of the Kurus!' mocked Gandhari. 'You and I are daughters-in-law of this house too. Haven't we accepted our fate? Why must she be different?'

'Panchali *is* a different woman. She does not blindly accept her fate but makes her choice and risks the consequences.'

'Her risk will be our ruin,' hissed Gandhari. 'She thinks too much of herself. Did you know that she challenged the Kuru elders in the sabha that day? Who brought her up to talk like that? If she had not argued so stridently, if she had only kept her mouth shut and her eyes lowered, all this would never have happened. Men cannot stand being humiliated by a woman.'

I remained silent.

'A woman's life is never in her hands,' she continued. 'Isn't this how it has always been? Isn't this what we were told? A woman's fate is decided by the family she is born into, the man she marries, the—'

'I am sick of this talk of fate and destiny,' I burst out. 'These are empty words behind which we hide our ineptitude and our lack of will. By tamely accepting our fate we prove nothing but our fearfulness.'

She drew herself straight. 'No one "tamely" accepts anything. We do what we must. What our dharma tells us.'

'Dharma!' I spat the word out. 'What is it but a weapon to bludgeon us into submission?'

'Kunti—'

'No. You've had your say, Didi. Now please allow to me speak. I, too, have tried to follow my dharma, but what's the good of it? All it ever does is offer a flimsy absolution against guilt. *We* are responsible for our condition, that alone is the truth.' Suddenly I felt such deep anger at her that I could not stop the words. 'Look at yourself! That piece of cloth over your eyes. That is dharma. Hasn't it left us all in darkness?'

'How dare you!'

I had been inexcusably rude, yet, the madness that made me lash out had not completely subsided. I had been angry for too long. I could not bring myself to apologize.

She broke the silence. 'This is not about me, Kunti, but about your daughter-in-law Panchali.'

I was weary to the bone. '*Don't*,' I said. 'Don't make excuses for your men…I am not making any for mine. If exile is what they've earned for themselves, *so be it*.'

❖

Though she had abandoned all the trappings of a queen, never had she looked more like one. Her face showed no sign of strain. Her hair lay open over one shoulder, falling to her knees—a blasphemy, an affront. She had vowed in the Kuru sabha not to tie it till she had bathed it first in Duhsashana's blood.

That blood will have to be shed. No wonder Gandhari is terrified.

'Dhrishtadyumna has come to take the children away,' Draupadi said, evenly. 'You can go with him to Kampilya. My father has invited you to live there.'

'What of Subhadra and Abhimanyu?'

'They are being escorted to Dwaraka. Would you prefer to go with them? The Vrishnis are your own people, it will feel like home.'

'My home was never with the Vrishnis,' I said. 'The only home I ever considered as mine was my husband's kingdom. I will stay in Hastinapur.'

'Are you sure?'

'I am,' I said. 'The mahamantri and his wife have invited me to stay in their house. I have accepted.'

We had grown to understand each other, Panchali and I. Over the years we had assessed one another's strengths and weaknesses. There was no need for either of us to pretend. She stared at me for a long moment. Her lips twitched briefly in amusement.

'Yes,' she said, with a nod that could have passed for admiration. 'Your mere presence in Hastinapur will remind that blind king every day of what he did to your sons. Pray to god that he will drown in his own guilt.'

❖

The blind king wanted to know from Vidur how the Pandavas departed for the forest.

'They went barefoot,' said the mahamantri. 'Yudhisthira led the way with his face covered; Bheem followed with his arms held out; Arjuna showered grains of sand on the ground as he walked away; the Madreyas covered themselves with dust and mud.'

The blind one asked: 'What do these different postures mean?'

'Yudhisthira, ever righteous, shielded his gaze so that its anger may not burn down your city. Bheem reminded himself that his arms were the strongest in the world and would one day tear Duryodhana apart. Arjuna swore that he would scatter a thousand arrows to destroy your sons. The Madreyas, handsomest men in the world, hid themselves so that the women of your city would not follow them.'

'And what of Dhrupad's daughter?' Gandhari asked. 'How did she look as she walked away?'

'She wore the blood-stained cloth in which she had been dragged into the sabha. She uttered a chant as she walked. *Thirteen years from now this will be a city of widows. Husbands dead, sons dead, friends and relatives dead. Their hair loose, like mine is today, shorn of adornments, the widows of this city will offer water to their dead men.*'

'What did the king have to say to that?' I asked Vidur.

'Nothing,' came the dry reply. 'He wept.'

10

Vidur's house was large, airy and cheerful. It faced the river at a place where there was a bend in the course. My room lay on the eastern side. The sun's pearl-pink fingers, tips dusted with gold, touched it first, tracing a delicate filigree through the latticed windows. The soft glide of the river was the only sound. Then a conch shell rang out, bold and piercing, as if grabbing the raw elements—the half light, the newborn breeze, the millions of droplets in the river, the sparkling sand grains—and blending out of them, a new day. A challenge. A burden.

Looking out on my first morning there, I had heard the sound of the conch first and only then seen the lone figure standing at the edge of the water. The sight sent a shockwave through me. It was Karna—offering prayers to Surya. His hair, lifted by the cool, playful breeze, was a like a nimbus. I was mesmerized. Something in his attitude, the raised head, the slope of his shoulders, the cupped hands, spoke of surrender. A human petitioning a god. After a while I heard his footsteps going past my window. In the time that I spent in Vidur's house, I learned to listen for them. For those thirteen years I saw Karna almost every day.

After his morning worship, it was said, he would give away cloth and grains to brahmins. It was Parashavi, Vidur's wife, who told me this.

'Every day?' I asked. 'Is Anga-desh so prosperous?'

'It is his personal wealth. Duryodhana heaps riches on him that he promptly gives away.' She shrugged. 'It's a mystery to me why he does it. They call him *Daanvir*. Maybe it's just for the name,' she added. 'To be known as Radheya is no longer good enough for him.'

'What do you mean?'

She hesitated, then said, 'It's well known now that the charioteer Adiratha found a newborn floating in the river past his village many years ago. There was some special jewellery, too, in the casket. Adiratha brought it to Hastinapur and showed it to Pitamaha. The craftsmanship was excellent, but when inquiries were made, no one could identify the goldsmith who had created it. Pitamaha concluded that the babe's mother was an unfortunate noblewoman from a country up river, a kanya probably, who had slipped up.'

'A slip-up?' I murmured, as if in a dream.

'High-born women, like their lesser sisters, have to bear the burden, isn't it? The male always walks away not guilty.'

❖

'The blind king does not sleep well,' said the sairandhri, as she massaged my inflamed joints with warm oil.

'What keeps him awake?'

'Regular bulletins from the Kaurava informers.'

Not satisfied with sending my sons into the forest, Duryodhana had sent spies to watch them. The news, however, did not seem to reassure him. First it was that Bheem had killed one more dreaded asura, Kirmira, the brother of Baka, who had lived in the forest known as Dwaita vana. Hearing it, Duryodhana had raged at his father. Returning their weapons to the Pandavas had been a mistake, he had cried.

'They quarrel every day,' said the sairandhri. 'The son rants, the father weeps and wrings his hands. They are both obsessed by the same fear.'

'And what is that?'

'As if you don't know!'

I sighed. 'Thirteen years is a long time, Sairandhri—ask me, I count the days.'

She shook her head. 'It may seem like that to you, Maharani, but it's not a long time if one has to prepare for a confrontation. The Pandavas may be in exile right now, but who can say that they will not emerge stronger than before? They've done so in the past. It is said that Dhrupad's son regularly visits them, as do your kinsmen, the Bhojas, Andhakas and the Vrishnis. Draupadi's kitchen feeds dozens of brahmins every day.' She laughed quietly. 'Even the Kaurava spies are fed from her *akshaya patra*, the magical cooking pot that produces unlimited quantities of food. It is said that the gods gave it to her. The Pandavas may be in exile, but their hospitality continues to be royal.'

'Is that what keeps the king awake?'

'With him, it is guilt,' the sairandhri said. 'There are enough people to rub it in. Every sage who visits the palace forecasts a terrible war fourteen years from now. They all say that he must do everything to stop it.'

'Yudhisthira is a peace-loving man,' I reflected. 'The king just has to return their kingdom to the Pandavas once the term of exile is over.'

'But will Duryodhana let him do that?' she asked. 'Though *he* feels no guilt, the fear of retribution dogs him as well. He, too, is imagining a war. Pitamaha, Acharya Drona and Kripa have all been reminded of their allegiance to the Kuru throne. And then there is Karna, whose hostility towards your sons is well known.'

'That cripple from Gandhara is behind it all,' I snapped. 'Why does no one take his name?'

The sairandhri shook her head. 'Shakuni is an out-and-out gambler. This is just a game for him.'

'But *why* does he play such a deadly game?'

The sairandhri was quiet for a while. 'Well, it's a matter of opinion,' she murmured. 'Pitamaha destroyed his sister's life, didn't he?'

This is Hastinapur, I reminded myself gloomily. Nothing had changed. It was rife with deception, uneasy rumours, bitter memories, distorting thoughts and discordant emotions. No wonder my aches and anxieties had increased. My thoughts turned to Pitamaha. Over the years, my distrust of him had not gone, but it had grown muted. He was very old now and the arrogance of his younger days, the sheer power he had radiated, had been replaced by an acquiescence, that I, no longer young myself, could empathize with. It was the submission of a dependant, I realized. Not a family bond any more, but a bondage.

Like Karna, he used to come to the riverbank, but in the evenings. I would see him strolling on the long stretch of sand beside the water. At that hour the golden light reflected off the wavelets. Temple bells, gongs and conches clamoured as the evening prayers were conducted in the city's shrines along the length of the holy river. The world prayed to the mother, and he, the son of that mother, what did he think of as he paced the glittering sands? A tall figure in white, flowing robes, hands behind his back, head bowed in thought. The river washed away all humanity's sins, but to me it looked as if he carried their burden on his back, so weighed down he seemed. Or was it merely the oppression of my own memories and the alchemy of the hour—the ceaseless flow of the river, land merging into darkening sky, past flowing into the future—that brought on these unsettling thoughts? That Pitamaha, like me, had begun to see the vainness of all our efforts. Nothing we had struggled for had remained. So what had it all been for?

❖

The puppy ran into my path out of nowhere. A single bell on a string tied around its neck alerted me. The creature, white with liver-coloured ears and a shiny wet nose, sniffed around my feet. It sat down and looked up lopsidedly. The velvet gaze melted my defences.

'Who are you?' I asked. 'Who do you belong to?'

There was a flurry of footsteps and a small figure crashed out of the jasmine bushes and dropped at my feet in a dive. I stepped back. The puppy went up to the fallen intruder and sloshed his face with pink tongued licks. The boy gave a gurgling laugh of delight and got on to his knees. He lifted the puppy and buried his nose into its coat. Then he looked up at me. The world around me shrank into the pinpoint of his gaze. Time turned back. I was looking at Arjuna. The same curly hair, the lithe compact body, the firm bud of his mouth. Arjuna at five, or was it six, years?

'Who are you?' I asked abruptly. The smile left his face. He eyed me warily.

'Is he yours?' I asked in a gentler voice. 'He's a naughty puppy, isn't he?'

The boy nodded slowly.

'Come into the house,' I said. 'He looks thirsty. Let's give him some milk to drink.'

He did not move. I walked on, aware that, after a brief hesitation, the puppy and his owner were following me. Parashavi had a visitor, the boy's mother. She came forward and touched my feet. She had a round, soft face that smiled easily. Her eyes were light brown. They gave her a placid look. Her name was Vrushali. She was introduced to me as Karna's wife.

'My father was Yuvaraja Duryodhana's charioteer,' she said. 'When I was born Radha Ma saw me and said she would have me for her daughter-in-law one day. It was as simple as that.'

I cannot remember what we talked about, but those moments—with the bright-eyed child playing close at hand—offered me a release. I forgot everything but the link we shared. It was difficult for me to take my eyes off him. His name was Vrishaketu. He was the youngest of eight brothers. When the time came for leave-taking, I ruffled his hair and said, 'Come and see me again.'

'He is starting school next week,' Vrushali said. 'That will keep him out of trouble.'

The hundred princes of Hastinapur had proliferated. The royal offspring were taught the basic kshatriya skills—riding, fencing and archery—in a school by the river. It was overseen by Kripacharya. Karna's sons, too, went there for training—Duryodhana had insisted on it. It was to this school that Vrishaketu had been admitted. The numbers were so many that if a student played truant it was not even noticed. This grandson of mine did so every now and then. I learned to keep the window open, to wait for the dog and his young master, to keep a platter of crescent-shaped modak, his favourite sweet, under a cloth napkin. Sometimes he wanted a story, at other times a song. I discovered that I had enough of both to keep him entertained. With him I stopped thinking about anything but the sweetness of the moment. For several years, these tacitly secret visits continued. He was my harbour in that difficult time, my joy and comfort.

11

After repeated invitations from the palace, that I had invariably refused, Gandhari came to see me. At her behest I agreed to revive some of the welfare institutions that had been started by Satyavati. When I had returned to Hastinapur from Shatashringa forest I had supervised them for a while, and now I welcomed the opportunity to keep myself occupied.

Hastinapur had grown in the years that I had been away in Indraprastha. Always thriving but orderly, it had recently become obese. It was an age of profligacy and abandonment. After sending the Pandavas into exile, Duryodhana had ordered the sacking of Indraprastha. A new treasury was constructed to store the wealth. The population of Indraprastha, bereft of home and livelihood, had turned towards Hastinapur. Its streets were noisy and chaotic, its air heavy and miasmic. The quality of age and refinement that I remembered had given place to a new strident gaudiness, an ugly swagger. There were many more slaves now to do the work, but the work never seemed to get done properly. Doorsteps were unwashed and bare of decoration while housewives had their faces painted and plucked. Household looms lay silent while gossip travelled from tongue to tongue. Kitchen gardens lay neglected while pleasure gardens for the fashionable thrived. Altars were ignored while taverns and gaming houses flourished.

There was enough for me to do. I started with the rehabilitation of widows who had been turned out by their families. The home that Satyavati had built for them was in a dilapidated condition as state funding had dried up. Rather than turn to the king, I decided to meet the wealthy merchants in the city and ask for donations. Before long, Gandhari descended upon me, agitated and angry.

'This wasn't what I expected from you,' she said. 'It is giving us a bad name...The king is most upset.'

'That was certainly not my intention,' I said smoothly. 'The idea came from the superintendent who, apparently, has sent petition after petition to the king, requesting funds. A widow is nothing, we all know, but even she needs money to live on.'

'Don't say that, Kunti! Must you seize every opportunity and milk it for your benefit?'

'*My* benefit?' I raised an eyebrow, feigning astonishment. 'But I was only talking about the homeless and destitute women of this kingdom.'

'You know what I mean.'

I said nothing.

'Come back to the palace,' she pleaded. 'Your home is with us. We are your kin. It looks so bad that you, the rajmata, choose to live on a *dasiputra's* charity, just a stone's throw away from your own home. It is terrible that you do not attend any of the royal functions even though we invite you every time. Whatever be our internal differences, Kunti, is it seemly to parade them before the world? As a mother you have kept your sons together, but have you forgotten that you and I are also related? We are both daughters-in-law of an old and respected family. This connection that unites us is undeniable. It is the common heritage which our children will take into the future. For their sake, at least, give up this rancour you nurse.'

I remained silent. She made a wringing gesture with her hands that conveyed her disappointment and despair. 'You'll get the money you asked for,' she said and left.

Following this exchange, my resolve to stay aloof loosened. Gandhari's words had made me uncomfortable. I began to attend some of the women's gatherings in the palace—the naming ceremony of a newborn, a seasonal festival. Gandhari was touchingly grateful. Some of our early rapport returned. Maybe it was just that we were close in age. There is a certain comfort in knowing, and being known, by another for nearly a lifetime. Sometimes she would request me to accompany her for a chariot ride into the countryside. I think we both liked the feeling of freedom that we got away from the palace.

That morning, we were returning from an old shrine to the Mother Goddess in the outskirts when she said, 'We are both mothers.'

I looked at her sharply. 'Are you trying to tell me, Didi, that you worry for my sons?'

'I worry for *my* sons,' she said frankly.

The breeze was teasing. The horses tossed their manes, jangling their harness bells. The route we had taken followed the line of the river.

'It is hard to say what is in Duryodhana's mind,' she said. 'Indeed, I do wonder if he ever had a mind of his own. When he talks sometimes his father speaks through him, and sometimes it is that sutaputra he has befriended. They are both using him and, in the process, confusing him. Then there is Shakuni.' She sighed. 'Ties of birth bind us, but I have long ceased to understand my brother. He used to be so protective of me, and I was grateful to him for being there for my sons, but now it feels like a—it's too late to look back!' After a moment, she added in a whisper, 'But when did I ever look to the future?'

Her perspicacity was no surprise to me. Sometimes I got the feeling that she had acquired the ability to read minds.

Twelve years had passed. They had been nowhere near as trying as the final one—the thirteenth year—was turning out to be. It was the year of concealment, the largest manhunt ever. Duryodhana's men had fanned out through Aryavarta, searching through forests, pilgrim spots, ashramas and royal courts to 'smoke out the Pandavas', as he put it. If he could manage to identify them, they would be exiled for another twelve years. A generous reward had been announced for information that led to their discovery. Week after week went by, bringing up tidbits of news, but to my immense relief, it was invariably false.

Gandhari sighed. 'Another few weeks and it will be over. Like you, Kunti, I pray that it ends well.'

Hastinapur came into view. The covered chariot rattled down the streets, flanked by the armed escort. Bystanders looked at it with curiosity. What was disquieting to me were the visible preparations for war. There was a recruitment drive on and young men were gathering in the open field next to the soldiers' barracks. I had heard that swordsmiths, lance- and shield-makers had been told to increase production. Animal traders had been sent out to other kingdoms to procure the finest war horses and elephants. Messengers, too, had gone out to all the friendly kingdoms to remind them where their loyalty lay.

Then, just a fortnight before the term of exile was to be completed, news came that Keechaka, the senapati of Matsya-desh, a kingdom to our west, had been murdered under mysterious circumstances. On hearing the details, Duryodhana was convinced that the Pandavas were behind the act. It had, he said, the stamp of Bheem's handiwork. He insisted on launching a cattle raid. If the Pandavas were indeed in Matsya-desh, they would come to its defence, especially now that the kingdom had lost its senapati. Once exposed, they would have no choice but to go back into exile. Soldiers marched toward Matsya and seized the cattle grazing in the pastures near the border. The captured herds were driven towards Hastinapur. Several days passed, the time that it took for news to reach Upaplavya, the capital of Matsya, where a king name Virata held court.

On a cold winter morning, as the two opposing armies waited for the fog to dissipate, a conch shell resounded across the battlefield. It was instantly recognized by the Kauravas as Devadutt, Arjuna's special conch, a gift from his birth father Indra. The Pandavas were out in the open. Duryodhana and his brothers cheered lustily, but Pitamaha grew thoughtful. The Pandavas were not fools, he said. If they had revealed themselves, it was because the term of exile was over. There were many ways to calculate a year. The acharyas and several astrologers were consulted. The thirteenth year had come to an end barely six days earlier, they said. The period of exile was over.

'Is it really over?' I asked Vidur when he gave me the news.

'It should have been,' he said, his face clouding. 'But I fear that it's just starting—the worst is yet to come.'

In the next few days the army returned to its barracks. An uneasy calm fell over Hastinapur.

❖

I listened to the brahmin sent by Dhrupad with a sinking heart. As an emissary of peace, he fitted the bill: advanced in years, dignified and self-assured. It was his words that were causing discomfort, not just to me, but to the Kuru elders as well. Pitamaha looked as if he'd just swallowed a fly, Drona stared fixedly into the middle distance, his brother-in-law Kripa studied the flag-stone floor of the ancient sabha. Only Vidur seemed to be listening intently.

The brahmin had come as an envoy from Panchala, he was Dhrupad's priest. He began well enough by respectfully greeting the king, but then he switched over to what could only have been Dhrupad's language. I recognized the hectoring tone, the hint of criticism and the simplistic logic of the argument that went thus: Everybody knows that Dhritarashtra and Pandu shared a common father. Ergo, they would also have shared the paternal property equally. The sons of Dhritarashtra, having got their share, usurped that of their cousins as well. Given the history of fraternal hatred that they had shown for years, including the several attempts to murder, this land grab was hardly surprising. However, the Pandavas, despite being powerful, were also men of principles; they did not start a quarrel despite repeated provocation. They had gone through the thirteen years of exile and met all the terms of the dice game. It was only fair that Indraprastha be returned to them and the matter ended peacefully. The alternative was war—make no mistake. It would mean the death of the Kauravas. In short, the brahmin concluded, don't let this opportunity to save your skins pass!

By the time the man had finished, his face was red with emotion, as no doubt Dhrupad's had been when he dictated that speech. For several moments no one said anything. Then Pitamaha cleared his throat.

'Your point is well taken, Brahmin, even though your tone is a bit too provocative for diplomacy,' he said haughtily. 'But that's probably because you are a brahmin and don't know the appropriate manner for a royal envoy. Nevertheless, all you said is true. Pandu's sons *have* suffered: they *were* robbed of their kingdom, their queen *was* humiliated, they *were* sent into exile.'

At this point Karna rudely interrupted. 'Let's not go into history,' he said. Ignoring Pitamaha's outraged glare, he continued. 'The facts are known to all. Yudhisthira lost the dice game, plain and simple. *He* lost his kingdom, therefore he had to go into exile. Though there are some who naïvely believe, on the basis of a dubious astrological calculation, that the thirteenth year is over, that point can be argued.' He curled his lip. '*I*, for one, don't think that the exile is over. The Pandavas should return to the forest and complete it. After that they can live as Duryodhana's dependants.' He paused and nodded in Duryodhana's direction. 'My friend is generous, I can vouch for it.'

Pitamaha stood up angrily. 'Radheya, be quiet! Have you forgotten who Arjuna is? Do you even know what weapons he has acquired? Challenge him and we are all dead.'

Karna stared at him, but did not reply. However, talk of war and dying had clearly frightened Dhritarashtra. He had turned quite pale.

'No one wants a war,' he said weakly. 'Pitamaha is right, of course. What good will come of a war?' Turning to the brahmin, he dismissed him, 'Please convey our good wishes to the Pandavas. We shall get back to them in a few days through our own messenger.'

In the queens' gallery, Gandhari abruptly stood up. 'That sutaputra,' she said. 'He's using my son to settle a personal score. *Damn him*!'

❖

The summons from the palace, asking Vidur to present himself, came late at night. The king's envoy had returned. If Dhrupad's brahmin had delivered his message with the clumsiness of an aggressive water horse, Dhritarashtra's response, carried by his charioteer Sanjaya, was as slippery as a river eel.

Cutting through the hyperbole, all it said was this: The king wants peace in his family. Yudhisthira, being intelligent and righteous as well as the eldest in his generation, should share this goal. If peace in the family is possible only by giving up the desire to regain Indraprastha, then Yudhisthira should follow that path. He will, thus, avoid the sin of killing his kinsmen.

'But when did I say that I did *not* want peace?' Yudhisthira had asked with asperity. 'Would any man in his right mind choose to go to war if what he desired was possible by other means? The Pandavas, like everyone else, wish to be happy, but they desire the happiness that comes from righteousness.'

In that case, Sanjaya argued on behalf of Dhritarashtra, the correct thing to do would be to stop hankering after the past. Indraprastha had been lost; it belonged to Duryodhana now. The sensible thing for Yudhisthira and his siblings to do was to go back into the forest and lead a life of virtue. They also had the option of being dependants on their kinsmen, the Andhakas and the Vrishnis.

'You are advising us to adopt the dharma of brahmins,' replied Yudhisthira sharply. 'But we aren't brahmins. Our forefathers were kshatriyas and it is that dharma that we are duty-bound to follow. Anything else would be adharma.' They went on in this way for a while. Sanjaya, the charioteer, parroting the homilies Dhritarashtra had coached him in, to an unimpressed and increasingly recalcitrant audience. Finally, Yudhisthira said, 'I listen to Krishna in all matters pertaining to dharma. Moreover, he has the welfare of both sides at heart. Let's hear what he has to say.'

Thus appealed to, Krishna, at last, spoke. In a nutshell, what he said was this: The Pandavas deserved an equal share in the Kuru kingdom, but the king allotted them only a certain portion—which was duly accepted. Even that was taken away from them through guile. Instead of censuring his son and the men who were behind this vile conspiracy, the king had all along aided and abetted them. It was he, Dhritarashtra, who sat as the head of the Kuru sabha when, in throw after throw of dice, his nephews were methodically divested of their hard-earned wealth. Because *he* remained silent when Krishnaa, daughter of Dhrupad, was dragged in and humiliated before the assembly, not one of the gathering, except Vidur, raised a protest. Had the king spoken then, had he made some attempt to stop Duryodhana, it would have made all the difference. Would Radheya have dared to tell the daughter-in-law of the Kurus that she had no one to shelter her anymore? Would he have gloated by saying that as a slave she could now choose a protector from among the men in the gathering? Those words cannot be unsaid, they are indelibly printed on the minds of the Pandavas. Thus, these messages of peace that the king now sends, through which he hopes to take the high moral ground, ring hollow. The Pandavas are left with no option but to fight for their right. If the king really cares about peace then he must make Duryodhana return Indraprastha to the Pandavas. That is the only way to secure peace. Otherwise, it is war.

Finally, Yudhisthira, much to the chagrin of his siblings, said to Sanjaya, 'Tell the king that I'll settle for five villages. That is all he needs to part with.'

❖

A strange mood seized Hastinapur. It walked the tightrope between despair and euphoria, dread and confidence, doubt and conviction. Nature reflected the turmoil. Flashes of lightning appeared in clear skies, wells threw up their water in sudden jets, streams reversed their flow, temple bells rang out in the dead of night. Spies had brought the news that Krishna himself was coming to Hastinapur with a peace proposal. Within the city there was a frenzy of preparation. Flower-covered arches had been erected all along his route to the palace. The royal guesthouse had been refurbished. The king took a personal interest in planning the banquet in honour of the guest and in ordering the gifts.

Vidur said in the sabha, 'Bribes may work with others, not with Krishna. If you really want to win him over, concede to his request.'

Duryodhana nodded. 'For once, I agree with you, Mahamantri. Krishna cares nothing for all the gems, gold, horses or chariots in the world. He will never betray the Pandavas.' He paused as though a new thought had just struck him. 'The thing to do is to welcome him with respect. However, instead of offering him the guesthouse, let's fix him up in a prison cell. When the Pandavas hear that their envoy is in our custody, they will tuck their tails between their legs and come running to surrender.'

At these words, Pitamaha walked out in disgust. Even Dhritarashtra was horrified.

12

'Do you hear the conches and the temple bells, Didi?' Parashavi asked. 'He has arrived. Devaki's son is here!' A smile of pure joy lit up her face. We were in the kitchen garden plucking greens for the midday meal. A brown hen and her four pale yellow chicks foraged for grain on the flagstones near the cistern.

'Why do you say Devaki's son?' I teased. 'He is Yashodha's son, too. Didn't she guard him with her life during those terrible years when Kansa's men were out to kill him?'

She lifted her head from her task. 'I have never met Yashodha,' she said. 'But I grew up knowing Devaki. I cannot think of any woman more unfortunate.' After a moment she added, 'Or more powerless.'

'Powerless? Krishna's mother?'

'Even Krishna's mother.'

Parashavi, in whose house I remained for thirteen years, had a brisk, unfussy air that was in complete contrast to her husband Vidur's studious, reflective and fuddy-duddy ways. From the beginning, she had treated me less as a guest who needed to be waited on, and more as a member of the family who could, when needed, be relied upon to provide an extra pair of hands.

It was a rather full household as Vidur's sons, too, stayed in the same compound with their wives and children; a mild sense of disorder was its chief characteristic. I had found its bustle reassuring, even comforting. The sea of clamorous activity—gossipy, giggling servants, children's games in the courtyard, the raucous crowing of the rooster, the clatter of kitchen pots—had kept me afloat for years.

A dasi came running. 'He's *here*!' she said, her eyes rolling with excitement, her hands flapping in confusion.

Leaving the basket of greens with the maid, we rushed indoors, past the household clustered near the main door, their faces agog with wonder.

Here? How? Why?

At first glance there seemed to be no change in him. The same Krishna, with his friendly, amused and relaxed half-smile greeted us. He was wearing his favourite colours, a yellow silk dhoti and shoulder cloth, with the trademark peacock feather in his crown. However, after a closer look I sensed that he was under some strain.

Touching my feet, he said, 'As soon as I could get away from the palace, I came to see you, Bua.'

'I am flattered that you found the time,' I said, pleased. 'The Kurus have a minute-by-minute protocol for your visit.'

'Not only has he thrown it to the winds,' Vidur said with mock resignation, 'he has refused to eat a meal with them.'

'But—but why?' I asked in alarm.

Krishna merely smiled. Vidur, too, did not offer an explanation. Some secret communication passed between him and Parashavi. In a slightly flustered voice, she asked Krishna, 'Putr, you will...?'

'Yes, Mausi,' he said humbly. 'But don't go to extra trouble for me.'

Her cheeks turned pink. 'Trouble?' she snorted. 'How can you say such a thing? Wait till you taste the *saag* I make for you.' To me she said, 'No, no, Didi...sit with him. Talk with him. Surely, he has much to tell you.'

We were alone. He waited for me to speak, but I could not trust myself.

'Bua,' he said, gently, as though he had fathomed the depth of my anguish. 'You have always been in my thoughts.'

My lips trembled. 'Krishna!' I cried. 'My children? Will I ever see them again?'

His face was touched by melancholy, but his eyes looked at me with a soft, sweet light. A feeling of deep compassion emanated from him. It washed away the bulwark in me, created over thirteen years, of hope, prayer and defiance. Tears blinded me. I wept without embarrassment, as though emptying myself out.

'How is my daughter-in-law?' I cried. 'When I think of what happened to her in the Kuru court, I am filled with anger at all my sons. Not the loss of the kingdom, not even that ill-fated dice game, *nothing* grieves me as much as their inability to protect her. How could my sons abandon her?'

He did not answer immediately. 'It is in no one's power to alter providence,' he said.

The words pierced my heart like a dagger of ice.

'Providence—I have come to detest that word,' I said. '*I* don't blame anyone for my present condition. Not Yudhisthira, not even Duryodhana. But if you say that no one has the power to alter providence, I don't agree. It was not providence, but my father who made the decision to give me away. He had that power over me. Indeed, if there is one human I *do* blame, it is him. He gave me away when I was a defenceless infant. He was the first to abandon me, Krishna, as though I was of no significance at all. Look at my life, Putr. Haven't I been in exile all my life? Where do I belong? What place do I call my rightful home? Whether man or woman, if one is forced to be a dependant, relying on others' charity for food and shelter, what is the purpose of living at all?'

He was listening intently. I had the feeling that all that I was saying, every word, was important to him.

'My sons were deprived of a father's protection when they were still very young,' I said. 'I promised myself that I would not forsake them. They would not be *alone*, as I had been. They would not be helpless.'

'You did not fail them, Bua,' he said quietly. 'You did everything for them in your power, which is all a human can hope to do.'

'And yet—yet, in this last year, I have heard, they were forced to work as *servants* in a king's household. My daughter-in-law became a maid...This is what the Pandavas were driven to. Who is responsible for it? Is it Dhritarashtra? He wanted his son to become king after him, so the kingdom of the Kurus was divided. He silently backed his son in the dyutasabha, so the Pandavas were cheated out of their kingdom.'

'Hush, Bua,' he said. 'Don't cry. You have borne a lot. There is no woman in the world like you. Your sons are the men they are because they are fortunate to have you for their mother. You are their shield and their sword.'

Looking into his eyes, I wanted to trust his words. I wanted so much to believe him, to fill that emptiness inside me with meaning. But I did not know what to believe any more. I was worn out.

'Please tell me what message I should give the Pandavas from you,' he said. 'It is the first question they will have for me, I know.'

'I have never differentiated between Dhritarashtra's sons and my own. But if there is any hope of justice, for dharma to endure, then *my sons have to get back their kingdom*.' The instant I said those words, I knew that they were the only words left to be said. I gripped his arm. 'Tell Yudhisthira this from me: Death is preferable to living on the charity of others. Tell Bheem and Arjuna that every kshatriya woman prays that her sons will act like heroes on the battlefield. If they let the moment slip, they will earn only contempt from others. And their own mother will have nothing more to do with them.'

He listened to every word. When I was done, he wiped the tears off my face and cupped my hands in his. He looked deep into my eyes. 'You will see your sons conquer their foes and live in peace and prosperity,' he said. 'You will see them soon.'

❖

Later that day, Krishna met the Kurus in the sabha. There, before the court, he placed the proposal from the Pandavas. If Dhritarashtra allowed them just five villages, they would gratefully accept. After he had spoken, the Kuru elders advised Duryodhana to do the right thing and give up

Indraprastha, but he paid no heed. He refused, too, the proposal of giving up just five villages. The threat of war and total destruction only made him push out his chest and swagger. His mother was called in to appeal to his better sense; he scowled at her. The kingdom should never have been divided, he said, but my father was forced to do so. What the Pandavas got as their share was lost by Yudhisthira, not once but twice. They do not deserve a kingdom if they don't know how to keep it. *Not even a needle tip of land will I surrender to the Pandavas.*

Vidur later remarked: 'With Karna by his side, Duryodhana could say it.'

'So it is…war,' I said.

'Unless Karna can be convinced to leave him,' he said.

13

The night was a cauldron on the boil. A powerful tempest brewed up, blowing gusts of sand from the river shore, snapping branches and lifting off roofs. The howling wind drove the rain, whipping it against the walls of the house and through the cracks below the doors. It raged all night, but it was nothing to the tempest in my heart. I struggled with my secret, crushed between the need to keep it and the need to let it go.

At dawn the world was an endless sea of calm, as though the devastation wreaked by the storm already belonged to a past life. Cresting the horizon, the sun's chariot blazed a trail of pink as it began its journey across the sky. Heart in my mouth, I made my way across the pale sands.

He stood up to his knees in the river, deep in prayer. I waited. The breeze was a lover's caress. A plain linen shawl, draped across his shoulders, lifted its edges. I had never before been this close to him. The time for secret glances was over, I studied him openly. His shoulders were narrower than I had expected, his arms longer. His hair was streaked with silver. Though I had cradled the secret of him within me for years, he was, I realized, a mystery to me. A boat with a single white sail plumped up by the breeze slowly passed us. He lifted his head and opened his eyes. The afterglow of worship was reflected in his serene expression. Then his gaze fell on me and his face stiffened into a mask.

Joining his hands together, he bowed his head. 'Lady, is there something you want from me?'

I shrank at the cold formality of his words.

He gave me an odd, wary look. 'Maybe you are looking for someone else,' he said. 'I am Radheya.'

'That is what you call yourself,' I said. 'But Radha did not give you birth.'

His face did not change. 'What you say is common knowledge,' he said, musingly. 'Nevertheless, she is the only mother I recognize. But why are you telling me this? What has it got to do with you?'

'Ask him,' I said, pointing to the sun. '*He* is your father, not Adiratha. You are Suryaputra.'

His smile was mirthless. 'In this life I have only been known as a sutaputra.'

'You are a kshatriya. Your name is Kaunteya.' A part of me was surprised at how easy it was to say it. 'You are my eldest son. I am your mother.'

Again he seemed unsurprised. 'Yes, Rajmata,' he said evenly. 'You have kept your secret only too well. I learnt of it just yesterday.'

The light in the sky became a bright shard, the world around me spun. 'I—who? Was it—'

His lips twisted. 'Maybe Krishna hoped to shatter me with this revelation.'

How did Krishna know? Who else knew?

'It was his parting gift to me,' he said with a dry laugh. 'The final joke that destiny has played in a life replete with ironies.'

'Don't be dramatic,' I snapped, annoyed at his flippancy.

He was silent, but his eyes mocked at me. 'Try to understand,' I said, half-pleading half-exasperated. 'I was *sixteen*. Kuntibhoja's foster daughter. Unwed. He put me in the service of Durvasa who—*who*—Oh, they used me, all of them, without any thought of what it meant for me!' I pointed to the sky. 'Even that god up there...I begged him to leave me alone not just for myself or my clan, but for your sake too.'

The look of contempt on his face deepened.

'You believe that being a sutaputra is a disgrace?' I cried. 'Being called a kanina is far worse...I hoped you would start life with a clean slate. Letting you go was—it was the only way.'

'Kanina, sutaputra,' he repeated, as though carefully measuring the weight of the words. 'Sutaputra, kanina. Those were my choices, but never a kshatriya. Never till today. Why is the world suddenly so keen to recognise me as a kshatriya?'

'You *are* a—'

He cut me off with an impatient shake of his head. 'The secret itself is irrelevant, but that you chose to reveal it *today* is what is of concern to me.' A hard glint entered his eyes, but his voice was smooth. 'Does it have anything to do with the fact that I've just been appointed the senapati of the Kaurava army and have sworn to kill your sons?'

I met his gaze steadily. 'They are your brothers.'

For a long moment nothing changed. Then an odd expression passed over his face. 'I *have* brothers, Rajmata. Adiratha's sons are my brothers. They would give their life for me—unlike your sons who have vowed to take it.'

'You have sold yourself to the Kauravas,' I said. 'They are using you.'

'And that arouses motherly concern in your breast?'

'Killing your own brothers is a sin, Karna.'

'Why don't you tell that to Arjuna?'

I took a deep breath. 'I will.'

He narrowed his eyes and studied me silently. 'Yes...I believe you will,' he said, at last.

'You are the eldest Pandava.'

He threw back his head and laughed out loud. 'An honour, I'm sure.'

'You have always wanted to be recognized as a kshatriya,' I said. 'Duryodhana was generous to you, but even he could not make you a kshatriya. Your brothers will see to it that you are honoured as one. They will wash your feet. All that they have will be yours...Give up Duryodhana.'

'Never,' he said quietly. He was silent for several minutes, then he added with sadness and resignation, 'You will not understand...Duryodhana gave me *everything*.'

'Gratitude is not love.'

His smile was grim. 'Coming from you, that is rich! What have you ever given me? Not so much as a glance, what to talk of love? Even today, when you stand here promising me the world, you are giving me nothing, but seizing what you can—for yourself alone.' He bit out the next words. '*You will go to any extent to save those sons of yours from certain death at my hands.*'

'I—I want to save *you*—from the consequences of choosing the wrong action.'

'Abandoning Duryodhana *is* the wrong action.'

Forcing myself to adopt a reasoning tone, I said, 'I agree with you that abandoning a friend is not right, but what is right is not necessarily what is good. When one is forced to choose between one wrong action and another, then one has to see it in the light of the possible consequences.'

A look of irritation passed over his face. 'I don't wish to get into this debate,' he said. 'Not with *you*.'

'Choices don't come in just two shades, black and white, right and wrong. The choice I made was between bad and worse. The god who fathered you felt nothing for anyone, but I was forced to think of what it would mean for me and for those who were responsible for me.'

'And so you discarded me! If we all did what you chose to do, there would be no value left,' he said grimly. 'No belief to uphold, no word to keep, no honour...If one does not live by one's principles, is it worth living at all?'

'Think for a moment of the consequences of *not* abandoning Duryodhana. His audacity, his sheer pigheadedness comes solely from your support. He is ready to go to war regardless of the fact that it will be the cause of thousands of deaths—his own included. No code in the world is worth the lives of innocents. The bloodbath will make widows of all women, orphans of all children. Doesn't the thought of their sorrow and suffering bother *you*? How can your support of him be right when the result is going to be disastrous for everyone?'

He had grown very still. The boat with the white sail

was nowhere in sight. At last, he said, 'I cannot leave Duryodhana. He is completely isolated. No one supports him, perhaps no one in his right mind should, but how can *I* forget that in all these years his friendship has been my sole sustenance? He was the one who broke through my isolation. Death comes to all of us, but its loneliness, too, can only be eased by the presence of a friend. I will fight by his side till the very end. And if I die before him he will know that I wait for him on the other side.'

My heart sank at the quiet finality in his tone.

'You called me the eldest Pandava,' he said. 'It sounds like an insult, my mind refuses to accept it. I am so close to Duryodhana that my mind knows Karna only as *Duryodhana's friend Karna*. The one cannot be separated from the other. It is the only self I recognize. I have never had the luxury of making a choice. Neither am I responsible for all the consequences.'

'That is your trouble,' I cried. 'You believe that you are ill-fated from birth. Life is a struggle for everyone, but one can, oftentimes, pick one's battles...Weren't there times in the past when *you* could have chosen to act differently? If you had not supported Duryodhana blindly, he would not have gone as far as he did in the dyutasabha.'

He looked away, but something about his expression told me that my words had found my mark.

'I owe you nothing,' he said. 'But I owe Duryodhana everything.' He passed a hand over his face. 'You should have stayed away,' he muttered.

'Will you kill your brothers for this obligation you feel towards your friend?' I said.

The next instant, from the change that came over him, I realized that they were the wrong words. His nostrils flared, eyes blazed. 'You have come here only to weaken my resolve. A word from you and suddenly I am Kaunteya and not Radheya, a kshatriya and not a sutaputra, brother to your sons and not their enemy. But that doesn't change the truth.'

'What truth?'

'That you are never loved for what you are, but only for what you can be. This is what Duryodhana taught me. You are only reiterating it...But Radha, the charioteer Adiratha's wife, loves me only for what I am to her—her child. She is the only mother I recognize. *I am Radheya.* Please...leave me alone, Rajmata.'

'The Pandavas are not gods but mortals, Karna,' I said, pleading.

'So am I, Rajmata.'

I shook my head. 'Not you—you have the gift of immortality. Your father—'

It was then I noticed that his golden earrings were missing. The shock of seeing them gone made me cry out. 'What have you done with them? Where is your kavacha? Why have you—?'

'I have,' he said, lifting the linen shawl to reveal the raw wounds on his chest. 'You aren't the only parent who fears for Arjuna. The lord of the skies, Indra, himself came to me a few days ago and took away my protection.'

'*Indra*? But how?'

'How?' he echoed, with an indifferent shrug. 'How else but through trickery? He came disguised as a brahmin with a request for alms—knowing, of course, that I would never turn him away.'

A sick feeling gripped my stomach. *These gods and their games!*

'I *told* him not to,' said a new voice. A shimmering pillar of light had appeared out of nowhere. Surya stood before me. Again, after a lifetime.

Karna had a queer smile on his face. He bowed in a respectful greeting.

The god raised his hand and blessed him. 'She is your mother, Putr,' he said. 'Respect her wishes even if you don't care for mine.' Karna did not respond, viewing the two of us with an uninvolved expression, as one might aliens who were speaking a different language. We three were nothing to each other but strangers. The god looked at his son with despair. 'You will not, I know,' he said. 'A name, an eminence all your own. You have dreamt of it all your life.'

Karna's face reddened, but he remained silent.

The father said, 'Death is not the only way to deathlessness. Have the courage to live. You were meant to rule, not a tiny kingdom handed to you as a bribe in exchange for your loyalty, but this whole land which is your birthright. Listen to your mother. You will be a glorious king.'

'Glory,' the son said, his shoulders slumping tiredly. 'Strange as it may sound to you, but I don't care for it. Do you want to know why? I am weary of the life you two gave me. Once I was greedy for victory, fame, a kingdom...but now, all I crave is an honourable end. Death on the battlefield would be a welcome thing.'

Death is important to a man, but survival is more important to a woman. I was his mother. I had to think beyond him. 'This will mean the end of everyone,' I said. 'Your sons too...Young lives.' My voice trembled.

'They were brought up as warriors,' he said stiffly. But at the back of his eyes there was something else, a faint shadow that could have been an ache, a longing, a secret fondness. I knew that he had heard me, what I had left unsaid. Looking intently at me, he said, in a very gentle tone, 'You have always only had five sons, Rajmata, and that number will not change, I promise you...If I live, it will be five, if Arjuna lives it will still be five.'

With that there was nothing more to be said. He turned to leave, trudged slowly for a few paces. Squared his shoulders, quickened his stride and was gone. There was just the silence now, and the unceasing flow of the river that had witnessed everything.

The god looked at me, not as a god but as the father of my son.

I have tried, his eyes said. *I have failed.*

14

She stood in the middle of the battlefield. The hem of her robe was darkened by the blood of her dead sons. A hundred. All dead. She raised her fist at the enamel sky where a few vultures wheeled lazily; the majority sat on the edge, too satiated to move.

'Mahadeva!' she cried. 'You gave me a boon that I did not ask for. This is what it brought me...Now give me a boon that I *want*. Raise one of them back to life. One son who will offer water when my husband and I are dead, just as we are about to do for all of them...Great god, give me back one of my hundred sons—if you can!'

No reply.

The day was windless, the sunlight pale over the wide plain. Kurukshetra, city of the dead, was filled with the ghosts of the living, women in white moving slowly, bending as they sifted through the corpses for their kinsmen so that the funerals could be performed without delay. The stench had become unbearable. Every now and then, one of the searchers would rush to a private corner, hand clapped over mouth. The sound of retching followed. There were sounds of grief too: muted sobs, a few whimpers, once in a while a loud wail. Victory and defeat belong to men. Kurukshetra was where the men had become heroes, but it was here too, that women had become widows. Sorrow is what women own.

It was hard to believe that all the warriors, lying side by side, had only days ago been each other's foes, albeit with a common goal: kill or be killed. Death had ushered in a new camaraderie. Facing each other, hands reaching out. Dying together. Mass funerals had been ordered—for kshatriyas, for others. Only those of royal blood would have separate pyres.

'Have you seen my brother?' The girl who stopped me with her question was young, no more than sixteen, slender, with a single plait. She could have been me—when I was that age. With her was an old man, milky-eyed.

'What does he look like?' I asked.

'Like me, of course. Taller by a few inches, though he is a year younger.'

Purujit, I thought. But Purujit was dead. As was Kuntibhoja.

The girl waited for me to say something. When I did not she turned away in disappointment. 'Come, Dadaji…Let us look elsewhere.' A short while later I saw her stop someone else, who pointed to the eastern corner of the field. Whose army had her brother fought for? How had he died? How did it matter? They were all dead.

My presence in the battlefield had been noticed; it was causing a stir. Several women were looking at me. But no one approached. They looked away, not ready to meet my eyes.

'Kunti?' I heard Gandhari say. 'Here?' After a moment. 'Whom has *she* lost?'

Yes, there was a comradeship between the mourning

women of both sides, but not between Gandhari and me. She, who had never ceased to be gracious in the past, had not spoken a word to me ever since she had heard how Bheem drank Duhsashana's blood. Strangely, it was Panchali to whom she had reached out, consoling her for the death of her five sons, and Subhadra, whose Abhimanyu had been murdered in a horrific manner...Weren't they my grandsons too?

'Rajmata, whom are you searching for?' a soft voice asked. I recognized it at once. Vrushali. Karna's wife. Her face was streaked with tears. I gazed at her for a long moment then, without speaking, held out my arms. She stumbled forward. Her body shook with fresh sobs. 'My husband... They've taken him away. My sons, Rajmata...All gone.'

'*All*?' I repeated. And then on a rising note of fear, 'How could you—he was but a child!'

She withdrew from my embrace. 'Who?'

My mouth was dry. 'Vrishaketu—my—your youngest.'

She looked blank. 'But he is at home...His father did not give him permission to fight.'

I hadn't known that I was holding my breath till I released it. Slowly. A voice called out, she turned. It was Adiratha and his wife Radha. 'I have to go,' she said. 'They are broken... All their sons are dead.'

There was a constriction in my chest. I merely nodded.

❖

The pyres had cooled, the ashes collected and immersed in the waters. Now only the prayers and final offerings remained. We were on the riverbank. The Pandavas entered the river to pray for the departed souls of their sons. Priests called out the names of the dead. Abhimanyu was followed by Panchali's sons: Prativindhya, Sutasoma, Srutakarma, Satanika, Srutasoma.

I stepped forward. 'Yudhisthira!'

He was about to leave the water. He looked up, surprised that anyone would have disturbed the gravity of that moment. He had aged overnight. The death of Draupadi's sons had shattered even his equipoise. There was a haunted look in his eyes.

'What is it, Ma?'

'Putr...There is one more name you need to remember.'

He frowned. 'What name would that be?' His brothers had come to stand closer by him. They were becoming aware that something was not right.

'What name?' Yudhisthira repeated.

'Kaunteya. Though no one ever called him by that name in his life, it was his...first name.' My courage failed. I pulled myself together. 'I am speaking of my eldest son, Karna—he was your brother.'

There was such a deep hush. Then the rushing of the waters returned to fill the void, this world. The sun grew back and light entered, white, bright and harsh. Concealing nothing. Their eyes were on me.

Only Arjuna's lips moved. 'Did he know?'

'Yes,' I said. 'I had to tell him.'

'*Had to*?' repeated Arjuna sharply. Suspicion clouded his eyes, there was a sense of betrayal. Had I, his mother, too, believed that Karna was the better archer? Had I gone to plead with him for his, Arjuna's, life? Now that the question had arisen, it would separate us forever.

'To stop this from happening,' I said.

The river laughed. The sun was low on the horizon. I said to Yudhisthira, 'Complete your duty towards your eldest brother. Claim him as your own. Include his name in your dead kin and welcome his youngest son into your number. He must know who he is.'

I beckoned the boy standing some distance away. As he approached, the Pandavas knew beyond the shadow of doubt. Arjuna at fifteen. I heard a moan. A cry from one of my remaining sons. Or maybe all. Only Yudhisthira remained frozen, his eyes blazing at me.

'You kept this a secret for so long. *How could you?*'

❖

Nothing was ever the same again. The secret that I had kept all these years to protect my sons had, by its revelation, drawn a rift between us. The Pandavas did not know how to behave with me. I had become a mystery to them. They tried not to judge me, but it was a struggle. Each one reviewed the new relationship in the light of the old, coming to an understanding of himself, trying to balance this new and complex equation, the shadow of guilt it cast, the demons that arose. Yudhisthira spent many hours beside Pitamaha who lay on his deathbed of arrows waiting for the days to pass, for the sun to turn. Pitamaha spoke to him at length. Krishna Dwaipayana, too, counselled him. So did Krishna. Yet Yudhisthira continued to suffer, from a fever and some deeper malaise that left him indifferent to all, but most of all to me.

For thirty days the Pandavas stayed on the riverbank.

Then, after offering the last prayers, they returned to Hastinapur. Though flower arches had been raised to welcome them and the citizens had turned out, the Pandavas were sombre. Were they remembering the last time they had passed through the Elephant Gates on their way to exile? They climbed the steps to the palace and I was reminded of that day when their father Pandu, too, had climbed these steps after a victory. How proud I had been then. How naïve, too. What had I known of life? What did I know now? It was an even deeper mystery than before; the only difference was that I no longer actively sought answers from it. They would come, if they were meant to.

❖

A decade passed before I left Hastinapur—for the last time. Unlike other journeys, this was not a banishment. Ever since I had heard that Dhritarashtra and Gandhari were going away to the forest, the idea had attracted me. Like an opening in a thick fog, it offered a glimpse of a free sky.

Hastinapur was not a prison, I was not ill-treated or neglected by the Pandavas and their wives, but it was no longer a place I recognized. Immediately after the war, there had been so much that needed to be done by way of rehabilitation and rebuilding. The women in the family, led by Panchali, had their work cut out. Meanwhile, Dhritarashtra tried to expiate his guilt through good works. Though the treasury was not his any more, he asked for and obtained generous grants that were spent in havans and rituals to appease the souls of his dead sons. Yudhisthira was unfailingly kind to his uncle, but Bheem was different.

It was as if after a lifetime of loathing Duryodhana, he could not give up the habit, and had transferred the hatred to Dhritarashtra. He never missed an opportunity to mock him. He created a furore over the expense involved in the acts of penance that Dhritarashtra indulged in, calling them useless. He shook his head and muttered rude words every time the blind king remembered his dead sons. In short, he all but forced Dhritarashtra out of the palace. Therefore, it shocked him and his brothers to know that I, too, had decided to go away.

'Why are *you* thinking of leaving?' Bheem asked.

'It is the appropriate thing to do at this age.'

Yudhisthira said, 'Your decision makes no sense...You urged us to win back our kingdom. What was that for if you never intended to stay?'

'It wasn't about your kingdom alone.'

'You sent us such a strong message through Krishna. *My sons have to get their kingdom back*. If that was not what you wanted, then what was it?'

'I also said that nothing had grieved me as much as the insult to Panchali.'

He gave me a long look. 'Are you saying that this war was fought over an insult—to a woman?'

'She was born from the yajna vedi,' I reminded him. 'You played with fire.'

A shadow crossed his face. 'But—'

I shook my head. 'Enough, Putr. For once in my life, let me do something *I* want.'

'All right, go!' Bheem exploded in frustration. 'But why with *them*? Have you forgotten how much grief he has caused you?'

'I have forgotten nothing,' I said. 'But I've known them both for many years. When an association is undeniable, the resentment simply becomes a feature around which the relationship must find a way to flow. Some of the bitterness fades, some of the scores are settled by time. The ill-will diminishes and the good memories gain ground. Maybe this is what forgiveness really is…They remember the day I came into this house as a bride. They welcomed me when I returned with you five after your father's death, no questions asked. This palace may have seemed unwelcoming to me, but it was always my husband's home and therefore mine. Gandhari Didi was never anything but kindness itself. Now when they have lost everything, I do not wish to turn my back on them.'

I stopped. How could I explain to them what I felt? That through Dhritarashtra I saw a pale image of his dead brother. Was it because he talked so often of the distant past, reflected on that childhood he had shared with Pandu? He cried when he told those stories, and so did I…I remembered my dead love and wept for all that I had lost. Whatever I had done, good and bad, hadn't I done it for him, *his* sons? He had always cared deeply for his blind brother and now I, too, had begun to see why: Dhritarashtra *was* pitiable, he had always been so. They needed me, Dhritarashtra and Gandhari. Or maybe I needed them.

'My decision is firm,' I said. In my mind's eye, I saw the open road welcoming me. Above it a free sky.

ALSO BY MADHAVI MAHADEVAN IN SPEAKING TIGER

BRIDE OF THE FOREST: THE UNTOLD STORY OF YAYATI'S DAUGHTER

'A lush, wondrous reclaiming that rightfully centres a long- neglected character in the Mahabharata: *Drishadvati aka Madhavi. A rich, pitch-perfect novel.'—Ashok Banker*

The myth of Drishadvati appears in the Mahabharata as the 'story of the salvation of kings by a maiden.' While tales of surrogacy abound in the Indian epics, this is the first known example of a womb-on-rent. This strange story—of a girl whose fertility was bartered repeatedly in exchange for priceless horses—has intrigued modern scholars, playwrights and authors for its cultural significance. While earlier adaptations have cast its theme as the exploitation of a helpless woman, Bride of the Forest presents it as the story of girl who is surprisingly radical in her ultimate rejection of patriarchy.

Staying true to the original myths and springing entirely from the world of the *Mahabharata*, the novel brings to life several other characters: Garuda, the divine bird who flies Lord Vishnu around the world; the proud kings of Ayodhya, Pratisthan and Kashi; the arrogant queen, Devayani, and her duplicitous maid—whose stories reveal an intricate tapestry of human and divine relationships. Intertwined in the tales of traditional rivalries is the age-old war between the asuras and the devas that gave rise to the perennial male quest for immortality, transmuted into the human desire for sons that lies at the root of commercial surrogacy even today. However, it is the story of Drishadvati, her sacrifice and her nobility, that will enchant the reader.